BORN AND RAISED IN A SECT

BORN AND RAISED IN A SECT

YOU ARE NOT ALONE

Lois Kendall PhD

PROGRESSION
PUBLISHING

DEDICATED TO

The second generation who dared to leave

To all our siblings, nieces and nephews who have yet to take that step

And to each and every second-generation child who never had the option

POEM DEDICATED TO THOSE READING THIS BOOK

Misunderstanding

As we speak and write, from our own perspective
With thoughts in our minds and good intent in our heart
We never fully know the wounds of another
How their heart has been scarred by life
How their culture has shaped them
How people, parents, peers and friends have added to their story
And how lovers have impacted their lives

And so, there is much room for error
As words which were meant to help
Touch on wounds and scars that, invisible to human eye,
Fester away unnoticed and uncared for
Raw and messy, the most sensitive of touch might cause an eruption

Buried deep or worn on the sleeve
Still these wounds and scars need care
They need love and comfort
For love will wait to see if the wound wearer gives consent
And soft, tender and delicate comfort can work its magic
Soothing and cleaning that raw place

And words can sometimes help
Or sometimes a look delivered in the right time and space
So please bear with me as you read this book
I've tried to stand in your shoes
My desire is that the words written here will soothe
But seeing life from your perspective and not fully knowing all
of your wounds
I may have missed the point or trodden wide shod on your
wounds
So bear with me as you read this book and feel free to write me
If you want to correct, and help me understand more
I am willing to listen and learn
I would welcome your feedback
And would feel honoured to hear your concern

Contents

Contents

Contents

CONTENTS

Preface

WHEN I WAS 21 years old I decided to go to the library and see if I could find out more about sects and cults. I remembered that someone had once told me that I was in a cult. I finally decided to explore whether the first 17 years of my life were in fact a sect experience and whether that might be why I was worried about the end of the world and hell. After all, no one else seemed concerned about these deep matters. Upon reading further, I awakened to the shocking truth that in fact I had been in a cult/sect and seven of my brothers and sisters as well as my parents were in fact still in a sect. I began a quest to further understand the environment in which I had been raised and I sought to assist others who had also had this experience. I went on to study psychology, hoping that it might be of use to a charity assisting those who had been in sects. In the spring of 1997, I was in the third year of a psychology degree, writing up my dissertation. I had become increasingly frustrated with those around me who seemed to have no understanding of sects or of how one might be affected by such an environment.

I decided that I wanted to research thoroughly the matter of those spending all or part of their childhood in a sect and write a book that others who had come from my background might find helpful. Therefore, in the autumn of 1997, I found myself studying for a PhD thesis in psychology, the title of which I decided would be 'What are the Psychological Effects of Former Membership of Extremist Authoritarian Sects?'. During the course of my studies, I delighted in discovering psychological theory which I felt directly related to those raised in sects. I conducted more and more research on the matter of sects, completing a series of studies. In 2006, I was awarded my PhD, but the end product was bulky and technical. This book is mostly taken from my PhD, with much of it being rewritten to make it easier to read and shorter in length.

During my research for my PhD thesis I found that even those research articles written about those raised in sects were very much written from the perspective of the first generation, those who had joined the sects in their teens or adulthood. This book seeks to address this imbalance in the literature, addressing the topic from the perspective of those born and or raised in cults.

It is my desire that those reading this book might find that they are able to relate to parts of it and in doing so, feel less alone. If this book is able to ease some of the pain that those raised in sects can experience, if it is able to assist others to feel more understood, to know that there are others who have had very similar experiences, then this author will be delighted. I hope that you relate to parts of this book but also bear in mind that we are all unique, have different experiences and one book couldn't hope to cover all these experiences.

Further books written on this topic are needed and perhaps one or two of the readers of this book might be inspired by the gaps here to write further on the topic.

Acknowledgements

IT IS GOOD to have the opportunity to again thank all those who participated and supported in all ways, shapes and forms the research for my PhD which formed the basis of this book. Ruth - I will never forget our eleven-day trip around the UK when I did a significant number of interviews. Over the years I have had many conversations with former members, both parents and those raised in sects. Your words and faces have stuck in my mind, and of course your stories have influenced me in the writing of this book, and especially in my poetry.

I'd like to thank the following people who assisted during the writing of my PhD and or this book: Livia Bardin, Dr Jason Crabtree, Dr Rod Dubrow-Marshall, Dr Lois Goding, Dr Trevor Hussey, Dr David Jones, Dr Michael Langone, Dr Lawrence Osborne, Christian Szurko, and my special thanks to my dear friend Claire. Thank you to Jennie who has been with me all the way through both the PhD and the writing of this book, I am particularly grateful for her support, encouragement and editorial skills. Thank you to Jane for working hard on ensuring that all commas, colons etc. are correctly placed in this book.

Thank you so much to the DialogCentre UK, ICSA (International Cultic Studies Association, formerly the American Family Foundation) and Wellspring (Wellspring Retreat and Resource Centre) without whom this project would never have got off the ground. During my PhD research, ICSA granted me \$500 towards expenses for my research interviews. Wellspring, specifically the late Dr Paul Martin,

Dr Pete Malinoski and Dr Ron Burks were supportive of my research in many ways. The DialogCentre UK has been an excellent resource not least by Christian Szurko's willingness to be interviewed for my PhD.

Because sometimes a bit of cheese is appropriate, I would like to thank my mum for teaching me to read before I went to school, and thank you to my dad for all the books!

Despite the numerous names above there are still more people who have contributed in some shape or form to either my PhD this book or both. Thank you to all of you. Perhaps the number of people that I could list and that I have referred to above is supportive of the view that creative work does not occur in isolation, rather it is passed down through the generations and is in essence a social endeavour.[1]

One life story, of someone who died many years ago, has been a particular encouragement, comfort and inspiration to me for nearly two decades. The life story is found in a book – The Bible – which in my 20's I found much of it very triggering (triggers and difficulties reading the Bible are discussed briefly in later chapters of this book) and troubling to read, although as I persisted in reading the book it got easier and much more enjoyable. However, this part of the book I never found triggering - quite the opposite, and I hope you won't either, but if you think it might, then perhaps best skip this page as I have included below a poem here based on that life story in the hope that at least some of my readers might be encouraged, comforted or inspired by the life of Joseph.

JOSEPH - THE ONE SEPARATED FROM HIS BROTHERS

As the symbol of his father's love was torn from Joseph's back
He saw the hatred in their eyes
As he knelt upon the ground
And begged his brothers for his life
But his pleading looks and cries
Fell upon deaf ears
And there was none to comfort him

Thrown into a pit by his own flesh and blood
He awaited his fate
Would death come quickly, or would it be slow and lingering?
But then a rope was lowered
And he was hauled up to the surface

Then sold to a passing Ishmaelite
Silver coins for Joseph's life
Taken to Egypt
Sold and bought again
Slavery became his lot

Sent from the bosom of his family
Taken to a far-away land
Where the culture and language were strange
It wasn't of his choosing

And as Joseph's mind played that day over
Each and every year
Etched in his memory
How he regretted his bragging
And remembered his last words
His dreams that they would bow to him
And yet it was him that bowed to them
But still his brothers' hatred was not soothed
Hatred of the love his father had for him
Symbolised in that robe that they tore from his back
Stripped down by brothers who were meant to protect
Oh jealousy, how fierce you are
Unyielding as the grave

But as the years wandered on
And God blessed Joseph in that far-away land
The land of his suffering
Joseph rose and fell, and rose and fell again
And decades passed
The injustice of false accusation screamed upon his soul
Forgotten, by those to whom he'd done good

But God's mighty hand lifted him up once more
To dizzy heights of power and influence
And God made his life fruitful
Famine the world over
God cared for the hungry
Using Joseph to work out his purposes
So that people would survive

And his brothers had need of him
And they came and knelt before Joseph
Though him they did not recognise

But with power in his hands
He checked on their remorse
And he understood God's plan
His past made sense
And he who received no earthly comfort
Gave comfort to his brothers

He told them who he was
And wept so loudly
No one missed his cry
And to those who once stripped him of his robe
He gave a set of clothing each, and to his youngest brother
To Benjamin, he gave not one, but five sets of clothes
As a symbol of his love

And Joseph's father was still alive
And they hurried to meet each another
Joseph flung his arms around his father
And as the flood gates opened
The weeping went on and on
And the pain of that loss
Broke the surface from the deep ravines
Of Joseph's soul
Just seventeen again

And later Joseph received his father's blessing
What a mighty blessing it was
And he gave instructions about his bones
You will carry them up from this place
And God will come to your rescue

And sure enough the generations to come carried his bones
Out of Egypt, then all around the desert

What comfort and encouragement
To know the life story of the bones they carried
And know what had been prophesied

And Joseph's trust was not misplaced
Because Joseph's bones were buried
After hundreds of years
By Joshua's peers
In the land promised by God
Yes, in the promised land.
Promised on oath
By a faithful God
Whose covenant cannot be broken
Who cannot lie to us
Our faithful God
In whom we trust

INTRODUCTION

PREAMBLE

REAL PEOPLE WHO ARE NOT ALONE

This book reports on research:

> 'Scientific research has a way of depersonalising . . . when read-
> ing research it is easy to distance oneself from the words on the
> page . . . It is important to remember, however, that behind
> every research finding there are real people.'[2]

REAL PEOPLE ARE behind the research findings reported in this book,
and the voice of real people is quoted in the form of both interview
and autobiographical quotes. I hope that this book will enable at
least some of those who have grown up in sects (the second generation) to realise that they are not alone and to feel more understood.
In addition, it is my hope that it will better equip different organisations and people coming into contact with current and former
second-generation sect members (second-generation adults) to support and encourage this group of people. The term 'second generation' refers here in this book to those born into sects, brought in as
children by their parents or those who joined as children under 16
years of age.

THE THIRD GENERATION AND BEYOND

I hope this book will inspire other second-generation former members to make a difference to this field. This book summarises some of the second-generation former-member research studies that exist, but little research exists examining the third generation. Although a few of some of the samples reported on in this book include the third generation (i.e., those whose parents were also raised in the sect), the number was too small to carry out any statistical analysis. It may be some years before academics and professionals have enough contact with the third generation and beyond to come to any firm conclusions regarding how sects affect them. Until such time as this research is carried out, it will have to be presumed (and perhaps wrongly so) that effects are similar to the second generation. Until that time, a full understanding of those raised in sects will be reliant on anecdotal and narrative evidence, such as life biographies written by former members and creative writing such as that written below by a third-generation former member who chose to call herself 'Out at Last':[3]

> It was snowing this morning. A mundane event for the people living here in the UK, but a momentous and special one for me. As most of my life in the Family was spent in South Africa, where it is rarely cold and almost never snows, I have not seen snow for over eight years. I left the Family a little over five months ago and naturally, moving on is difficult. Every day is a battle as I try to come to grips with the new world I have thrown myself into. From a job to education, from using public transport to learning social rules, everything is different and adjusting is hard. People can be cruel, and they are unforgiving when their social conventions are stepped upon. Finding work and trying to obtain a college diploma is a struggle, when one has no real academic experience at all. I often feel overwhelmed with how much I have to learn and how many amendments I must make to my attitudes and even the way I interact with people. Often the temptation comes to just give up.

Catching up on work at college and making it back in time for work and studying for my graduation were the only things on my mind this morning as I shrugged on my coat and headed for the door. The enormity of the task before me dragged down my spirits as I drank the remnants of a cup of coffee and prepared to brave the cold outside.

And yet, as I stepped out of my front door and saw the snow falling gently, transforming the scenery from a dirty grey to a magnificent white, it struck me how very far I now am from my former situation. I can now make my own decisions and do what I want to do; make my own mistakes if need be, but I am now allowed to be my own person. The fact that even the terrain and the weather was so different now to what I am used to brought home the fact that I am not in those conditions any more.

I walked down the small country lane, and saw the landscape being covered in a glittering blanket of snow, I smiled. The little white flecks fell silently, until, with a tiny hiss, they hit the warmth of my face. A tear rolled down my cheek as I whispered two words into the cold, morning air – 'I'm free'.

This book is about such experiences of children in sects, and after they leave. I am writing this book so that those who have been raised in sects will know that they are not alone, that there are others who share the bond of having had similar experiences.

Overview of Introduction

In this introduction, I firstly briefly discuss reasons for doing research in this area, including reasons for studying sects from a psychological perspective. I outline where the information contained in this book comes from including, brief discussion of some of the key research studies referred to. I explore the different assumptions that those writing about cults and sects make and discuss the controversies in terms of their impact on children in sects.

WHY STUDY THIS AREA?

DIFFERENCES BETWEEN FIELDS IN STUDYING SECTS

The study of cults, sects and new religions is a field in which the questions asked, their area of study (e.g. whether they are from an anthropologist's, psychologist's, sociologist's or theologian's point of view) and the approach taken by researchers, and therefore the outcomes of their research differ widely. Sects, their existence, operation and effects, are commonly associated with religion, one of the most deeply personal and core level experiences of human nature. Therefore, perhaps it is not surprising that such tension and differences exist within this area of work. What does this mean in terms of this book, which is about the children raised in sects?

STUDYING SECTS FROM A PSYCHOLOGICAL PERSPECTIVE

As a starting point, I accept that perhaps not all sects are 'bad' or 'harmful' to existing or former members. However, there is a credible body of research indicating that some sects do produce damaging and pathological experiences among some current and former members. The association of 'sect' with religious experience and belief does not prevent the psychological examination and understanding of these experiences and the potential means of support and treatment. The acknowledged possibility that child abuse is part of these damaging experiences also makes this area of study imperative. Further, some people who leave these groups feel very affected by their experiences and these people need to know that others care about what has happened to them and there are other people who have had similar, though obviously not identical, experiences.

Where does the information referred to in this book come from?

Study of Jonestown and Centrepoint

In addition to quoting from autobiographies, and occasionally journalists, this book includes much of the research available at the present time on those raised in sects. For example, a book entitled 'The Children of Jonestown' by Kenneth Wooden[4] is referred to, which documents the lives and deaths of children in this sect. Sadly, this sect ended as a result of the murder of the 260 children and, the cyanide poisonings of over 900 people, in total, which were carried out under the direction of Jim Jones in Guyana in 1978.

This book also discusses key research, including a study conducted in New Zealand on Centrepoints, a so-called spiritual and therapeutic community. Researchers[5] interviewed and produced a report on 29 of the 200–300 former members who had spent all or part of their childhood in this group.

Author's PhD thesis

Harry's Sect and Ted's Sect
Much of this book is taken from my PhD thesis[6], which involved a series of studies including those of two groups, which were given the pseudonyms 'Harry's Sect' and 'Ted's Sect'. Harry's Sect was a Bible-based group with around 100 members. Ted's Sect was a small Buddhist-based, hand-reading (reading the lines on your hand to tell you who you are and what you are like[7]), yoga and karate group. Quotes from former members of both these groups are used throughout this book. For more information, please refer to the original thesis' entitled: 'A Psychological Exploration into the Effects of Former Membership of 'Extremist Authoritarian Sects.''

Data from Wellspring Retreat and Resource Centre
For my PhD, I utilised data from a sample of individuals who had
sought help at Wellspring Retreat and Resource Centre in the US.
Wellspring is based in Ohio in the USA. It was one of the few residential rehabilitation centres in the world for former members of sects.
Wellspring delivered a one or two-week residential programme, which
included individual counselling and group educational workshops.
Those entering treatment at Wellspring fill in psychometric tests
(chosen to measure the types of symptoms that former members have
been reported to have) upon their arrival, when they leave Wellspring
two weeks later and again six months after leaving. My PhD also involved utilising psychometric testing with former sect members who
had come out of groups in the UK.

WHAT HAS IMPACTED THE WRITING STYLE OF THIS BOOK?

ACKNOWLEDGING IN MY WRITING THE PAIN AND HURT SUFFERED BY MANY

While this book is based on scientific studies, research and first-hand
accounts of experience, and while I tried to write my PhD in an objective fashion, it has also become apparent to me that in the face of such
suffering, it would be callous of me to continuously write purely from
a disinterested academic perspective without acknowledging the pain
and hurt suffered by so many. Thus, while maintaining the integrity
of the academic content of my work, I have both tried to write in an
accessible fashion, and I relate to the words of Louis Theroux,[8] who
says this about his second documentary on a group that he refers to as
a church, which many would consider a sect:

> 'Another surprise was how much I had personalised the story
> by this time. My role in returning to the church had changed
> somehow. I was no longer a disinterested journalist. I'd seen

too much. It was more like going to see family members with whom one has fallen out, with the same sense of rawness and exasperation.... I am fair in the film, but it is no good me pretending I don't understand the human cost of what they are engaged in.'

Growing up in a sect

Even more so than a journalist, I feel an affinity with second-generation former members because I am one. I think of second generation former members as my peers, often I see them as my friends, as a group of people who understand where I come from. A number of those reading this book will want to know of my personal experiences growing up in a sect. In the preface, I discuss briefly how I came to write this book. I grew up in Harry's Sect, and as such, some of what is written about in this book I have personal experience of. However, this book is not an autobiographical account, and if it was, it would not represent the breadth of experiences of children raised in sects.

The poetry in this book

The poetry included in this book is written by me, but is an amalgamation of what I have heard, read and seen, over the years. This is even the case sometimes when I write in the first person. Therefore, while I do on occasion in this book refer to some of my own experiences, including in parts of the poetry, I do so sparingly and in the hope that they will assist the reader to understand what I am trying to communicate.

Academic controversies that affect children

Polarisation

The study of sects has been plagued by polarisation of the field among academics, with both sides claiming human rights as their cause[9] and with children sometimes stuck in the middle as collateral damage. One side, mostly sociologists, maintains that freedom of expression must be guaranteed to any group[10]. The other side states that the members' human rights are violated.[11] This is partly because of the different perspectives from which such sects are studied. It is mostly psychologists and mental health professionals who work directly with former members, and who claim that sect members are recruited into sects using undue influence, and that sects are harmful.[12] These academics and professionals have been labelled 'anti-cultists'. Conversely, there are those who, examining the perceived benefits of sects – mainly sociologists – who have been labelled 'cult apologists', 'cult sympathisers' 'pro-cultists' and 'defenders of the sects'. However, different individuals mean different things when they use the term 'cult apologist'.[13]

DEPROGRAMMING AND EXIT COUNSELLING
Some of the initial concern of academics stemmed from the 1970s when some members of sects were being kidnapped from groups and held against their will to ensure that they relinquished ties to the sect. (Although this method seems extreme by today's standards, parents often took this step because of the radical changes that they were seeing in the behaviour of their children.) More recently, *exit counselling*, which includes voluntary participation by a current sect member, is based on respectful communication,[14] and has been advocated by those concerned about individuals' involvement in sects.[15]

FURTHER COMPLICATIONS AND EXAGGERATIONS
The appearance of both sides in courts of law has further complicated this area.[16] It is simplistic to portray sects as either purely harmful or good.[17] While much has been written on the topic of sects from both perspectives, most of the discussion involves opinion rather than actual research.[18] According to Thomas Robbins, 'Some of the allegations against "destructive cults" may be exaggerated'.[19] I would add that, conversely, it is also possible that some of the claims to psychological

well-being and an absence of harm during and after sect membership may also be exaggerated.

EVIDENCE OF HARM AND DISTRESS

If one looks at research on post-traumatic stress disorder, for example in war veterans, we find that individuals interpret evidence of harm found after these events as harm occurring due to the experience rather than to personality types or problems that existed prior to them entering the armed forces. It would be unethical to set up a controlled experiment examining the distress and harm caused to an individual who has experienced adverse life experiences. It is possible to explain evidence of harm after sect membership as evidence of harm due to the processes occurring in sects (which might also make existing problems worse), and yet research can also examine risk factors for individuals who develop psychological distress after sect membership. Children born into sects have no pre-sect environment. Harm found in sect members after leaving may be a result of the sect experience, the experience of leaving, experiences after the sect, or a combination of all three.

HOW THESE DEBATES AFFECT CHILDREN

Children raised in sects are probably, for the most part, completely oblivious to these debates. However, what happens in sects, and how communities and societies respond to sects, may affect the children the most. Further, children and young people who leave a sect may chance upon a book written by an academic about the group in which they were raised and if they have had painful experiences as a result of a group, experienced separation issues, abuse and/or neglect, it may be very unhelpful or even harmful to discover that academics are producing research that fails to reflect theirs and their peers' experience of the group. One of the reasons put forward for the harm occurring to veterans of the Vietnam War was the response they received when they returned to the US. Similarly, the types of responses that those raised in sects receive from the mainstream society, which they enter after leaving a sect, may affect how difficult or straightforward it is for them to process and move on from the experience of having been raised in a sect.

SUPPRESSION OF RESEARCH

Reliability of research in this field may be thwarted by the fact that some sects use less-than-ethical means to suppress adverse publications about themselves or control researchers' access to information as a condition of access to the group and its members. This means that scholarly research, including research about the experience of children in a group, may not be published or even begun due to intimidation or other less-than-savoury reasons[20] Sometimes groups attempt to suppress the freedom of speech of both former members of the group, including those who have grown up in the group, and of social scientists.[21] There is a great need for 'agenda-free research' to be conducted[22], since without it, little progress will be made in increasing understanding of how sects affect children.

SUPPRESSING THE VOICE OF CHILDREN/YOUTH WHILE THEY ARE IN AND AFTER LEAVING SECTS

Children raised in some sects have silence restrictions put upon them while they are in the group, and may well have lacked freedom of expression. This is explained in more detail in the later chapter on abuse and neglect of children in sects. If they leave the sect in which they were raised, and again experience a lack of freedom of expression because a group attempts to suppress their freedom of expression and because of the non-belief by those around them or by social scientists writing in the field, it could be harmful to them, and this painful experience may echo their childhood. Due to its impact on children, young people and others, censorship cannot continue, and researchers must ensure that they do not become merely those who repeat the propaganda, or become academic supporters of sects.[23]

Censorship must stop

In addition to the voice of children and young people being suppressed by academics there are sometimes other problems with censorship and bias in academic work. Some researchers have received funding from the groups they are studying and have not stated this when presenting their findings.[24] If funding relies on the groups being studied, then conclusions drawn from these studies may be biased towards the group in question, in turn this may impact the children of the group, both while they are involved in it and if and when they leave. The issue of not being clear about where the research funding has come from is even more problematic, as it does not allow a reader to judge to what extent receiving funds may have affected the research. Ethical problems such as these have only served to polarise the field further and to create even more mistrust and suspicion.

Summary of the introduction

This is a book written about the second generation for the second generation. It is a book based on research; a rewrite of my PhD with some of the more technical parts omitted, other research and quotes from autobiographies, as well as a little of my own poetry added. I too was raised in a sect, and while this book sparingly refers to my own experiences in my poems, I also utilise poetic license and my knowledge and understanding, gleaned from my reading, interviews and many other interactions with former sect members.

The book is written so that those who have grown up in sects and left and who feel very affected by their experiences will know that they are not alone, there are others to relate to who have also suffered. I have briefly referred to the suppression of research and polarisation which has occurred in studies of this field. However, this book is not a focus on debates of this kind, as in the most part, those who have been raised in sects are probably unaware of these discussions. These issues might impact the second generation, if they chance upon a book written by an academic that does not reflect their experience, particularly when their group experiences include, separation, neglect or abuse. Addressing this imbalance within this book I include a focus on these issues in later chapters. I also make clear that those raised in sects often lack freedom of expression and it is imperative that both former members and social scientists are able to put into the public domain information about the experiences of those who have been in sects.

What comes next in Chapter 1?

The next chapter provides a more in-depth look at how different people define the word, sect or cult. While use of these terms can be helpful for some, for others the use of these words can be very difficult, as is clear from the quote from a former member who was raised in Harry's Sect below:

> *I can remember one particular occasion, talking to my older brother, who also left as well. He had not remained a Christian, but he had left, and I remember talking to him. Suddenly it became crystal clear that it was a cult, and I could allow myself to think that without invoking the wrath of God or something for thinking that.*

So how long after you actually [left]?

> *That was probably about two years.*[25]

CHAPTER 1

WHAT IS A SECT?

1994 was when Ted's Sect went into a phase where it was most obviously a cult.[26]

OVERVIEW OF CHAPTER 1

IN THIS CHAPTER I will discuss the different terms used in this area and describe why I use the term 'sect'. The chapter will also provide a number of psychological definitions used by others for the word 'cult', and briefly describe what is meant by the term 'thought reform', which is sometimes incorporated in those definitions. I will then look at the Group Psychological Abuse Scale and discuss whether some groups might be abusive in some respects, but in other ways may be positive. Finally, I will take an in-depth look at the definition of the term 'extremist authoritarian sects' which is discussed here with reference to relevant psychological literature.

WHY USE THE WORD 'SECT', RATHER THAN 'CULT' OR 'NEW RELIGIOUS MOVEMENT' IN THIS BOOK?

CULT

Researchers have used a variety of terms to describe extremist authoritarian sects (abbreviated to sects in this book). These include 'cults', 'new religious movements', 'isolated religious communities' and 'high-demand groups'. Former members, including children raised in groups, may well not initially identify their group as a sect, cult or New Religious Movement.

Despite popular usage of the word 'cult' by the general public, many who work in the field view it with some misgiving.[27] Academics often regard it as an emotive word, loaded with negative meaning and stereotypes[28]. In a study of 98 undergraduates in the USA, Jeffrey Pfeifer[29] found that most undergraduates had very little direct knowledge of what a cult actually was and based their negative evaluations on sensationalised media reports. Nevertheless, any term used to categorise groups such as Jonestown or David Koresh's Branch Davidians would quickly gain a very negative association due to the highly disturbing events that have happened in these groups. John Saliba[30] goes so far as to say that the word cult is 'so laden with diverse meanings and replete with emotional content that it might have lost one of the major functions of linguistic designation, that is, to convey accurate and useful information'. Michael Langone[31] points out that, while the concept of the word 'cult' is fuzzy, the same could be said for many other terms in our language (e.g. 'child abuse'), yet we continue to use these terms.

NEW RELIGIOUS MOVEMENTS

One popular alternative to the word 'cult' in academia[32] is the label 'new religious movements' (NRMs). However, some groups fitting a psychological definition of a cult could hardly be described as new[33]. For example, the Exclusive Brethren (including the Taylorite Branch, the Plymouth Brethren and the Closed Brethren; in USA, classified as Plymouth Brethren IV[34]) had its origins in Dublin in the late 1820s and cannot be considered new. Defining the word 'movement' also presents difficulties. Michael Langone[35] states that most cults are small: a group with no more than a few hundred members worldwide can hardly be described as a 'movement'. The term 'new religious movement' also presents a problem, as do the phrases 'new religions' and 'isolated religious communities', in that not all cults are religious in nature.[36]

Researchers often use different definitions for sects, cults and NRMs.[37] This makes comparisons between studies difficult at best and may mean that those engaged in discussion of cult phenomena are sometimes talking at cross-purposes. For example, Eileen Barker[38] uses the term 'new religious movements' (NRMs) as referring to 'those groups, movements or organisations that have been called 'alternative religions', 'non-conventional religions', or contemporary sects. James Beckford and Martine Levasseur[39], though acknowledging problems with the term NRM, define NRMs as 'organised attempts to mobilise human and material resources for the purpose of spreading new ideologies and sensibilities of a religious nature. They are therefore intentional, collective and historically specific'. Margaret Singer,[40] however, would define only some of these groups as cults, and her definition of a cult includes groups that are completely non-religious, including some that could be described as political, self-help, self-improvement, lifestyle and racial types of groups.

On the difficulty of definition, John Saliba[41] states that, when defining a cult or new religious group, the broadness and range of religious and non-religious phenomena that the definition is likely to encompass is immense. He suggests that we stop using the word 'cult' as these groups' 'nature, characteristics, significance, and implications cannot be summarised in, much less determined by, a single definition'.[42] Arguably, a new set of words is needed with observable and measurable boundaries to define the broad range of cult-type groups present in societies. Until such a time as we have a new set of words, then we have to continue to use existing words, no matter how imperfect they are.

SECT

The word 'sect' is often used among English speakers to describe these groups. 'Sect' does not have the negative connotations of the word 'cult'. Therefore its use will, hopefully, allow this book to be read with less pre-existing prejudice than may occur if the word 'cult' is used. 'Sect' is a short form of the term 'extremist authoritarian sects'.[43] A downside to this term is that it has been traditionally used to refer to religious groups, however, I also use the term to refer to groups that may have a non-religious ideology but whose ideology is held in such a way that it is similar to a religious belief, as in the case of some of the so-called therapeutic communities discussed in this book. My use of the term 'sect' is defined at length in the latter part of this chapter, however it is worth noting here that the term is not used in the traditional sociological sense [e.g. a fervent splinter group from a church[44]]; rather, it refers to extremist authoritarian sects that are often known as cults, new religions or high-demand groups.

WHAT IS A CULT OR A SECT?

The core defining feature of cults and sects is control.[45] How exactly that control manifests itself will differ from one group to the next. Definitions of sects and cults outside the field of religious studies[46] do not generally include the belief system of the sect, but do require evidence of undue influence, and sometimes also incorporate psychological, physical, emotional or financial harm.

DEFINITION OF CULTS FROM A PSYCHOLOGICAL PERSPECTIVE

Michael Langone's definition
A psychological definition of sects or cults that does not depend on the beliefs of a group has been put forward by Michael Langone. He defines a cult as a group or movement that, to a significant degree:

4

'(a) exhibits great or excessive devotion or dedication to some person, idea, or thing:

(b) uses a thought-reform program to persuade, control and socialise members (i.e., to integrate them into the group's unique pattern of relationships, beliefs, values and practices[47]):

(c) systematically induces states of psychological dependency in members:

(d) exploits members to advance the leadership's goals; and

(e) causes psychological harm to members, their families and the community.'[48]

Margaret Singer's definition

Margaret Singer[49], a psychiatrist who did a lot of early work and writing in this area, states that for her purposes, a sect (she uses the word 'cult') refers to three factors.

Firstly, she looks at the origin of the group, and specifically the role of the leader. She argues that sects have leaders who claim to have extraordinary knowledge and a special mission in life. They are self-chosen, persuasive persons who are also single-minded, domineering, charismatic, and centre veneration on themselves.

Secondly, she points to the power structure in sects, i.e. the relationship between the leader (or leaders) and the members. She notes that sects are authoritarian, exclusive, novel and tend to employ a double standard of ethics.

Thirdly, Margaret Singer states that sects use a coordinated programme of persuasion, which she identifies as 'thought reform'.[50] She argues that sects have a propensity towards being totalistic and are all-encompassing in controlling their members' behaviour. She explains that they demonstrate extremism in their world view as well as usually requiring members to undergo a major disruption or transformation of their lifestyle.

Robert Lifton's view of thought reform
Many definitions of cults have incorporated the concept of thought reform-sometimes referred to as mind control or brainwashing. Thought reform was a theory originally proposed by the psychiatrist Robert Lifton[51] as a result of his research in prisoner-of-war settings. He found eight conditions that define thought-reform, resulting from what he called 'ideological totalism' which is where everything has to be experienced on an all-or-nothing-at-all basis.

Robert Lifton's notion of thought reform has proven to be enormously useful to former members of sects trying to understand the environments that they came out of. Leona Furnari[52] has applied Robert Lifton's thought reform themes to the development of children in sects. Her ideas are particularly relevant to the purpose of this book:

1. 'Milieu Control – The control of communication within an environment; builds unhealthy boundaries. Parents may be given directives about parenting do's and don'ts: Don't hold children; don't respond to their cries; Do keep them quiet; Don't be attached to them. The message children receive is "my needs are not okay" or "I am not important" "I am not safe" which is essentially dispensing of existence. Infants learn that they cannot trust that their needs will be met.

2. Mystical Manipulation – "Divine authority" mandates dysfunctional and/or abusive parenting. This authority allows any means towards a "higher end" or goal. Verbal and non-verbal messages are given to infants that interfere with the development of trust.

3. Demand for Purity – Absolute separation of good and evil within self and within the environment. Good children behave in proscribed ways and do not "act" like children.

Children are often forced to participate in rituals that are not age-appropriate. Shame and doubt interfere with development of autonomy or the belief that it's okay to think and feel for oneself.

4. The Cult of Confession – One-on-one or group confession (by child or on behalf of child) for the purpose of humiliating the confessor and creating dependency upon the leader for one's definition of goodness. Humiliation discourages risk-taking; the child develops a sense of guilt and is fearful of exhibiting initiative.

5. Sacred Science and Doctrine over Person – The teachings of the CHDG [closed high-demand group] and/or leader is the Ultimate Truth that allows for no questioning. The individual is always inferior to the Ultimate Truth of the group or leader(s). This necessitates denial of self and self-perception. When parents or caretakers encourage a child to become self-directed the child develops a sense of competence. The inability to question or to value one's own ideas lead to the development of inferiority. The child is always secondary to the doctrine or leader(s).

6. Dispensing of Existence – Anyone not in the group or not embracing the "truth" is insignificant, not "saved," or "unconscious"; the outside world or members who leave the group are rejected. The developmental tasks of adolescents are to separate from their caretakers and create their own identity. This cannot be done without thinking for oneself and adopting one's own set of values. Yet to do so in a cultic environment is tantamount to rejecting "Truth". The only way to survive is to dispense of self.

7. Loading of the Language – Use of terms, jargon that have group-specific meaning; phrases that will keep one in, or bring one back into, the cult mindset. In the case of a child growing up in a thought reform environment theses

meanings are the only ones the child will learn. The loaded language is the child's first language. Upon leaving the group an adolescent or adult questions his or her competence at understanding the language, behaviours, and customs of the culture.'[53]

Debate about the thought-reform model

Some have criticised the concept of mind control and thought reform as non-scientific.[54] Others have strongly defended the concept (or variations of it).[55] While some (but not all) of those raised in sects see explanations of thought reform as helpful, it may also be potentially useful in terms of understanding our parents and why they behaved in certain ways. However, some of those raised in sects see the model of thought reform and mind control as used by the parents and first -generation to abdicate responsibility for their actions while in a sect. However, if mind control is seen as the main mechanism present in sects, then it is clearly not 100% effective, 100% of the time, as many people still leave sects. In terms of responsibility, there are probably a great deal of differences between how much or how little people are responsible while they are being influenced in sect environments. The concept of diminished responsibility might be useful to consider in trying to understand the actions of those who were or are heavily influenced by totalistic environments.

The Group Psychological Abuse Scale: a continuum

The Group Psychological Abuse Scale was developed by researchers to try and measure the factors in groups, as well as which specific groups were evidencing group psychological abuse. Groups can be very positive places since no person operates well in isolation, and many people have excellent experiences of groups. Groups can also be innocuous in some respects, yet display sect-like characteristics in other respects, and be positive in other respects.[56]

Some researchers in psychology place abuse or harm (particularly, what is termed 'group psychological abuse') at one end of the range, and very positive results at the other end.[57] Further, groups don't stay static, but may move in one or the other direction on the scale, or continuum (range) as shown in Figure 1.1.

Figure 1.1 Showing continuum for group abuse or harm

For example, groups discussed in this book include Centrepoint and the Hare Krishna. In both groups there was sexual abuse of some children. However, both of these groups are recorded as having changed significantly in more recent years.[58]

THE DEFINITIONAL APPROACH TAKEN IN THIS BOOK
The definitional approach which I will use in this book is that of Christian Szurko, who defines Extremist Authoritarian Sects as having three characteristics that are most likely to have a harmful effect on those closest to them: extremism, authoritarianism and sectarianism. Each of these will now be discussed in turn.

Extremism

'is the tendency to reduce all situations to simple black-and-white decisions that reinforce the "rightness" of the group's leader and the "wrongness" of dissent. As a part of this the sect often presents its teaching in a context which suggests that uncertainty = unbelief, and unbelief = sin. This has the effect of stifling questions and driving members towards unconditional and unreasoning commitment. It also can produce intolerance of others, especially outsiders.'[59]

Children naturally ask questions, and to be in an environment where they experience this repression of freedom of expression and the stifling of their minds can be very difficult.

The leader's control and dominance of the members of the group emerges at the heart of the dynamics of both Harry's Sect and Ted's Sect (more details on both these sects can be found in the Introduction section of this book), and has been found in many sects. Control has been found to be strongly linked to anxiety.[60] Mike Finch, a first-generation former member, who wrote an autobiography entitled '*Without the Guru: How I took my life back after thirty years*[61]', explains well the cycle of reinforcement between a guru and his followers, and the seductive nature of adoration. Domination and control link into the idealisation of the leaders. The idealisation of leaders and the control of followers by leaders can be explained in the context of being traumatised and the subsequent idealisation of an abuser by a victim.[62]

The successful implementation of a swathe of social influence processes and abuse, including dependency on the leader, maintain the control and dominance. One former member explained that their leader: '*demanded 100% loyalty*'.[63]

Authoritarianism

'is the tendency by members to depend solely upon the leader(s) for the data by which decisions are made, and convictions are arrived at. Initially this may be subtly encouraged by holding up as examples those who never question the leader(s), but in a number of groups authoritarianism is openly enforced by blatant condemnations of "independent thinking", "individualism", and similar expressions. Hand in hand with this is the frequent practice of certain groups of withholding information which new recruits need in order to decide intelligently about the nature and extent of their involvement in the group.'[64]

A child's parents may not have full knowledge of the group they bring their children into. Further, the children's intellectual development may be stunted if their thinking is condemned and they are encouraged to believe illogical arguments. This problem is expanded on in Chapter 7.

Obeying leaders is a common theme in sects, but this has also been studied in the general population. Stanley Milgram wanted to understand how and why the Nazis were able to exterminate so many people during WWII. He therefore set up psychological experiments to test the extent, if any, to which different people would obey authority figures. He had people (participants) deliver higher and higher levels of electric shocks to an actor (learner) under the orders of an authority figure (no shocks were actually delivered) (experimenter). Milgram and other researchers have found that individuals would cause harm to others when given the order, even when they had the opportunity to consider the implications of their actions away from the actual presence of the authority figure.[65]

Milgram's study has been reproduced in at least seven different Western countries, also Japan[66]. Results of this cross-cultural research, which incorporated various modifications of the experimental design, found that levels of obedience can differ considerably, and slight changes in the environment that define the meaning of the orders given by the authority figure, will mean people obey them to varying degrees.

More recently Milgram's findings have been challenged, rather than people just blindly following authority figures an "individuals' willingness to follow authority figures is conditional on identification with the authority in question and an associated belief that the authority is right."[67]

Present in both Ted's Sect and Harry's Sect members was the tendency not just to obey authority figures, but to also see authority figures as being right, which links into the concept of extremism. Examples from Ted's Sect of the extent of the obedience to leadership and leadership underlining the view that they are right and that members should have an elevated view of the leaders are given below:

> ... *I was given a list of rules by which to live, and one of them was I'd have to be exactly what Darren says, because I don't know....* [68]

> *Darren knew, apparently that Ted made some of his students do prostrations to Ted– not the shrine. Not to Buddha. That's a bit odd.* [69]

This may contribute to post-sect findings of felt guilt and harm experienced by former members, particularly after they spent some time outside of the sect, when they may change, and no longer see the leader as right or in the case of the first generation, they may again morally restructure (reverting back to the view that the immoral is actually immoral as discussed further in chapter four). Those who have caused harm to others and have violated their own moral code have been found to suffer ill effects themselves, in the form of Post Traumatic Stress Disorder symptoms induced by toxic levels of guilt and shame.[70]

In fact, such was the distress experienced by those who participated in Milgram's studies, despite their being debriefed regarding the research, that new ethical guidelines were introduced to avoid future research participants experiencing this. Because of the harm caused to participants, the deception of participants, and issues around participants right to withdraw from the study, Milgram's study is often used when teaching ethics to psychology students as an example of an unethical study[71]. However, Alexander Haslam and Stephen Reicher who have challenged Stanley Milgrams findings, state that in Milgrams study:

> 'rather than being distressed by their actions, participants could be led to construe them as "service" in the cause of "goodness"'[72].

I.e. through moral restructuring the immoral became moral. This was because scientific progress was seen as justification for the electric shocks that participants thought they were delivering to the learner. Thus rather than simple blind obedience it was important that research participants believed in the importance of what they were doing. This may have similarities to the way parents of those raised in sects may genuinely believe that they are saving the world and achieving a greater good by their time in the sect. What follows is a quote from Alexander Haslam and Stephen Reicher[73] about the study by Stanley Milgram which is very interesting in light of children and parents in sects:

> 'Furthermore, close analysis of the experimental sessions shows that participants are attentive to the demands made on them by the Learner as well as the Experimenter[74]. They are torn between two voices confronting them with irreconcilable moral imperatives, and the fact that they have to choose between them is a source of considerable anguish. They sweat, they laugh, they try to talk and argue their way out of the situation. But the experimental set-up does not allow them to do so. Ultimately, they tend to go along with the Experimenter if he justifies their actions in terms of the scientific benefits of the study (as he does with the prod "The experiment requires that you continue")[75]. But if he gives them a direct order ("You have no other choice, you must go on") participants typically

refuse. Once again, received wisdom proves questionable. The Milgram studies seem to be less about people blindly conforming to orders than about getting people to believe in the importance of what they are doing.'[76]

While some parents in sects are able to provide a caring and supportive environment for their children, some do not. Of those who do not, some parents after leaving do not express a sense of remorse either for what they did or failed to do, and parents still involved in sects may feel no remorse at all. This may result in difficulties in the relationship between parents and the second generation when both have left the sect. Moral restructuring is discussed further in Chapter Four. Some parents after the sect have an overriding sense of guilt about the treatment of their children in the sect. The difficulties in relationship between parents and their adult second-generation children are discussed further in the final chapter of this book.

Developmental regression describes how an adult or teenager might start acting a much younger age, thereby resembling how a child might behave as opposed to an adult. In Ted's Sect and Harry's Sect, the obedience was coupled with developmental regression that seemed evident in the members. Both obedience and regression are potentially mutually reinforcing. Obeying leaders to the extent that the members obeyed in these sects may relate back to their earlier ways of relating to parents. Simultaneously, regressing to earlier developmental states is likely to mean that the members will obey the leaders.

Sectarianism

'is the tendency of the leadership to exercise its considerable authority to isolate members from a wide variety of people whom that leadership may stigmatize as "unspiritual", "demonic", "backward thinking", "left brain", "Piscean", "reactionary",

14

and other dismissive terms. Side-by-side with this they will often use negative language about outsiders (which may include immediate family unless they are sympathetic to the sect), and exalted language about the group, like "God's SAS". "True Family", "the Initiates", "gods", "the Inner Circle".[77]

The isolation of children from the wider society can make it particularly hard for young adults and children who step into mainstream culture when they leave sects. This is further discussed in Chapter Seven.

People can be dependent on alcohol, drugs, etc. In the case of sects, people (followers) are dependent on leader(s). Systematic induction into states of dependency occurs in sects.[78] An example of this is given below:

> *If he smiled at us, it was almost as though, through him, God was smiling at us, so he was effectively acting as a priest, a very powerful priest in a sense, that my state of well-being was influenced to quite a large extent by my perception of his feelings towards me, so he could actually wield quite an influence, you know, and get me to do what he wanted to, because one felt one wanted to please him . . .[79]*

What appeared to result in a particularly high level of dependence in members was that reported abuse would be followed by love and attention, as discussed by a Ted's Sect participant discussing the behaviour of a leader:

> *Extremely harsh, followed by love and attention. You never knew where you were, you never knew what mood he was going to be in, and his approval was everything.[80]*

These interview reports support theories of traumatic bonding.[81] Those relationships were characterised by an imbalance of power and the alteration of 'good' and 'bad' treatment, resulting in the subordinate and dominant person becoming increasingly dependent upon each other. The feeling of never knowing how one was about to be treated in the sect can continue after the sect, and may contribute to high levels of anxiety in former members, when interacting in the wider society outside.[82]

Unhealthy dependency is also present in women who are battered by their husbands, and that bonding between a woman and her partner has also been referred to as 'traumatic bonding'.[83] In the case of battered-women syndrome, physical and emotional abuse by the dominant partner results in the maintenance of the power imbalance.[84] Parallels have been found between domestic violence and sects.[85] Children in sects are, however, dependent on the adults around them for their survival, and they cannot leave, therefore in some sects, rather than children experiencing the alteration of 'good' and 'bad' treatment, they may only receive 'bad' treatment.

> The extent of the dependency of members in Harry's Sect and Ted's Sect on the leadership is perhaps best shown by the fact that some individuals in both sects ended up not believing what their own eyes had seen.

In Harry's Sect, one woman described disbelieving what her own eyes had seen and just thought it was her own nasty mind.[86] In Ted's Sect, some members challenged the *dojo* (a *dojo* is a place designated for training) leader and he convinced them they had not seen what they had thought they had seen.[87] Both these events involved acts of sexual intimacy between the leader and a female sect member.

Links between dependency relations and the developmental regression of individuals have been identified. In a prison experiment, study researchers described a network of dependency relations that not only promoted helplessness but also resulted in an 'emasculation' of prisoners. In turn, these relations led to a prisoner's tendency to regress to earlier child-like ways of being.[88]

SUMMARY OF CHAPTER 1

There are a quite a number of definitions of sects and cults that exist, one of their defining features is control. There are a number of psychological definitions of the word 'cult' and sometimes thought reform or mind control forms the basis of definitions. In this instance, however, thought reform is addressed from the perspective of children and their development and then from the perspective of the second generation and how they sometimes view it in connection to parents and responsibility.

Every group is different. The Group Psychological Abuse Scale seeks to measure group abuse and how groups differ in this regard. The definition that I used in my PhD thesis for these groups came under the term Extremist Authoritarian Sects, which in short was:

> Extremism 'is the tendency to reduce all situations to simple black-and-white decisions that reinforce the 'rightness' of the group's leader and the 'wrongness' of dissent...'[89]

> Authoritarianism 'is the tendency by members to depend solely upon the leader(s) for the data by which decisions are made, and convictions are arrived at.... Hand in hand with this is the frequent practice of certain groups of withholding information which new recruits need in order to decide intelligently about the nature and extent of their involvement in the group.'[90]

> Sectarianism 'is the tendency of the leadership to exercise its considerable authority to isolate members from a wide variety

of people whom that leadership may stigmatize. Side-by-side with this they will often use negative language about outsiders... and exalted language about the group...'[91]

This definition can be placed and discussed in the context of existing psychological literature, such as dependency and Stanley Milgram's studies on obedience to authority figures.

What comes next in Chapter 2?

In this book I use the term 'second generation' to refer to those born into sects, brought in as children by their parents or those who joined as children under 16 years of age. Chapter 2 will look at how the parents of those raised in sects come to be in them, what attracted them to the sect and why they raised their children in the sect. There are also parents who unwittingly send their children to sect schools. This happened to Sarah Jones,[92] who records in her autobiography 'Call Me Evil, Let Me Go' that she was sent many miles from home to a church school by her parents. Talking about her parents in her description of the book, she states that:

> They had no idea they were sending Sarah to a place where she would be forced into obedience - a place that sanctioned force-feeding and beating in order to smash a child's will. They had no idea she would end up marrying a boy from the cult, and cutting the rest of her family out of her life. Or that she would begin to treat her own children in the same way - believing there was no other option, and that everyone in the outside world was evil.[93]

CHAPTER 2

How did I get here?

Patricia Hochstetler describes in her autobiography 'Delusion':

My parents wanted the best for me and tried to protect me from the evil in the world around them. They wanted a better life for their children than the ones they had. That choice meant exile for me and my siblings in a colony far away from what my folks considered to be an ungodly society (Patricia Hochstetler, 2007, p16).

Overview

I, like many others, because of my parents' sect membership, was born into a sect. Some children, like Patricia Hochstetler above, are brought into a sect by parents. As parents are usually instrumental to how children come to be in sects, this chapter will look at why adults become involved with sects and whether there is a particular personality type who join, and will also consider whether parents could be described as psychologically damaged in some way before they get involved in sects. The chapter will highlight the absent 'second generation' and will explain the reasons as to why, in some groups, there are no children, despite many of the women being of child-bearing age.

How many people are in sects at some point in their life?

In the 1950s, there was a reported upsurge in the number of sects, with numbers of members of these groups increasing in the 1960s and 1970s, including through the birth of children to members.[94] In 2005, one individual estimated that there were 1.25 million children being raised in sects in the US.[95] There are a number of differing estimates regarding the percentage of people who have spent time in a sect at some point in their lives. Two studies were carried out in Montreal using a very broad definition of the terms 'new religious' and 'para-religious' movements (i.e., they included some groups not fitting the definition of sect as used in this book). These studies[96] concluded that around 18% to 22% of the adult population had been involved in these movements at one time or another, but typically, individuals were only involved for short periods.

A review of the studies looking at sect membership concluded that around 2% of the US population have been involved in sects at some time in their lives.[97] A summary of the limited European and US prevalence studies that have been conducted over the past two decades conservatively concluded that around 1% of the population are involved in sects at some point in their lives.[98] However, the number could be significantly higher than this, particularly when micro groups are taken into consideration which may not come to anyone's attention.

WHY DID MY PARENTS BECOME INVOLVED IN THIS GROUP?

This and related questions may arise at some point in the minds of children, adolescents and adults raised in sects. Not all of those raised in sects have the opportunity to ask their parent/s this question, and often we give simplistic answers when the true answer involves multiple reasons.

FIRST GENERATION BECOMING INVOLVED IN A SECT

Some parents state that they did not join the sect by choice, rather they were recruited into the sect. The sensitivity of the first generation to the issue of whether they were recruited or joined a sect becomes clearer when we consider why a response like the one below might come from a former member:

I belonged to the . . . [Sect] for about 10 years. I have seen and experienced many remarkable things but the most remarkable thing for me has been the discovery that I have been the butt of a devastating hoax. The pain was so deep, and the realisation that I have been taken for a ride, so embarrassing,…[99]

This former member went onto describe his sect experience as a '*major life disaster*'.[100]

THE PARENTS OF THE FIRST- GENERATION

It may also be a sensitive area for the parents of the first generation. Parents of the first generation may respond in a variety of ways to their adult children joining a sect, and they may witness their adult children changing significantly. For example, adult children may drop out of university, become very judgemental, constantly quote the teachings of the group, and become alienated from their parents. The parents of the first generation may feel a whole mix of emotions, including feeling very distressed, anxious, powerless and concerned for their adult children and grandchildren in the sect. There may feel a strong sense of frustration and hopelessness. If contact is cut by the adult child in the sect, they may wonder if they will ever see their children and grandchildren again, or indeed they may long to meet their own grandchildren, but never have the chance. They may feel humiliated and embarrassed by the attitudes and behaviours of their first- generation children; they may feel very angry and yet also feel a great depth of compassion for their adult child. They may wonder if they have been 'bad parents', and the opposite of comfort might be forthcoming from those close to them who are all too ready to subtly or not so subtly express the view that they must have been 'bad parents' for their adult child to join a sect and raise children in that sect.

The children of the first generation

It's tough for those raised in sects who go on to leave, to meet with the realisation that their parents are in fact in a sect. Both the parents of the first generation and their grandchildren - the second generation - may have a common question regarding 'why the first generation became involved in a sect, and why they raised their children in a sect?. Consequently this area will therefore now be addressed in some depth.

Did our parents have emotional problems before they entered the sect?

Where harm is found in those entering sects in adulthood, after someone has left a sect the question remains: How can we be sure that the harm is as a result of the sect membership and not, for instance, a pre-existing condition or the conditions that attracted the individual into the group in the first place?[101]

Review of the literature on Jehovah's Witnesses

One researcher[102], Jerry Berman, carried out a scientific literature review of eight studies on Jehovah's Witnesses. The review included studies of all admissions to psychiatric hospitals in Western Australia; a random sample of Swiss citizens imprisoned because of objection to military service; admissions to all state and private hospitals and local mental health clinics in Ohio from 1972 to 1986; and another four more recent studies, which incorporated a few PhD theses. Problems with the studies regarding the validity of the results comprise the tendency to either over- or under-report the true number of Jehovah's Witnesses with mental health problems. However, where we have a number of studies with different methods, and samples all pointing in one direction, it supports the conclusion that current Jehovah's Witnesses did have a rate of mental illness considerably above average-rates of mental-health illness. The in-depth analysis concluded that 'Although persons with emotional problems tended to join the Jehovah's Witnesses, the Watchtower teachings and its subculture clearly adversely affected the mental health of those involved.'[103]

The Unification Church

One group of researchers[104] asked current members of the Unification Church to fill in a long questionnaire about psychological distress before they joined the sect and how they were now functioning. They found that the current sect members had greater neurotic distress before conversion, which improved after they joined their sect.

Eileen Barker[105] found that 10% of those who attended an introductory Unification Workshop (run by the Moonies) joined the sect (she uses the term NRM), and of those who joined, 50% left within two years. Researchers cite her work as evidence that the 'mind control' or 'thought reform' theory is a fallacy. Otherwise, it is argued, more people approached on the streets would eventually join the Moonies.[106] This is also relevant to the debate regarding pre-sect psychological functioning. Eileen Barker rarely cites Taylor's study of the Moonies[107], which found that slightly more than 50% of the prospects chose to stay beyond the first week.[108] One researcher states that the 10% of those who attend a Moonies' workshop and go on to join the group represents a significant percentage. 'The Moonies approach total strangers on the street, persuade some to come to a free lecture and get a free meal, and then, within a matter of two to three weeks, persuade 10% of those persons to radically alter their lives and become full-time missionaries and fund-raisers for the Unification Church!' [109] This can be compared with the relatively small number of non-believers who attend Billy Graham crusades and subsequently make a decision for Christ.

The chicken-or-the-egg dilemma

Speaking of treatment of former sect members, one clinician put it this way:

'The clinician may be faced with a chicken-or-egg dilemma in attempting to discern whether psychopathology is a function of cult involvement or vice versa. There are no studies which exist which have measured for emotional problems both before someone joins a sect and then measures the same people for emotional problems after they have left the sect. Therefore the question of whether or not the parents of those raised in sects had emotional problems prior to joining the sect may never be fully resolved.'[110]

Some researchers[111] dismiss this tendency to attribute psychological effects found post-membership to reasons for joining the sect as nothing more than blaming the victim. However, it is still the case that if individuals demonstrate higher-than-average levels of psychopathology and mental illness during their pre-sect psychological functioning and experiences, then psychological functioning after individuals have left a sect may be affected.

Results of research on distress prior to becoming involved in sects
There are, in fact, mixed research results regarding whether those who become involved in sects are more 'distressed' or vulnerable than those who do not join sects. One study[112] found 6% to 9% of the Divine Light Mission's and the Unification Church's current members included in their sample had been hospitalised with previous mental health problems prior to joining their groups. Another study[113] traced the history of 520 mostly borderline and schizophrenic patients who had been hospitalised 25 years previously for mental health reasons. Of these, 6% had joined a sect, cult or other religious group at some point after hospitalisation. Research[114] also shows that about one-third of current help-seeking former members had received counselling or therapy before joining, which is slightly higher than the general population in the USA, of whom one-quarter have received counselling or therapy.[115]

The family of origin of those becoming involved in sects
One study[116] that looked at families of origin retrospectively found that the families of sect members had higher-than-average scores on measures of independence, but on other measures they were similar to families with no family member in a sect. Research I conducted found that, overall, those becoming involved in sects did not have significantly different family backgrounds from those joining non-sect-like groups, although the averages were different (as measured by the Family Environment Scale which was a questionnaire about the family environment in which individuals grew up). They score their family environment by looking back at their childhood. Thus, those becoming involved in sects reported a family background that was higher in terms of conflict, as compared to those joining non-sect like groups, but lower in terms of cohesion, expressiveness, independence, achievement, intellectual cultural, active recreational, organisation and control. (For more information on cohesion, expressiveness, etc., please refer to Chapter 3). These differences were not significant.

The first-generation former sect members did, however, score their family background as significantly lower in terms of the amount of moral religious input that they were given, compared with those not joining sects. First-generation joiners also scored psychological maltreatment from parents significantly higher than those who had not joined sects. Nevertheless, there are wide differences in the religious backgrounds and parents of the first generation. Further, family history, prior trauma and prior adjustment have been found to comprise the smallest predictor of Post-Traumatic Stress Disorder and its symptoms.[117]

Clinical observations, in addition to research studies, have found that pre-existing psychological factors or family background did not predict sect involvement.[118] It may also be the case that those joining sects are vulnerable to recruitment and deception, not because of psychopathology, but because of the stage in life at which a sect approaches them. One therapist reports that, in the vast majority of cases, those who become involved in sects are at a stage of life transition.[119] These life transitions include having just begun college; the break-up of a romantic relationship; moving away from one's parents' home; the death of a loved one; the loss of a job; or graduation. However, the reasons for people joining or being recruited into a sect may be more wide-ranging, and further reasons are addressed in the following section on how former members of Harry's Sect and Ted's Sect first heard about the sect and made contact.

The research above indicates that, on the whole, those becoming involved in sects are not more psychologically distressed prior to their sect involvement, and mostly do not have significantly different family backgrounds as compared to those with no family member's in a sect, although more of those who become involved in sects appear to have received counselling than in the general population. Furthermore, the methods of sect recruitment might partially account for sect membership, along with the stage of life an individual is currently at, specifically if someone is at a life transition.

FAMILY BACKGROUND, AND EXPERIENCES OF THE FIRST GENERATION AND PARENTS PRIOR TO BECOMING INVOLVED IN TED'S SECT AND HARRY'S SECT

Looking specifically at two groups, Harry's Sect and Ted's Sect, and the family background of those becoming involved in one of these sects, it appears that certainly there are some who have what they would consider to be a normal family background. Ted's Sect and Harry's Sect were similar to each other in that some of those who became involved reported having a very good relationship with their family of origin before becoming involved in the sect, which may have acted as a buffer for subsequent negative sect experiences. Therefore, they may have been less harmed by experiences in the sect than those who did not have a good relationship with their family of origin before joining the sect.

Some spoke of experiences or relationship difficulties prior to becoming part of the sect that they felt made them susceptible to joining and staying in a sect. For example, of those who joined Ted's Sect, some reported having difficulties in their relationship with their father before joining:[120]

> *My relationship with my dad wasn't good at all. It hadn't been since I hit puberty.[121]*

> *I think a lot of people in Ted's Sect had funny relationships with their fathers, that's my personal opinion, that there was a need for that ... male authority figures in charge, quite paternal as well, it had a particular effect and also when they offer caring and support and direction and understanding and kicks up the bum (laughs). It's funny, because I always in a way wanted my Dad to be angry with me – I wanted some kind of definite response ... [122]*

It may be that those in Ted's Sect were more likely to speak of negative parental experiences prior to sect involvement which attracted them to the sect because of Ted's Sect' focus on criticism of parents. Additionally, a Ted's Sect former member reported that while in the sect, they became critical of their parents because of the sect.[123]

One former Harry's Sect member reported having a depressive personality. Others did not specify any experiences or relationship difficulties that made them likely to join a sect, although this does not mean that this was not the case for some of them. Other former members reported having no emotional problems prior to joining: This was also stated by some former members of Ted's Sect as the following quote from a former Ted's Sect member indicates:

Personally ... people might disagree with me, but I don't think there was that much wrong with me. I was just kind of normal, really, and I just quite naturally got involved.[124]

Is there a particular personality type that become involved in sects?

A major study of current sect members found that there was not a particular personality type that joins sects. Rather, those joining sects had a wide spectrum of personalities before joining. The study[125] by Flavil Yeakley looked at 835 current members of the Boston Church of Christ (part of the International Churches of Christ), as well as other sects and their personality scores on an often-used personality test called the Myers-Briggs Type Indicator (MBTI), which is a personality assessment tool that distinguishes 16 different personality types.

One of the major criticisms of this group had been that they employ methods that produce unwholesome personality changes. The study attempted to show, using psychological testing, whether this was the case or not. Current members of the Boston Church of Christ were asked to fill out the MBTI. Each individual filled in the MBTI three times from three different perspectives – themselves in the present; how they felt they would have answered five years ago; and how they thought they would answer five years into the future, to see if falsification of type (change of personality, so that you become something you are not: a personality type put on over the top of your existing personality to conform to an expected or acceptable personality type) was occurring. Falsification of type occurs when an environment so pressures a person that they change type to become frustrated copies of other people.[126]

Analysis of this data found that members were converging towards a single type, which was the same as the group's leader; although they were a normal group five years earlier (i.e. the same personality distributions as the general population), their present and expected future scores indicated a clear convergence towards a single type. The MBTI was also administered in the same way to 304 members of the Churches of Christ, who are considered not to be a sect and are not part of the International Churches of Christ. Analysis of this data revealed only minor changes in type and no observable patterns in changes. Similar results were found in 150 individuals from five local Christian congregations of different denominations.[127]

The researchers also looked at 30 members from each of six sects, namely, the Church of Scientology, The Hare Krishnas, Maranatha, The Children of God (The Family, The Family of Love), the Unification Church (Moonies), and The Way. A clear pattern emerged. In each of these groups, there was a high level of change in personality types, with members converging towards a single type – that of the leader – in a similar way to the Boston Church of Christ.

A criticism of this study is that the members are filling in personality characteristics for how they perceived themselves five years earlier. Research on memory, and particularly long-term memory, indicates that it is difficult for a person to remember the past clearly.[128] In this instance, those in the Boston Church of Christ are taught to reinterpret their history. They are taught to 'demonise' their past, i.e. view their past in a very negative way. This means that results for the perceived personality change in Boston Church of Christ members may not be entirely accurate. However, such 'demonization' would rely on stereotypical models of the 'unbeliever', and such stereotypes are unlikely to produce the range of personality types that showed up when they were asked to fill in the personality questionnaire for how they felt they would have answered it five years ago.

If personality change really does occur, as the study above seems to suggest, this could affect the psychological health of former and current members of groups. For example, the extent to which one's personality differs from that of the group's 'norm' personality (or, the desired norm within the group), may be significantly related to the amount of negative effects the individual suffers as a result of sect membership. Those whose personality type before membership in the sect is significantly different from the converging type may be more affected than those whose personality type is similar to the sect norm or the sect's desired personality type. However, even a change further into extroversion for an extrovert might have a detrimental effect on the individual.

While members of an average church or group may be expected to display similar attitudes and beliefs about the world and themselves, they also had a wide range of personalities. Indeed, even after religious conversion, mainline denominations typically encourage individuals to become what they are uniquely capable of becoming, although that individual may have changed his or her attitudes and beliefs radically. This is in stark contrast to the findings in the Boston Church of Christ, a sect.[129] Therefore, it could be argued that the term 'personality' incorporates more than just attitude and belief.

Who joined and who was recruited into Ted's Sect and Harry's Sect?

To further understand becoming part of a sect, I now turn to two groups and look at the similarities and differences between the two sects in terms of the types of people who become involved in them. At the time of becoming involved in Ted's Sect and at the beginning of the existence of Harry's Sect, those becoming involved were young adults who were working or were students. In Ted's Sect a few were unemployed. As Harry's Sect has aged, those becoming involved have included whole families; some mothers were already raising children full-time when they became involved in Harry's Sect.

Typically, those who become involved in sects are unmarried.[130] Ted's Sect always tended to attract young adults. Prior to starting this sect, the leader of Ted's Sect, Ted, had instigated similar organisations. Ted's Sect, which has now disbanded, mainly attracted young, single individuals. This suggests that even if Ted's Sect had not disbanded, families would still have been unlikely to join. Unlike Ted's Sect, Harry's Sect could be said to be untypical in its later years as it has also attracted whole families into its membership as opposed to those without children. This difference between sects highlights the problems of overgeneralisation and the importance of looking at individual sects and differences between them.

Most first-generation Ted's Sect and Harry's Sect members interviewed were well-educated, many with degrees or (in Harry's Sect) professional qualifications in other areas. This is similar to research findings in the USA,[131] although some sects attract those with lower levels of education.[132]

Religious beliefs and geographical location prior to becoming involved
Those who became involved in Harry's Sect were found to be almost always Christians and regularly attending a Christian place of worship. Conversely, many of those who became involved in Ted's Sect had no prior experience of Buddhism, but reported being open to learning more about Buddhism or just interested in doing yoga, hand-reading (reading the lines on your hand to tell you who you are and what you are like[133]) or a martial arts course. Those becoming involved in Ted's Sect generally came from the local area to participate in classes. In contrast, those in Harry's Sect usually came greater distances to join, and thus had to relocate to join.

Differences because of sect influence or pre-sect personality
Ascertaining any differences between former Ted's Sect and Harry's Sect members before joining is very difficult due to sect influences.

Nevertheless, interviews with former Ted's Sect members indicated that they were more sociable before joining their sect than Harry's Sect members. The latter were possibly more introverted and had less interest in cultural and social activities. Attempts to make such a distinction are complicated by the fact that Ted's Sect was the more participatory of the two sects, while involvement in Harry's Sect would have encouraged introversion. Thus, this result should be viewed with caution since it could be due to sect involvement rather than pre-sect differences in the personalities of those who became members.

HOW DID THEY FIRST HEAR ABOUT THE SECT AND MAKE CONTACT?

THE IMPORTANCE OF CHANCE!

A number of individuals first encountered Ted's Sect and Harry's Sect because of friends and in the case of Harry's Sect, family members who got involved. Some individuals first heard of Ted's Sect through advertisements in publications such as *Time Out* or through a stall at their university's 'fresher's' fayre.' This was similar to some Harry's Sect members, who first came across the sect through their university's Christian Union. Since this would depend on whether or not the sect happened to be active at the individual's university, chance played an important part in such initial contacts.

Initial contact with Ted's Sect generally occurred because individuals were interested in Buddhism or in taking up yoga, hand-reading or martial arts. Again, chance played a major role in such contacts with Ted's Sect, since contact would depend on the individual responding to an advert placed by Ted's Sect rather than some other martial arts group. Psychology cannot foretell these chance encounters, and yet they may lightly touch a life, have a lasting effect or contribute to individuals' life paths moving in a completely different direction.[134]

Chance also appears to play a role in the life course of Harry's Sect members whose initial contact with Harry's Sect also emerged as being related to chance. For those who joined Harry's Sect at the beginning of its existence, their first contact with the leader of Harry's Sect, Harry, occurred because he was a visiting speaker at the church they attended. Later, initial contact with Harry's Sect was through Harry's books, tapes and preaching. Harry's books were available from Christian bookshops and a few secular places or Christian book fayres. Some members of the public with Christian affiliations, but with no prior knowledge of Harry, were sent a copy of Harry's magazine.

Some individuals' first contact came through attending his preaching at a public hall, which Harry's Sect hired so individuals could hear him preach. Harry's public preaching was very widely publicised by current members. Current members often spent holidays and the time when they were not at meetings or work putting up posters advertising the preaching. After initial contact with Harry, individuals visited the chapel in the UK to be present at a few meetings. Following this, they moved into the local area and began attending all the meetings at the chapel.

Enjoyment of being in Ted's Sect, particularly the initial enjoyment

Those who attended Ted's Sect described it as being very interesting, exciting, active and dynamic in terms of both the mixture of people and the discussions. The other members were also described as being very nice, which contributed to attraction to the sect. Interviewees also spoke of the appeal of both the *dojo* (a *dojo* is a place designated for training) leader, Darren, and the main leader, Ted. They were both charismatic individuals, supportive and insightful, and with very good oral skills. Interviewees stated that they had really enjoyed being in Ted's Sect, particularly at the initial stages.[135] For many, this enjoyment continued to some extent throughout their membership.

Reasons given for joining and being attracted to the sect were that it gave them permission to be different; it filled a vague gap in their lives; they were searching for meaning in their lives; it challenged them; and there was a sense of togetherness.

ADDITIONAL REASONS AND MOTIVATIONS FOR BECOMING INVOLVED IN TED'S SECT INCLUDED:

- altruism
- physical benefits
- sorting out health problems, including depression and physical ailments
- seeking answers to existential questions
- expansion of the mind
- learning
- loss of a friend and
- loneliness.

In general the weekend away, which was called a *gashaku*, was the turning point for many interviewees, leading to further involvement in Ted's Sect.

ATTRACTION TO HARRY'S SECT LEADERS PERSONALITY AND OTHER REASONS FOR BECOMING PART OF HARRY'S SECT

Those who became part of Harry's Sect also described being attracted to Harry by his personality and his charisma. Some reported very positive initial experiences of him, including his teaching and preaching. A number of interviewees felt that they had spiritual problems before joining Harry's Sect and hoped that Harry, the leader of Harry's Sect, could assist with this. Quite a number described spiritual experiences, specifically conversion experiences, as a result of their contact with Harry's Sect, particularly in the early stages of the sect's existence. Those interviewees who became part of Harry's Sect more recently described less contact with Harry. However, when they first contacted the sect, they liked his teaching.

Some interviewees felt that it was God's will for them to join Harry's Sect, and some persevered in this belief. However, once they had joined, interviewees did not describe an enjoyment of being in Harry's Sect. Some individuals explained that part of the reason for their attraction to Harry's Sect was their dissatisfaction both with the church they were in and with themselves. Research participants (apart from those appointed to leadership positions after joining) communicated that they had limited participation in the group; it was more a case of listening to Harry or reading his books before moving to the main Harry's Sect location and then attending the meetings.

INTERACTIONS BETWEEN MEMBERS

While Ted's Sect interviewees described their sect as being very participatory from the first attendance, Harry's Sect did not involve a great deal of communication or interaction between members. Those who became members generally did so after visiting the meeting chapel one weekend or after visiting for a number of meetings. Harry was not usually present at the meetings, but senior members of Harry's Sect led the meetings in his absence. Interviews indicated that Harry's Sect was comparatively conservative and dull compared to members' experience of Ted's Sect. The second generation who moved with their parents to Harry's Sect did not really know what they were getting involved with, and often did not want to move. They commonly described Harry's Sect as boring[136] and were not attracted to it. Many of the second generation in Harry's Sect were born to parents in the group.

WHY CENTREPOINT CHILDREN WERE PRESENT IN THE SECT?

A study conducted in New Zealand on Centrepoint, a so-called spiritual and therapeutic community found that second-generation former members recorded a number of reasons for how they came to be at Centrepoint, some having been sent by their parents and some coming of their own volition, but in the main those coming as younger children were brought by their parents, despite the reluctance of the children to be there.[137]

THE WELL-MEANT DESIRE OF PARENTS TO PROTECT THEIR CHILDREN

Protecting children can be precisely the reason why some parents join sects. They want a better life for their children, as shown by the quote at the start of this chapter. Sadly, the well-meant desire to protect their children often does not transpire into reality, as evidenced in Chapter 4 (on abuse and neglect of children in sects) and as expanded on in Patricia's preface:

> *Parents set out to find truth, to draw closer to God. In their wayward search their children become scarred, sometimes eternally scarred.*[138]

THE HARRY'S SECT SECOND GENERATION AND THE TED'S SECT 'ABSENT SECOND GENERATION'

THE HARRY'S SECT SECOND GENERATION

A large proportion of the existing and former membership of Harry's Sect consists of those who were born into the sect or those who were brought into the sect by their parents. Therefore, the second generation had a complete lack of control and choice over their sect membership. Nevertheless there is evidence from one of Harry's books that he did correspond with a minor whose parents were not part of the group to encourage involvement in the group. This individual joined Harry's Sect in their late teenage years.

THE TED'S SECT 'ABSENT SECOND GENERATION'

To the best of the researcher's knowledge, only one child was in Ted's Sect in the whole of the sect's existence. In Ted's Sect, members did not have children, they were discouraged from do-ing so. The desire to bear children was seen as selfish, and having children was not seen as a good course of action. This was perpe-trated through the teachings of the group as expanded on by an interviewee below:

> *Ted's take on the 'five hindrances to spiritual enlightenment' were: house, wife, car, job, children. The more of these you had, the more obstructions to the spiritual life. A job was just about OK – it provided money to pay for classes . . . of course, the 'worst' of these were definitely wife and children.*[139]

Another interviewee said the following about children in Ted's Sect:

> *having children is a selfish thing in Ted's Sect. It gets in the way of training, and there are enough people in the world already, you can go and adopt some if you really want to, but why don't you just concen-trate on the students. Most kids get born, messed up by their parents, so help to un-mess some of these adults or something.*[140]

I consider the 'second generation' to be mostly absent within Ted's Sect particularly for this reason. Its mode of operation led to changed birth plans and patterns.

The case of Ted's Sect and the absent second generation links into previous research on abortions in some sects, which states; 'their lead-ers attempt to prevent women from getting pregnant or to pressure them to terminate their pregnancies. Regardless of the specific pat-tern, the leaders – not the couples, the women, or the men – decide about and control pregnancies and abortions.'[141] A psychotherapy sect that thrived for nine years did not have even one child born in that time to any of the 350 members, although most of the women in the sect were of child-bearing age.[142]

Other sects have part of their second generation absent due to medical neglect, which results in the death of children as discussed in Chapter Four.[143] If the literature relating to the deaths of children due to physical abuse, or the murder/suicide of the members, is also considered, it is evident that a number of sects have part of their second generation absent due to the deaths of these children.[144] Some sects then have a completely missing or partially absent second generation.

In Ted's Sect it is likely that, with so many sect members of child-bearing age, some at least would under usual circumstances give birth to and raise children. This suggests that Ted's Sect was a group with a 'missing' or 'absent second generation'. On some level, this is a form of developmental destruction for the first generation. Adult development generally includes an 'interest in establishing and guiding the next generation'[145] without which there may be boredom and a lack of psychological growth. This 'developmental destruction' is likely to impact the post-sect harm experienced by the first generation, particularly those who leave their sects after child-bearing age having had no children.[146] Daniel Levinson, a psychologist who specialised in adult developmental stages, refers to women who remain childless and experience a 'painful developmental process of dealing with the loss'[147], and also to the difficulty that many women have in coming to terms with the fact that they will not bear and raise children.

First-generation former members not having children

The finding of one of my studies of participants of former members of a variety of sects and non-sect like groups was that 49% of first-generation former members did not have children, despite the sample being on average 40 years old, with 54% of the females aged 34 or over. In the comparison group, 21% had no children (average age of 47 years, with 84% of the females aged 34 or over). Considering that the first-generation former members are on average nearly 40 years of age, and 60% of the sample is female, this represents a large number of individuals who had not yet produced offspring. Survey and census data indicates that well under 10% of mothers have a first child after the age of 34,[148] though that percentage may have increased in recent years. This does though support the assertion that for quite a large proportion of former first-generation members, the 'missing' second generation may continue after sect membership, i.e. a larger than expected number of those leaving sects do not have children even after having left their sect.

Parents in some sects have many children

Some parents are in relationships arranged by the sect and the decision to conceive children may be arranged by the sect leader or require their permission[149]. In some sects, it is usual for parents not to utilise birth control and have many children. For example, one researcher[150] studied second-generation former members in fundamentalist Mormon communities whose key belief is their adherence to polygamy. She found that only three of her research participants were from families of fewer than 10 siblings, and seven were from families of 26 or more siblings. Here is an excerpt from Elissa Wall's autobiography, *Stolen Innocence*:

> *...It hadn't always been so tense in the Wall household. Growing up, I remember many good times with my family. There were camping trips, picnics in the mountains, and countless visits to the FLDS communities in Canada and Southern Utah for festivals, celebrations and group events. There were struggles, but I remember so much happiness, and how much I loved my dad. Sixteen of Dad's children were still living at home when I was born on July 7, 1986. I was the eleventh of my mother's fourteen children, and number nineteen of Dad's eventual twenty-four...[151]*

SUMMARY OF CHAPTER 2

A review of the limited studies conducted in Europe and the US conclude that around 1% of the population have spent time in a sect at some point in their lives. Some questions regarding the involvements of parents in sects may be particularly pertinent for second generation adults, such as: Why do people join groups? Is there a personality type who join sects? What are the family backgrounds of those who joined sects like? How do people hear about sects and make contact with them? For those raised in sects, understanding why one's parents joined a group and related questions may become pertinent at some point. Similarly, these questions and mixed emotions may be pertinent for the grandparents of the second generation, as it was their adult children (the first generation) who joined or were recruited into a sect. Strong feelings might be present surrounding questions of whether the parents of the second generation had emotional problems or were distressed before they joined a sect.

First-generation parents might have had a well-meant desire to protect their children, in fact this can sometimes be a reason for parents to join a sect, although sadly the reality for children can be that they were anything but protected in the sect. In some sects there is no second generation, rather there is what I call an 'absent second generation'. In still other sects parents have a large or very large number of offspring and there is a huge second generation.

WHAT COMES NEXT IN CHAPTER 3?

The chapter that follows looks at what families can be like for children in sects. The quote below comes from Jayanti Tamm's autobiography, and describes her and her brother Ketan's efforts to acquire a pet bunny:

With Ketan as the leader, I eagerly agreed to his plots, curious to see how far we could push our boundaries. No longer satisfied with just our TV triumph, Ketan began scheming for our latest, and most dire, rule manipulation: Operation Get-a-Pet. Guru forbade disciples from owning pets, and so Ketan wisely decided that on such a critical matter, the way to go was to exploit my Chosen One status to the fullest. The assault would have to come from me. Even the idea of having an animal made me shiver with glee. Ketan and I talked constantly in front of our parents about owning a pet, but we realized that we were wasting our efforts. The way things worked in my family was that my parents did not make any decision.

"Ask Guru," they would say when it was a matter of anything from our bedtime to having a rope swing.

Though I knew Guru prohibited pets, my desire for a small, fluffy friend seemed to outweigh my desire for spiritual progress. We decided that if I asked for an animal that Guru hadn't mentioned by name during his talks about not having pets, then maybe it would be all right. Dogs and cats were officially on his bad list, but we had never heard of his policy on rabbits.[152]

CHAPTER 3

IS THIS A BAD DREAM?

DR BRUCE PERRY treated the children released during the cult stand-off in Waco, Texas, the group's leader was called David Koresh. Below is a quote from Dr Perry and Maria Szalavitz's book, detailing what happened when Dr Perry interviewed a 10-year-old boy and asked him to draw a self-portrait:

> *What he drew was virtually a stick figure, something that a four-year-old could produce. Even more shockingly, when I asked him to draw his family, he paused and seemed confused. Finally, he created a page that was blank but for a tiny picture of himself, squeezed into the far right hand corner. His drawings reflected what he'd learned in the group: the elaboration of things that Koresh valued, the dominance of its supreme leader, a confused, impoverished sense of family and an immature, dependent picture of himself.[153]*

OVERVIEW

Children in sects may spend very limited amounts of time with their immediate family, or in other groups they may spend time with very few people apart from their immediate family. The group might be opposed to close contact between parents and children, seeing parent–child attachment as a negative attribute.[154] How children are affected by their attachments to adults is explored in a later chapter, particularly in terms of sects that separate children from their parents.[155]

This chapter will discuss how the structure and hierarchy of a sect impacts families, and what families may be like. It will examine how children in the same sect may be treated very differently. It will look at the parenting styles of the first generation and identify the basic needs that all children in all cultures have. Because a sect can have such a huge influence on families, this chapter finishes with a discussion of how social influence occurs in sects.

The impact on families from the sect's structure

Communal living and the concept of biological family

In some sects, the very concept of 'family life' as a distinct and separate entity, may be inaccurate because children are raised communally. Bhagwan Rajneesh (alias Osho, now deceased) was an Indian mystic and controversial spiritual teacher. From the 1970s he initiated disciples, including many Westerners, and set up ashrams (spiritual communes). In 1986, a school was set up in England for children and a few grandchildren of disciples. Bhagwan Rajneesh saw the spiritual commune as a substitute for the nuclear family.[156] He stated that:

> 'The real family is not your father, your mother, your brothers, your sisters, your wife, your husband, your children; they are just accidental. Your real family is the family of a Buddha.'[157]

Winfried Hempel was born into a sect called Colonia Dignidad, located in Chile. Babies were taken to a communal nursery and raised not knowing who their parents or siblings were. All adults were referred to as uncles or aunts and the sect leader was referred to as the 'permanent uncle'. Winfried found out who his parents were when he was 10 years old[158], and he describes the children working out who their parents were in the following way:

With time one starts to notice that one of the people that one referred to as uncle had more contact with one, always secretly, and when they came to kindergarten to see the boys on one side and the girls on the other, they had a certain concealed preference. And that's how one re-alised, after a while, that this uncle and that aunt were my father and my mother.

The general culture and structure of a sect is likely to impact families because the culture and demands of sects are often at odds with the needs of the children in the group. Nevertheless, it is important to remember that, like families in mainstream society, families in sects also differ.

HOW LOYALTY TO THE SECT LEADER UNDERMINES FAMILY ATTACHMENTS

Christian Szurko[159] outlines below how in Harry's Sect, the members' loyalty to the leader undermines attachments to family members:

It seems as though members of the family are not expected to express their primary loyalty to one another. Their primary loyalty is to him [Harry]. And the family is, if you like, an area in which they demonstrate that loyalty. Now that's only justifiable if you see him as being such a direct expression of the mind and will of God that he's infallible and is not going to, in any circumstance, abuse that extreme role.

So you can justify, within most religions, giving God absolute pre-eminence and priority over every other loyalty, because in those religions there is a balancing principle that God will protect every other valid relationship even better than we would ourselves,… In Harry's teaching you have no balance. You have simply undermining of the family fabric, an over emphasis on loyalty to God, by which he means loyalty to himself ultimately, which undermines every other affection, every other loyalty.

HIERARCHAL AND AUTHORITARIAN STRUCTURES

Both Harry's Sect and Ted's Sect had authoritarian structures. In Ted's Sect, Ted was the leader and founder of the sect. He had a 'right-hand man' (Darren) and area leaders, beneath whom were seniors. Belts were awarded in an order from white belt (the lowest) to black belt, and then to higher grades. The hierarchy of the sect was according to the belt status of the members, right down to fringe members. In Ted's Sect, as in some other sects, men and women have roughly equal status.

THE STATUS OF WOMEN IN HARRY'S SECT

There was a patriarchal, all male, 'time-served' ['seniority-based'] hierarchy in Harry's Sect, with Harry as the founder and main leader. Under him were other men who had been in the sect for a long time (although new arrivals were sometimes promoted quickly). Women were clearly low in the 'chain of command' and children below them, with female children being right at the bottom. The data reveals that women were viewed as second-class. For example, women were not allowed to speak in meetings. The current member interviewed said the following about women and men in the meeting:

So is there a difference in the way men and women are treated?

Oh yes, the women are downcast, the women are to look up to the men, and the men have to be the boss.[160]

THE LEADERS' IMPACT ON MARRIAGES

It became apparent from the interviews that, to some extent, Harry stood in the middle of marriages. The primary loyalty extended to marriages and children (discussed later in this chapter). The non-wearing of a wedding ring[161] may have symbolised the finding that Harry stood in the 'middle of marriages'.[162] This is similar to research on other sects, for example research on Jonestown, which found that the leader Jim Jones also sought to loosen the bonds between husband and wife.[163]

One first-generation member explained how she felt about this after leaving Harry's Sect:

> 'Cos Harry had always been, you know, sort of stood in the way, and it was really lovely... like a sort of honeymoon all over again, and I thought, 'I've really got my husband now, and this is a proper relationship now, rather than him being between us'[164]

AUTHORITARIAN STRUCTURE: FEAR AND ANXIETY

The authoritarian structure in Harry's Sect appeared to result in fear and anxiety being present in members as the following second-generation quote shows:

> There was sometimes an atmosphere of tension or stress with my parents, even when they were talking about issues connected to the meeting, and about Harry himself, and frightened to go to meetings, that kind of thing, tension. . . . I think I remember there being stress when they were talking about new rules or whatever that Harry would bring in... They were scared of him, I guess, and as a kid I picked up on that.[165]

This authoritarian culture in Harry's Sect and Ted's Sect and its resulting fear is consistent with a study[166] of 1,200 American, Australian, Chinese and Nigerian children aged between seven and 17 years, which found that cultures favouring inhibition, compliance and obedience (which are all related to authoritarianism) lead to increased levels of fear in these children. This might explain some of the high levels of anxiety found in some second-generation adults after sect membership.[167]

Hierarchical structures are commonplace, but when a hierarchical structure also includes harshness, humiliation and a lack of compassion, fear becomes the norm. Children in some sects have been described as being 'marinated in fear'.[168]

A research study[169] on the general population looking at very young children aged 22, 33 and 45 months found that children who were more fearful in typical fear-inducing paradigms also displayed more guilt. Further, girls displayed more guilt than boys and a fearful temperament contributed to a greater guilt-proneness, which then inhibited the young children's tendency to violate rules.[170] A study of levels of fear in the general population in children and adolescents aged seven to 18 years found that gender and initial fear scores were better predictors of fear levels than the ages of the children.[171] However, any genetic predisposition to fear may account for just a small percentage of the variance that might exist and the environment may account for a significant percentage of the variance in fear levels for children. For example, a cross cultural research study[172] with a sample of 1200 American, Australian, Chinese and Nigerian children and adolescents aged seven to 17 years found differences in the pattern and content of fears for girls and boys across countries, suggesting that cultures which favour inhibition compliance and obedience serve to increase levels of fear.

Two studies of second-generation former members showed that 70% (in a sample seeking help at Wellspring Retreat and Resource Centre) and 19% (sample mostly acquired via the internet) respectively had clinically significant levels of anxiety, which endured over time and in a variety of situations. The fear generated in some sects is extreme. The children who had left Waco had pulse rates at rest, six weeks after leaving, well above normal.[173]

Harry was a very important person in the lives of Harry's Sect members because how they saw themselves was very much linked to what they perceived he thought about them. Harry was described as a father figure by some former members of Harry's Sect. At times it is evident from Harry's Sect publications that members referred to Harry as a father.[174] In some cases, it is difficult to know whether members' letters to Harry reflect how they really felt or express conformity to expectations. For example, is the following an expression of conformity or of genuine feeling?

> *Mr. Harry, you are a father in Christ to many, and even to one as valueless as myself.*[175]

Similarly, those in Ted's Sect commented that at the time of membership they viewed the leaders as 'all-knowing'.[176] Members' obedience to the leaders[177] illustrates an authoritarian style of leadership. Parents in sects who themselves have experienced this style of leadership from the sect leader might also display this style of parenting with their own children.

THE CANNIBALISATION OF FAMILIES

Christian Szurko comments on the impact of the sect on families in Harry's Sect:

> 'It's characteristic of a group that cannibalises families, and I would use that kind of picture of Harry – families cannibalised into something else. Families become food for Harry. What I mean by that is that the family is not a thing in itself to be respected as a primary value. A family is a way of preserving and sustaining and helping to grow the Harry group. The family is a tool.

> And in that sort of situation, it's important, it's vital to pit family member against family member. It's important to set up structures within the family that reflect the ultimate goals and priorities of Harry. ...

That means that the family has to reflect that. It reflects that by a very rigid hierarchy within the family. The father is, you know, seated at the right hand of Harry, the leader almighty. And after that, everybody else is jockeying for position. And that sets up a high degree of competition within the family, against one another. Instead of the family working as a unit, it works as a unit except when there's any kind of strife within it, at which point it enters into competition, because it then becomes necessary to become more orthodox than orthodox. More orthodox than one another. But at the same time, you've got all these personality things going, and there is so much strife that is created within the family unit where you have that kind of structure. And there's so much potential for hurt.'[178]

PRIMARY LOYALTY TO THE SECT LEADER

The parents' primary loyalty in sects may be to the leader, as opposed to each other or their children. In some sects, parents' behaviour towards their children is carefully monitored.[179] Furthermore, children in sects may also be encouraged or forced to give their primary loyalty to their sect leader as opposed to giving it to other members of their family, including their parents. For example, in some sects they may be required to report parents' or siblings' violation of group rules to the leader. This, however, is not always achieved as in the case below[180].

Perhaps the most startling instance is the case of a boy in Jonestown who demonstrated ingenuity in saving the life of his mother, who had temporarily left the settlement. He wrote to her at his uncle's house and used a symbol that his uncle would understand, but that those reading the letters going out of Jonestown would not understand. The letter made it out of Jonestown and arrived at its destination. Due to his mother being warned by her young son, she did not travel to Jonestown and her life was ultimately saved, although sadly the boy perished alongside nearly everyone else at Jonestown.

In some sects, non-compliance by parents can result in the harsh treatment of their children. This can be exceptionally painful for everyone and is a way of ensuring the compliance of parents.

THE FAMILY ENVIRONMENT OF THOSE GROWING UP IN SECTS

To look in more depth at the families of those in sects, I used the Family Environment Scale (FES) in my research. The FES[181] sections include: relationship, personal growth and system maintenance.

1. Relationship dimension: assesses how involved people are in their family and how openly they express both positive and negative feelings.
   - 'cohesion: the degree of commitment, help and support family members provide for one another
   - expressiveness: the extent to which family members are encouraged to act openly and to express their feelings directly
   - conflict: the amount of openly expressed anger, aggression and conflict among family members'[182]
2. Personal growth dimension or goal orientation: measures the family's goals by tapping into the major ways in which a family encourages or inhibits personal growth.
   - 'independence: the extent to which family members are assertive, are self-sufficient and make their own decisions
   - achievement orientation: the extent to which activities, such as school and work, are cast into an achievement-orientated or competitive framework
   - intellectual-cultural orientation: the degree of interest in political, social, intellectual and cultural activities
   - active recreational orientation: the extent of participation in social and recreational activities

- moral-religious emphasis: the degree of emphasis on ethical and religious issues and values'[183]
3. System maintenance dimensions: assesses the family's emphasis on clear organisation, structure, rules and procedures in running family life.
   - 'organisation: the importance of clear organisation and structure in planning family activities and responsibilities
   - control: the extent to which set rules and procedures are used to run family life'[184]

It is interesting to read what researchers have said about minority religious groups and the control of adolescents:

> Minority groups tend 'to enforce selective contacts or minimal contacts with the wider society around them. They would carefully control social interaction. When a group is smaller and more distinct culturally, as compared to the majority, the more the limitations it puts on young members… Minority religions are more likely to employ social barriers and close control of adolescents.'[185]

In two studies I carried out, former sect members filled in retrospectively the Family Environment Scale. I found that the second-generation average scores were lower than the first-generation average scores on the FES sub-scales of 'cohesion', 'expressiveness', 'independence' and 'active recreational'. The first generation did not grow up in a sect, whereas the second generation did – as such, this gives us an indication of the sect environment. Again, both the studies found that the second generation had higher average scores than the first generation on the sub-scales of 'conflict', 'moral-religious', 'organisation' and 'control'. These differences were at a statistically significant level in one of the studies on measures of 'conflict', 'independence', 'moral-religious' and 'control' in the family.

These findings indicate that the second generation in these samples veer towards the family pattern of distressed families.[186] In other words, they grew up in families that were like the families 'of alcohol abusers; of general psychiatric patients, and of families in which an adolescent or younger child was in a crisis situation, had run away from home, was identified as delinquent, or was being placed into a foster home'.[187]

The differential treatment of children

Children in some sects are treated differently, dependent on their (or their parent's), positions in the hierarchy. In some, children may be elevated to a place of authority above their parents. They may be labelled as 'special' children. The first 'blessed' child of the Western Unification Church was Donna Collins. She[188] explains that 'blessed' children were born to parents in the Unification Church. They were viewed by the group as free from sin and, unlike their parents and others, they did not have to pay 'indemnity'. Indemnity is about a process of doing something, e.g. fasting, fundraising, recruitment and other such works, through which human beings and the world are restored to God. Within the Unification Church (the Moonies), there were also 'unblessed' children who were not born to Moonie parents. Flore Aaslid describes her experiences growing up as an unblessed child. She experienced stigmatisation and the sense of not fitting in anywhere, either inside or outside the group.[189]

Donna Orne-Collins reports that[190] during her time at the Unification Church, she experienced a shift from 'blessed children' being viewed as special to being treated as resources for the Unification Church and Sun Myung Moon, the leader (now deceased). Many of the second generation were leaving the group and were less devoted than their parents. In recent years, leadership has focused on getting these children and young people married or matched to others in the group so that they remain in the group to be 'work-horses.'

Donna also added:

> *Never underestimate the power the UC holds over its youth. They use it hard and fast, and many more stay than leave now, whereas just a few years ago, it was the other way around.*'[191] She also states that, '*One doesn't see Moon's own children going door-to-door selling trinkets, nor any high level leaders' kids. They're usually too busy going to Yale or Harvard, or taking Ballet lessons with private instructors, or being in horse-riding competitions. However, they do graciously find the time to give speeches to the second-generation children to "fire them up," for clearly their opulence depends on convincing these children/young adults to serve and devote their lives to Moon and his family.*'[192]

This demonstrates differences in the experiences of children in sects dependent on their parents' status in the group.[193]

However, being the child of a sect leader, or the son or daughter of another leader, doubtless has its own trials and difficulties including after leaving. Not least the fact that they live with the knowledge that they have 50% of their genes. In and of themselves genes are neutral, what we do with those genes and who we are, is not determined by either of our parents. Nonetheless, it may be difficult to work through the complex emotions that the child of a sect leader/s may experience after leaving. In some sects the children of leaders do not get preferential treatment. An example of the lack of preferential treatment is expanded on by Winfried Hempel (a second-generation former member who now works as a lawyer) and Faris Kermani (a journalist) in the Aljazeera documentary[194] about a sect in Southern Chile created by Paul Schaefer:

Faris Kermani: Such was the extent of Schaefer's power that not even the children of some of his closest colleagues were spared. Some of the children who were abused by Paul Schaefers were actually the children of the leadership, weren't they?

Winfried Hempel: *They did nothing. They knew and did nothing.*

Faris Kermani: Why did they allow it?

Winfried Hempel: *Cowardice, cowardice and the privileges that they had in exchange.*

Parenting styles

How parents behave and how they treat their children have huge implications for children's lives and adulthood. Psychologists have studied parents and their children, and have come up with what they call types or styles of parenting. Parenting styles are based on the fact that parents vary in the consistency of their rule setting, in their responsiveness to their children (warmth or nurturance), in their level of expectation from their children (maturity demands) and in the quality of their communication with their children (high or low communication).[195] Variations on the different dimensions interact with each other to form a style or pattern of parenting.

Authoritative parenting style

One of the parenting styles is authoritative parenting, where standards for behaviour are within the capabilities of the child and match their level of development. Rules are firmly enforced and explained to the child, yet flexibility is maintained. An authoritative parenting style has consistently been associated with positive child outcomes such as children with good mental health.[196]

Authoritative parenting is generally accepted and supported by research as the most helpful development style for the child[197]. The characteristics it fosters are those that are particularly valued in our society. Even a study looking at the parenting style of parents coming from cultures that value interdependence over independence lend support for the authoritative parenting style linking into high self-esteem and satisfaction.[198]

Permissive parenting style
Another style, called 'permissive', indicates that indulgent parents place few demands on their children while granting them considerable freedom. Such parents are highly affectionate, communicative and accepting of their children. This style of parenting has been associated with negative child outcomes. One research study[199] found that, for boys, a permissive parenting style was associated with negative attitudes towards parents, lower self-esteem, and increased identity, anxiety, phobia, depression and conduct disorders.

Authoritarian parenting style
Authoritarian parenting as a third style, on the other hand, involves discipline that is punitive and absolute, without discussion. There is little affection, nurturing or communication. Disobedience is met with resistance and force. An authoritarian style of parenting is associated with negative child outcomes, such as children who are more dependent and aggressive.[200]

In Harry's Sect, the position of fathers is discussed by Christian Szurko in the following way:

> 'It seems to me from what I've heard from Harry ex-members, is that there is a very easy way of turning any failure to be a mature Christian into a suggestion that you need to obey [Harry] more in order to be a Christian at all, and that becomes highly

manipulative. It means that if a father doesn't dominate his children and his wife into total obedience to Harry, that he himself – as part of the hierarchy, the chain of command – has to ask himself, 'Am I a proper Christian?' It means that if he is doing his best to try and bully his family into submission but the family's not being right, not only does he have to question himself, but then the family has to be in fear that maybe they're not Christians.'[201]

Authoritarian parenting has been found to be significantly related to parent–adolescent conflict.[202] However, a study on Palestinian–Arab adolescents in Israel found no significant relationship between authoritarian parenting styles and mental health issues.[203] The researchers who did the study of Palestinian–Arab adolescents propose that parenting style is linked to the particular culture someone is in, and whether the children and parents are male or female, rather than impacting in the same way across the world.

WHAT ALL CHILDREN FROM ALL CULTURES NEED

However, a researcher[204] who has studied cultures and children stated that 'all children from all cultures require:

- basic physical care;
- affection, including physical and emotional intimacy;
- security, which includes consistency in routines, stability and continuity of care;
- the stimulation of innate potential through encouragement and praise;
- guidance and control;
- age-appropriate responsibility; and
- age-appropriate independence to make their own decisions, tailored to the child's ability and understanding of the consequences of such decisions.'

DISTINGUISHING BETWEEN PARENTING PRACTISES AND PARENTING
STYLES

There needs to be a fit between the child's needs and the parental
response. More recently, psychologists have distinguished between
parenting styles and parenting practices.[205] 'Parenting style is defined as a stable complex of attitudes and beliefs about parenting,
whereas parenting practices are specific behaviours engaged in by
parents.'[206] Studies have confirmed direct links between parenting
practices and child outcomes.[207] For example, poor monitoring and
supervision, inconsistent discipline and corporal punishment of
children have been found to be predictive of behaviour problems
in children.

RISKS AND PROTECTIVE FACTORS IN THE LINK BETWEEN PARENTING
AND CHILD OUTCOMES

One researcher has developed a model which addresses risk and
protective factors in the link between parenting and child outcomes.[208] Risk factors for negative child outcomes included family
stress, family conflict (as measured by the Family Environment Scale
[FES] sub-scale conflict), parental psychopathology and low socio-
economic status. Protective factors included family cohesion (as
measured by FES sub-scale cohesion), family social support, family
moral-religious orientation (as measured by the FES sub-scale moral-
religious). It should be noted that this is by no means a universal predictor. Children of abusive alcoholics may end up highly successful
and children of child development experts may end up alcoholics.
Nevertheless, my research supported the risk and protective factors
model, with the second generation scoring significantly higher on
the FES sub-scale 'conflict' (study 1), significantly lower on the FES
sub-scale 'cohesion' (study 2) and having significantly higher levels
of psychological distress after sect membership than those not raised
in sects.

The leader's example and its influence on the parenting style and practise in Harry's Sect

As well as supporting the view that the style of parenting in sects is a risk factor for possible development of psychological distress in adulthood, my research also indicated that in some sects, parenting styles and behaviours might be acquired not through the parents, but through the sect leader, who also appeared to be seen as a parent figure for all members of the sect. Harry influenced the parenting style of actual fathers in Harry's Sect, as shown in the following quote from a former father in Harry's Sect:

Did Harry influence the way you brought up your children?

Yes he did . . . not in the way of giving instructions of how to do things, but it was an example I suppose. I think he set an authoritarian example of discipline... being very definitely the head and the boss, and disciplining, even physical discipline of various kinds.[209]

Christian Szurko describes the following:

'In the New Testament, fathers are encouraged specifically to love their children and not vex them, so that their use of authority, while valid, is not meant to be a humiliating ... or a demeaning use of authority. We're not meant to corner our children into total frustration and a sense of helplessness and worthlessness, and yet Harry's followers report that this is exactly what's happened to them. The father was forced to choose between Harry and his own children in ways that left the children feeling worthless ...'[210]

Direct links between parenting practices and child outcomes have been found.[211] Authoritarian parenting is associated with negative child outcomes, such as children who are more dependent on others.[212] This could interfere with a child's ability to deal with possible stigmatisation from those not in the sect (discussed further in Chapter 6).

UNINVOLVED PARENTING STYLE MAY BE PRESENT IN SECTS

While an authoritarian parenting style was found in Harry's sect, some groups are characterised by an indifferent (uninvolved) parenting style, which in its extreme is neglectful. These parents are non-controlling, over-permissive and aloof from their children. Life and discipline are centred on adult needs. The child's interest is not considered and their opinion is not sought.[213] Bhagwan Shree Rajneesh's theories on parenting and children are described thus:

> 'The first expression of love towards the child is to leave his first seven years absolutely innocent, unconditioned, to leave him for seven years completely wild, a pagan... It needs guts and it needs immense love in a father, in a mother, to tell the children, "You need to be free of us. Don't obey us, depend on your own intelligence. Even if you go astray it is far better to commit mistakes on your own and learn from them, rather than follow somebody else and not commit mistakes."'[214]

An example of an uninvolved parenting style in sects is shown by Tim Guest's autobiographical account 'My Life in Orange', which describes his life growing up in Bhagwan Shree Rajneesh's communes. He recounts an event as a young child where he phoned his mother to ask if he could stay in her room with her that night (as opposed to sleeping in the Kids Hut), but after the phone conversation finished he stayed on the phone and overheard her mimicking him sarcastically. He then writes:

> *Now on my daily travels – as I crunched over the gravel, slid down corridors and hallways, ran across the grass – I carried a cold heavy lump around with me, this new secret knowledge heavy in my heart.*

*My mother did not want me. Heavy – but at least it was mine. No one
could take it from me. I began to imagine this new sorrow as something
priceless inside me, as valuable as it was weighty and cold: like a frozen meteorite, invaluable to science.*

*After that day my mother and I saw less and less of each other. She
would sometimes catch hold of me in the hallways and ask me how I
was; I smiled to keep her happy, then wormed my way out of her arms
to go and read a book or play with the other kids. I never asked to stay
in her room again."*[215]

Communal living arrangements, and particularly the tenets (doc-
trines) and attitudes of some sects, result in children who are not
looked after directly by their parents. Where they do receive parenting, it comes from adults in the group generally. Uninvolved parenting was recorded as a consistent feature by psychologists who studied
those who had grown up in Centrepoints. These psychologists stated
that most, but not all the relationships between parents and their children were regarded by the second-generation former members as a
form of neglect. They go on to state that:

'In spite of the practically distant relationships between children and their 'direct' parents the community itself seemed
to give 'parenting' in general and the value of children, a high
priority in their belief system. This notion is perhaps most
clearly exemplified in the Centrepoint belief as told to us by
participants, that those who have grown up there are 'children
of the community'. This belief that the community itself was
the 'parent' of its children may have been part of what diluted
biological parent's direct accountability to their children for
practical care'[216]

An indifferent parenting style could be present in a sect, not in the
sense that children are not supervised, but in that children are only

supervised to the extent that they are seen to look good to those outside the groups.[217] Supervision of the children may be for the group's best interest rather than the children's. In this sense, it could be a parenting style that could be considered indifferent and, at the same time, authoritarian.[218]

POSITIVE RELATIONSHIPS BETWEEN PARENTS AND THEIR CHILDREN IN SECTS

While an authoritarian parenting style and parenting practices were evidenced in first-generation parents, some children in families reported positive relationships with their parents while in Harry's Sect, and described an atmosphere of love in their family, as the quote below shows:

> *Oh, I'd definitely say it was a loving family. I'd say there was a real atmosphere of love there. And security. Which probably helped me to be insulated from the weirdness of the meeting, really. Looking at it objectively now, I can see how weird it was, I think being in a family that had a fair atmosphere of love and my parents generally . . .* [Provided] *the basic good foundations of a stable home life... Like having parents with a good relationship that helped us kids. With an atmosphere of love, there wasn't anything weird or sort of brutal-like, you know, particular punishments or anything like that.*[219]

The individual above demonstrates that the family in which this individual was raised served as a buffer to the sect environment. Interestingly, Alexandria Stein,[220] in an article about the influence of cults on the relationship of mothers to their children, after describing all sorts of incidences of children receiving abuse and/or neglect, reports that:

> 'What comes across in these stories is how the mothers felt that they were doing the best thing for their children. Perhaps in this way, mothers strive to reconcile the internal conflict that is at work. They do, clearly, still love their children deeply. In that sense, the bond between mother and child remains intact.'[221]

She goes on to state that some mothers left the group because of the treatment their children received, following on from thoughts such as *'You can hurt me, but...not my kids, not anymore.'*[222] For those growing up in an authoritarian structure both within the family and sect, one wonders how dissent (opposition) is reduced or eliminated. It is to this perplexing area that we now turn.

ELIMINATING DISSENT: FEAR, SOCIAL INFLUENCE, JONESTOWN SUICIDE AND MURDER

In order to better understand the influence of sects on families it is important to better comprehend the environment of sects as a whole, particularly social influence. Social influence involves the exercise of power by a person or group to change the attitudes or behaviour of others in a particular direction.[223] Research interviews that I carried out supported the view that numerous social influence processes were in operation in Ted's Sect and Harry's Sect: in the joining process, continued membership and the type of treatment individual members endured in the group.

In an article entitled 'Making Sense of the Nonsensical: An Analysis of Jonestown', the author Neal Osherow, identifies and discusses a wide range of processes that influenced, persuaded and manipulated members of Jonestown and that help us to understand the deaths of over 900 people, including babies and children. He explains how describing the personality of the perpetrator (the sect leader – Jim Jones) and portraying the vulnerability of the victim (members of the Jonestown sect) does provide an explanation, but at the same time limits our understanding of what happened.[224] He goes on to discuss the importance of understanding the social influences that were present at Jonestown. In particular, he discusses how conformity and obedience were strongly in evidence in Jonestown. For example, members obeyed

Jim Jones and conformed to what was expected of them even when that resulted in harm to themselves and their children.

Neal Osherow identifies the most perplexing questions as: 'Why didn't more people leave the Temple? How could they actually kill their children and themselves?'[225] He describes Milgram's finding that a disobedient person greatly reduced the extent to which most people in the experiment obeyed the authority figure and how, in Asch's[226] study, disobedience of a single person made others much more likely to disobey. One member who dissented from the majority led others to dissent as well. He related this to how Jim Jones, the leader of Jonestown, got rid of those who disagreed.

Dissent in either Ted's Sect or Harry's Sect might result in a verbal telling off. Indeed, former Ted's Sect members described in depth the degree of pressure that they were under regarding actions or thoughts much less significant than dissent. For example:

> I was anxious all the time, slightly fearful, [thinking]... what's going to happen next? What have I forgotten to do? What am I going to get bollocked for now? What am I going to get in trouble for next?[227]

Former members, reported being in constant fear of being in trouble for something. To dissent would invite even more fear. Ted's Sect adult members might also expect physical punishment. Many of the social influence processes identified by Neal Osherow – for example, obedience to authority[228] and Solomon Asch's[229] conformity social influence processes in relation to Jonestown – were also evident in both Ted's Sect and Harry's Sect. The key ways where both Ted's Sect and Harry's Sect differ from Jonestown is that Jim Jones had a fascination with suicide, whereas neither Ted (nor Darren, the sub-group leader) nor Harry is reported to have had this dangerous fascination. Additionally, neither Ted's Sect nor Harry's Sect was as geographically or socially isolated as the Jonestown group eventually became, when members moved from the US to a jungle location in Guyana, a sovereign state on the northern coast of South America.

A number of authors[230] have shown that social influence is at the heart of the functioning of sects. While social influence is in operation to some extent in all groups, it is extreme in sects and as such can be considered harmful to individuals.[231]

Despite the social influences in sects, there are accounts of those who attempted to stand up against authority at Jonestown both for their lives and the lives of others. The following petition was found crumpled in the mud near Jones' house after the murder and deaths at Jonestown:

We, the undersigned mothers, have been shown a dream. We left our homes to follow it. Now we fear that it is about to turn into a nightmare... Dad, we beg of you, don't finally embark upon the step that you have spoken of. Please spare our children. If we must die, let them live. There is nothing noble in dying, nothing fine about killing our children.[232]

The death of one of the teenagers of Jonestown, Julie Ann Runnel, who refused to take the poison, is described in the book 'The Children of Jonestown'.[233] She was restrained by her court-appointed guardian and a nurse who held her head back while they tried to pour the poison into her mouth, but five times she spat out the poison. Finally, they beat her, and this time they covered her mouth and nose so that she could not spit out the poison. Despite all the manipulation, the psychological coercion and pressure to conform, this teenage girl clearly desired not to drink the poison. In the end, those who should have cared for and protected her were the very people who took her life.

Summary of Chapter 3

In some sects, children have a shocking lack of understanding of what constitutes family. In other sects families are impacted by their primary loyalty being to the leader which undermines their attachments with each other. In a few sects, this can be to such an extent that it is only after they have left the group that they have the opportunity to know who all their families members are and, in some cases, to begin to build relationships with one another. For married couples who simultaneously leave a sect, a honeymoon period might be experienced where the sect leader no longer figuratively stands between the couple.

In Ted's Sect and Harry's Sect there was an authoritarian structure which clearly resulted in Harry's Sect members experiencing both fear and anxiety. The fear present in children raised in sects can be extreme and this links into high levels of anxiety found in studies of second-generation former members.

In Ted's Sect males and females had roughly equal status, whereas in Harry's Sect women were viewed as second class. The unequal status and low regard for both women and children, while commonplace in some societies, represents an area that those leaving some sects may be particularly sensitive, too. If those interacting with these former members pay special attention to this and reflect the former members' value to them in terms of their treatment of them, it may enable the former member to take great strides in terms of valuing themselves and improving their self-concept.

Reports on studies of the family environment of those in sects compared to those who were not raised in sects indicate that these sect families veer towards a pattern of distressed families. The experiences of children within the same sect may differ dependent on the parent's status within the group. Children with especially low status may experience a great deal of stigmatisation and may not feel that they fit within either the group or the outside world, therefore finding a sense of belonging is important after leaving a sect.

An authoritarian style of parenting was found to be present in Harry's Sect, though an indifferent or uninvolved parenting style may be present in the context of particular sects. All children in all cultures have needs and also there are both risk and protective factors present in families. Sometimes there are positive relationships between parents and children in sects. Sects can have a huge impact on those families who are within them. Social influence processes that have been deemed to be present in Jonestown are also identified and highlighted in relationship to both Harry's Sect and Ted's Sect.

WHAT COMES NEXT IN CHAPTER 4?

The next chapter deals with the sombre topic of child abuse in sects and includes statistics on the percentage of children abused in sects. The quote below gives an indication of why it can be very difficult for children in the sect to dissent:

> You've got no means of self-expression', you've got no, you couldn't dissent against anything or not overtly so; you just felt locked into a corner.... In the end, you just lost the fight if you ever had any, because... from an early age you believed this was the only possible way of living, so you know [that] even if you began to think for yourself and everything else, you did not. You were cowed in one sense by... the whole set-up. You couldn't step out of line because of the awful punishments and isolation that would result.[234]

CHAPTER 4

IT'S NOT YOUR FAULT!

THOSE WHO DIDN'T MAKE IT

I love the devoted determination of people
Who against the odds
Have found a way to conquer
Aching abandonment, numbing neglect, things too terrible to
mention
But we must not forget our peers,
Someone's brother, sister, someone's child
Let's spare a thought today for those who didn't make it.

They won't take part in research,
Or look an academic in the eye,
In that they haven't missed much
But they can't play ball with a child
Or wonder at a baby's fingernails
They don't see the swirling colours of hoards of flashing fish
Or watch a spider stepping side to side
Releasing its silky thread

Friendship, vin rouge, laughter,
A look held close within one's heart
Words, enjoyed later

Memories
This and so much more,
No longer with us or part of what we share

A boy, beaten, bruised, broken, suffering
And death reared its gruesome head, in the name of God
I heard of a sister, her young brother died in a group
But she said it was a blessing, as he had suffered so

I've read of children fed poison, by those meant to nurture
The authorities hid their faces
They'd signed the adoption papers
For those meant to nurture

And children who died in pain
No morphine to hasten their path
Or turn the dark shadows to day
But for whom death was a release
They didn't see a doctor or have timely medical care
They died from sickness, for which there was a cure

And what of those who left their group at tender age
Just 17 or younger still, or maybe 21
They ran away,
They could not stay.
Or perhaps they were booted from all they'd ever known
Into a culture which they had never known
Their naivety stood out, their vulnerability
Five years going on 50, they got the wrong attention
Then murdered in a park

The loss of a sister
The ache, the pain of smouldering grief
Held in a secret compartment in the heart

And we remember those who killed themselves
Who could not continue, for whom life was too much
And hope died within them

While they haven't missed much,
By not looking in an academic's eye,
Will the academics notice, will they wonder why?
Will they understand: informed consent cannot be given
A questionnaire won't be filled

Will they remember those who are missing
From whom nothing has been heard
Are they alive or dead in distant lands?

And those who have no clue
They battle through
Confused, tormented
No doctor will they see
Rejected by their group
Living in the devil's playground
Rejecting those with outstretched hand
Spiritual is my problem
There is no help for me
Their needs unmet, they have turned recluse

Or too ill
In the psych hospital

How many of our peers are homeless?
How many sit upon our streets?
What of those in a deluded space
The needle is their friend
Will they ever return, will they look to be helped?
Will they find support?

69

And let us remember, those of us who are here
Who just struggle onwards,
Or who celebrate our lives
Live them to the full
We are the lucky ones.
Somehow we made it through
We are here today to tell a little of our tale
And learn something new

We will not take part in survivor guilt
But as far as we are able, within our limited means
We will look for those who are missing
Support those who want our help
We will breathe out hope
And give kind looks to the recluse and those who are unwell
For we know they are our peers
Ours or someone's sister, brother, someone's child
But we won't forget
And we will spare a thought today for those who didn't make it

And we hope the academics will also spare a thought today
And tomorrow when they write a paragraph or chapter
Will you help give meaning, will you honour them?
Show their worth and value
Search for those who are missing
Please will you remember those who didn't make it.

A sect leader's reality:

'It's really then just a question of how does he want to manifest his domination. How does he want to act out his domination? Does he want to brutalise them? Then he'll brutalise them. Does he want to rape them? Then he'll rape them. Does he want to take their money? Then he takes their money. Does he want to control their career choices? He controls their career choices. Does he want to interfere with their relationships? He interferes with them. Doesn't matter. If he wants to do it, he does it. If he doesn't, he's got better things to do, you know? So many options for abuse and so little time! So he makes his choices, again, as I've said before, according to his own pathology. What does his pathology need him to do in order for the abuses to be sustained in some way?' Christian Szurko, Co-ordinator of the Dialogue Centre UK, who works with former members, current members and those with loved ones in extremist authoritarian sects.[235]

Many sect leaders have been found to display evidence of mental illness.[236] What then might happen to the children in such a group who, by reason of their physical size and emotional maturity, are vulnerable?

Overview

The quote above suggests that the abuse reports that follow are dependent on the potential psychopathology of the leaders, and as such will differ according to the leader of the particular sect, sub-sect or family in which a dominant leader exists. This chapter looks at child maltreatment, neglect and abuse, as well some of the experiences of adults abused in sects. It will describe how witnessing the abuse of others is a form of abuse in its own right. It should be borne in mind that not all children in sects are abused, neglected or maltreated, and to assume such would be a grave error. Nevertheless, those who are may be profoundly affected by those experiences, and thus it is imperative that the topic is dealt with in some depth in this chapter. It is also worth noting that often a child who experiences one type of maltreatment, abuse or neglect also experiences other types as well as negative or dysfunctional family environments[237] (if they live in a family environment which they may not be the case for some children in sects, in which case they may experience another environment which is negative or dysfunctional).

Neglect

Child neglect refers to one or more of a child's basic needs not being met as a result of which a child suffers harm or is at risk of harm[238]. The basic needs of children are wide-ranging and as a result child neglect includes: neglect of health care or personal hygiene, poor nutrition, inadequate household safety, lack of household sanitation, inadequate shelter, abandonment or supervisory neglect, educational neglect, emotional neglect and encouraging criminal behaviour.

The effects of child neglect, characterised by omission of care, should not be underestimated. Research has found that child neglect can have a greater negative impact than other forms of abuse and maltreatment.[239] Children have basic needs. Failure to meet these basic needs of children can have profound effects on children, which are carried on into their adolescence and adulthood.

Medical neglect

Michael Langone and Gary Eisenberg[240] reported on a study[241] on 70 former sect members, which found that:

- 27% of the respondents said children in their groups were not immunised against common childhood diseases;
- 23% said children did not get at least eight hours sleep a night;
- 61% said families were encouraged to live together and share responsibilities; and
- 37% said that children were seen by a doctor when ill.

Neglect of healthcare in groups may arise from the desire to avoid wasting time or money on anything considered non-essential to the group's goals. For example, a sect devoted to public proselytizing (the act of attempting to convert people to another opinion, particularly a religious one) may teach that taking a few day's bed rest for a cold or 'flu is self-indulgent or uncommitted in the light of the urgency of their cause. Some groups may shun certain kinds of medical treatment on the grounds that it is wrong according to their doctrine.

Christian Science is well-known for members having denied medical care to both adults and children who subsequently die,[242] and so far over 50 people have been charged in connection with these deaths. Caroline Fraser,[243] who herself was raised in Christian Science, writes the following:

> 'It is heartbreaking to see children in hospital beds, suffering from cancer or leukemia. But ill and frightened though they are, such children at least have adults to minister to their physical and emotional needs with medical care, pain killers, counseling, and empathy. Imagine those children at home, being told by their parents that their illness is not real and that the pain they feel is not a part of the real world-- God's world. Imagine yourself at six or nine or twelve being very sick and hearing your parents read to you Eddy's definition of man, which begins, "Man is not matter; he is not made up of brain, blood, bones, and other material elements." Imagine what happens to a child when her cancer goes untreated for months. And then imagine how it feels. If you can bear to imagine that, you will be imagining what actually happened to Ashley King. Ashley King died in 1988. She was twelve years old, and she had bone cancer.'

There are a number of sects that teach dependence on God for all one's needs, while other sects emphasise correct thinking or mental purity as a way of controlling or transcending the laws of the physical

73

universe. In either of these kinds of groups, neglect of healthcare may take the more extreme form of consciously refusing some or all professional medical help or treatment, regarding it either as a lack of faith or as a failure to overcome delusion, i.e., they regard illness as a delusion of the mind, and therefore do not believe it should be treated.

Research in the US[244] looked into 172 child deaths where parents withheld medical care because of reliance on religious ritual where documentation was available to determine the cause of the death. In total, 144 of the 172 child fatalities were from conditions for which survival rates with medical care exceed 90%. An expected survival rate of over 50% was present in 18 more had they received medical care. They report that: 'When faith healing is used to the exclusion of medical treatment, the number of preventable child fatalities and the associated suffering are substantial and warrant public concern.'[245]

> When refusal of health care is chosen by adults for themselves, it may be regarded as an unfortunate exercise of their rights, but when it is applied to minors, it constitutes unacceptable child neglect and is abusive in that it may endanger the child's well-being.

In some parts of the world, it is specifically outlawed, and the right of children to adequate medical care has been recognised by the international community.[246]

Brent Jeffs, who grew up in the Fundamentalist Church of Jesus Christ of Latter Day Saints, insightfully states the following:

> *I think our avoidance of outside medical care developed out of our desire to be a separate people, but I can't help but think that it also was a way to hide child abuse.*[247]

Further, in countries where medical care is not financed by the state, the cost of medical care may also play a part in children in sects not receiving adequete, or even at times any, medical care.

EFFECTS OF CHILD NEGLECT

Children are affected by child neglect in a variety of ways, including the development of social and intellectual difficulties (e.g., they may have great difficulty in interpersonal relationships, including with attachments to caregivers), emotional and behavioural problems; furthermore, the physical consequences are numerous and can even include death.[248] Child neglect has been found to be more serious than other types of child maltreatment both in terms of the numbers of children who are at risk of being harmed and the number of children who are harmed as well as how serious the harm is, it can include loss of life.[249] Part of the responsibility of parenting is providing appropriate boundaries which children need in order to feel safe. A woman who spent her childhood at Centrepoint in New Zealand describes her experience in the following way:

> 'There were no rules, there was no safety.'[250]

Lack of appropriate care which amounts to emotional neglect and educational neglect is covered in a more detailed way in Chapter five which looks at the development of children.

PHYSICAL VICTIMISATION

PHYSICAL VICTIMISATION OF CHILDREN

The study referred to by Langone and Eisenberg[251] in the section on child neglect also found that:[252]

- '60% said their groups permitted physical punishment of children;
- 13% said that the children were sometimes physically disabled or hurt to teach them a lesson; and
- 13% said that the punishment of children was sometimes life-threatening or required physicians' care.'[253]

A survey of former members raised in 'The Family' (an international sect) found that over 98% of the respondents considered that the discipline they experienced in the group was 'much too severe' or 'too severe'.[254] A study was done on the children raised in The House of Judah following the beating to death of a child in the sect.[255] Despite having nutritionally healthy bodies, male children in the sect had at least a 75% chance of showing signs of severe physical abuse to their bodies by the time they reached adolescence. The author states that:

> 'The children of the House of Judah have been reared in a manner unacceptable to any and all standards. Their bodies seriously and permanently injured... What limited responsibility for one's own action that has been formulated is now in question by their witnessing the death of John at the hands of their elders and the laying of the responsibility of John's death upon God.'[256]

Sometimes the extent of children's physical and emotional abuse in sects is downplayed by academics, as has been the case with the children of Jonestown,[257] who suffered horrific abuse and terror in the years prior to their murders.[258]

Results from data I analysed from a sample of individuals who sought help at Wellspring Retreat and Resource Centre, where former sect members receive therapeutic care, showed that 44% of the second generation reported physical child victimisation leading to bruises, scars, broken bones or bleeding, as compared to 11% of the first generation.

A further study I conducted in the UK had remarkably similar findings, with 11% of those joining sects as adults reporting physical child victimisation leading to bruises, scars, broken bones or bleeding as compared to 13% of the comparison non-sect-like groups and 42% of those raised in sects.

Two examples of physical violence towards children in Harry's Sect are given below from female interviewees:

> *He would punch us and hit us over very stupid things, and as I told you, he'd whip us with a horsewhip, which he kept just for that. . . . He knocked me, when I was about 10, he hit me really hard and knocked me down the stairs, and I got an ear infection from the blow to the ear.*[259]

> *There was one time when my gym mistress saw me when I had to have a shower after games, and I had six black stripes across my bum and down my legs, and she called me in and she wanted me to report who had done that to me, and I wouldn't. She made quite a big thing of it.*[260]

Some second-generation former member interviewees from Harry's Sect did not report being physically abused, and individual differences appeared to be present between families according to the degree to which the leader's teaching was implemented at home. The leader's teaching encouraged physical discipline, so where this teaching was implemented there was likely to be a greater degree of physical abuse of children. Additionally, parents may have been under considerable stress themselves, particularly if the leader had recently verbally abused them. Fathers were seen as at the top of the family hierarchy,

and part of their responsibility was to ensure their 'family's good behaviour' in line with the standards of the sect.

Physical abuse in childhood may cause long-term effects in adulthood,
including contributing to criminal or violent behaviour, substance
abuse and socio-emotional problems.[261]

PHYSICAL VICTIMISATION OF ADULTS

There were no reports of physical abuse of adults in Harry's Sect referred to above. Within the same sect, adults and children may have
different abuse experiences. Children being the least powerful individuals in a sect by reason of both their physical size and emotional maturity may experience higher levels or different types of abuse
than adults. However, interview reports from other sects indicate that
adult physical victimisation does occur. Further at times both adults
and children may be the victims of physical violence as reported by
Winifried Hempel[262], who was in a sect in Chile:

> *This was the religious meeting room where people confessed to Schaefer
> publicly and people prayed in public, and you had to confess your sins
> every night in front of Schaefer and everyone else. It was something re-
> ally horrifying. Sometimes he put people in the middle and beat them.*

Faris Kermani: *You saw that yourself?*

Winfried Hempel: *I saw that many times. Then the person who
would be beaten had to pray to God in front of everyone and ask for
forgiveness for being such a sinner and for having brought punishment
upon himself that in itself was a sin.*

If adults including parents are suffering such treatment, then one wonders how children might fare in such an environment. In the UK, as in
other countries, it is considered a crime to physically assault another

adult without their consent. The key defining factor of physical victimisation of adults is then that the adult did not consent to being hit.
Non-consensual hitting occurred in the Buddhist sect, Ted's Sect, as
reported below:

> *He was a higher grade, and then he did this thing which is basically
> all-out sparring, and she was there, her belt falling off, 'No Darren,
> don't hit me, Darren don't hit me!' but he still went and sparred with
> her. Then he made someone else go and spar with her, and then some-
> one else go and spar with her, and afterwards, and then she was cry-
> ing, she was battered into the wall. This is definitely the closest thing
> I ever saw to physical abuse, definitely. She was battered into the wall,
> she was crying her eyes out, begging them to stop, and he was going,
> 'Fight back! Come on, we're not stopping this 'til you fight back.' And
> eventually she did, but her face, this whole side of her face was red and
> swollen, and I mean she'd been beaten up basically, and that was the
> worst that I ever saw it get.*[263]

Although adult physical abuse was reported by interviewees to be severe at times, it did not seem to be a frequent occurrence. Not all
participants reported receiving or witnessing this, particularly if they
were on the periphery of the sect. At other times, there was a problem
not with the fact that individuals were hit, but with the way in which
they were hit. Victor Frankl, a psychiatrist, said this about being hit
while in a concentration camp:

> 'At such a moment it is not the physical pain which hurts the
> most (and this applies to adults as much as to punished chil-
> dren); it is the mental agony caused by the injustice, the unrea-
> sonableness of it all'.[264]

However, there are indications that individuals view the abuse of others and themselves in sects as for their good. Additionally, where an

individual is beaten up or physical abuse is severe, fear of injury or fear of loss of life also needs to be considered, as it could constitute a traumatic stressor for the individual.[265] Furthermore, it might occur while individuals are also experiencing psychological maltreatment and psychological abuse such as humiliation causing shaming. One former member of the Buddhist-based sect referred in this way to the physical violence: *'It's not so much physical, but it's very, very scary. Mental scariness is really a lot worse than physical violence. '*[266] This backs up other research that found that in women whose partners were participating in a group treatment programme for physical abuse, the psychological abuse rather than the physical abuse the women had experienced was more strongly and uniquely associated with post-traumatic stress disorder symptoms.[267]

Parallels between situations of domestic violence and sects have been observed;[268] this also links into battered-women syndrome.[269] The consequences of violence for battered women include fear, learned helplessness, emotional trauma, intellectual impairment, motivational impairment, stress, physical illness and post-traumatic stress disorder.[270] Consequently, physical abuse in sects or comparable settings is also highly likely to have an impact on post-sect harm and recovery.

Psychological victimisation, abuse and maltreatment

Psychological abuse is defined as where: 'A group or an individual (e.g. a psychotherapist, religious leader, police officer) in a position of differential power over an adult uses psychologically manipulative and coercive techniques – for example, rejecting, terrorising, isolating to control that person's behaviour, effects, and cognitions, usually to the influencee's detriment'.[271] Psychological abuse can also happen to children.

Research conducted with those seeking help at Wellspring found that children received significantly more psychological maltreatment from one of their parents than the first generation in childhood. The first generation did not grow up in a sect. A further study of former members who were raised in sects in the UK also found that they received significantly more psychological maltreatment from their parents than their parents did in their childhood as well as more than those who had left non-sect-like groups. It is important to recognise that psychological maltreatment of children in sects can occur from individuals other than parents, as the following research about Harry's Sect and Harry the sect leader shows.

Harry rarely attended sect meetings. However, interview reports indicate that his authority and status as sect leader meant his presence and effect had a disproportionate impact relative to the actual time he spent in meetings. Additionally, there was evidence that Harry sometimes met with individuals and/or phoned them, including those raised in the group which was another avenue for influencing child and adult group members.[272]

Different types of psychological child maltreatment that have been consistently identified by authors in the field[273] include rejecting; degrading (verbal abuse); terrorising; isolating; mis-socialising; exploiting; acts of omission such as a lack of stimulation and responsiveness; close confinement (restricting a child's movement by binding limbs); and other types of maltreatment not already specified such as withholding food, shelter, sleep or other necessities as forms of punishment, or continually applying developmentally inappropriate expectations (sometimes referred to as over-pressuring). Six of these types of psychological maltreatment[274] were identified from research on Harry's Sect and are therefore listed below. These include interview quotes from former members, which serve as examples of these occurring in Harry's Sect.

1. Rejecting: Verbal or symbolic acts that express feelings of rejection towards the child. For example, singling out a child for criticism and/or punishment. This happened in meetings.[275]

2. Degrading (i.e. verbal abuse): Actions that depreciate a child. For example, publicly humiliating a child. This also happened in sect meetings.[276]

3. Isolating: Preventing the child from engaging in normal social activities. For example, refusing interactions with individuals outside the family or refusing interactions with other relatives. This occurred in Harry's Sect and is discussed in more detail in the section on lack of relationship with others in or outside the sect in Chapter Six.

4. Denying emotional responsiveness (i.e. ignoring): Acts of omission whereby the caretaker does not provide stimulation and responsiveness. For example, failure to express affection, caring and love towards the child. An interviewee described Harry as emotionally 'crushing' children in the meeting, which indicates the abusiveness of his behaviour.[277]

5. Terrorising: Actions or threats that cause extreme fear and/or anxiety in a child. An Harry's Sect participant's quote is given below to demonstrate the fear present in the meetings in children in Harry's Sect:

    And then when Harry came, that was even' worse 'cos you'd be scared. Well, I thought if I knew he was coming, I'd feel myself shaking and my heart beating. And I'd think of all the things I'd done wrong that week, they'd be running through my head, because once he told us that he was there and he could read our thoughts or something – not that he could read our thoughts, but when he prayed, God told him what we were thinking, and if we were doing anything wrong. So I used to think, 'Oh no, he knows about me, and he's come to tell me off.' I used to [think] for the whole meeting. I'd be scared that he'd look at me,.. You know, he dragged his eyes across me and look at something, and his eyes, as they passed me – aarrggh – I think everybody felt that way.[278]

6. Other: types of emotional maltreatment not specified under other categories. For example, chronically applying developmentally inappropriate expectations (sometimes referred to as over pressuring). In Harry's Sect, very young children (e.g. four-year-olds) had to sit very still in meetings,[279] and of course they also weren't allowed to speak or make any noise (other than singing when that occurred).

Interview reports indicated that this psychological maltreatment was present in Harry's Sect from Harry himself usually in the meetings. Harry's 'lead' and the example he set of treating children also influenced parental treatment of children both in and outside the meeting. Negative effects associated with psychological maltreatment include interpersonal maladjustment, intellectual deficits and affective behavioural problems.[280]

Other sects may have still other types of emotional maltreatment. For example, some children in The Children of God had to endure weeks of silence restriction, whereby they were forbidden to talk to others and even had to wear signs hung from their necks, so that other children are aware that these children are not supposed to talk or be spoken to except by an adult in charge.[281]

Sexual abuse

Child sexual abuse

The National Center on Child Abuse and Neglect (NCCAN; 1978) defined child sexual abuse as:

'Contacts or interactions between a child and an adult when the child is being used for the sexual stimulation of the perpetrator or another person. Sexual abuse may also be committed by a person under the age of 18 when that person is either significantly older than the victim or when the perpetrator is in a position of power or control over another child.'

The effects of child sexual abuse are numerous, including emotional, cognitive, physical and behavioural difficulties such as sexualised behaviour in children. Long-term effects associated with child sexual abuse include emotional, interpersonal, post-traumatic- stress-disorder symptoms, sexual adjustment and behaviour dysfunction.[282]

A paper written[283] about child abuse in the Hare Krishna movement records that not only was severe abuse, including sexual abuse, taking place for a period in excess of 15 years, but also how that abuse was justified and came to occur in parts of the group. It is now widely recognised that sexual abuse directly and indirectly influenced the lives of a sizeable number of children in the Hare Krishnas. While the frequency or lack of frequency of the occurrence of child abuse in sects does not negate the pain and suffering of individuals, it does allow us to address the issue of child abuse in sects to see if the occurrence is greater than in the general population.

In some sects, sexual abuse is sanctioned. In the Davidians, girls as young as 10 years old were being groomed to be David Koresh's sexual partners.[284] In the Fundamentalist Latter Day Saints, girls as young as 13 were given as brides to much older men.

At Centrepoint, 'The living arrangements made it likely that sex could be easily observed by anyone passing by, and we were told that it was common for children to see and hear sexual encounters.'[285] Centrepoint actively encouraged child sexuality, and it was common for boys and girls to have sex somewhere between the ages of 11 and 13. Researchers stated that:

'The Centrepoint community normalised open attitudes to sexual behaviour, valued exploration and non-monogamous relationships, practiced nudity and used therapeutic techniques to break down social inhibitions and boundaries related to sexual identity and behaviour. While the underage sex described by half our participants would legally constitute sexual abuse, it was not always identified as abuse by participants because they understood it to be consensual and normal. But around a third of our sample specifically identified themselves as having experienced sexual abuse during their time at Centrepoint.'

Looking at current children in The Family (formerly known as the Children of God), Lilliston[286] found no evidence of physical or sexual abuse. However a more recent study[287] found that 76% of the respondents reported yes to the question, 'Did you ever experience children being directly involved in sexual practices in TF?'

Research analysis that I did on the Wellspring help-seeking data sample looked at child sexual victimisation. Study 1 found that 61% of the second generation reported sexual victimisation in childhood, compared to 28% of the first generation. Further research was carried out in the UK. Differences in worldwide ages for consent to have sex legally, exist.[288] Unfortunately, in the questionnaire used in the UK study, individuals were asked to report sexual abuse up to the age of 14 instead of 16. It found that 26% of the second generation reported sexual victimisation in childhood compared to those not raised in sects, including 23% of the first generation and 25% of the comparison group who had left non-sect-like groups.

In Study 1, where very high levels of sexual victimisation were reported, the percentage of males to females was low for both the first and second generation. However, this is reversed in Study 2 for the second generation sample which had a much higher percentage of males to females. Given that previous research[289] indicates that females are far more likely to be sexually abused than boys, while boys are far more likely to be physically abused than girls, the differences in levels of child victimisation between Studies 1 and 2 might be partially accounted for by differences in the ratios of males and females between Studies 1 and 2.

Sexual abuse of boys does occur in some sects. Brent Jeff's autobiography[290] the 'Lost Boy', describes some of the sexual abuse that he experienced and how the evidence of sexual abuse went unnoticed by the adults.

In summary, sexual abuse of children in some sects occurs in high levels and at times is even part of the teaching of a few. Experience of sexual abuse is very harmful to children, and can continue to have profound consequences on into adulthood and throughout the lives of individuals.

SEXUAL ABUSE OF ADULTS

What follows is a discussion of sexual abuse in an English, Buddhist, karate, hand-reading, yoga sect whose leader Ted was described as a 'dirty old man'[291] and a 'womaniser'.[292] Interview reports also indicate that Ted sexually abused women in Ted's Sect. To further understand the sexual abuse of adults, it is necessary to first understand the unethical nature of psychological abuse. Michael Langone[293] argues that psychological abuse is an ethical concept because it suggests wrongly using someone; it refers to situations in which techniques of persuasion and control are used to exploit and/or otherwise mistreat people. Similarly, sexual abuse can be viewed as an ethical concept. Marie Fortune[294] states that it is wrong for a pastor to have sexual contact with someone he or she serves or supervises, because sexual activity in this context is exploitative and abusive. She states that it is:

1. a violation of role;
2. a misuse of authority and power;
3. taking advantage of vulnerability; and
4. an absence of meaningful consent.

Similar arguments can be put forward in the case of Ted's Sect, as shown below:

1. A violation of role – Ted was the head teacher of Ted's Sect, and this presupposes certain role expectations. The expectation is that a head teacher makes available certain resources, talents, knowledge and expertise (in this instance, that referred to martial arts, yoga, hand reading and Buddhist knowledge) that serve the best interest of the student. Sexual contact is not part of the role. If sexual contact was supposed to have been part of this role, then students should have been forewarned upon their first contact with the group.

2. A misuse of authority and power – The role of head teacher carries with it authority and power, and the attendant responsibility to use that power to benefit the students. Engaging in sex on the basis of that role is a misuse of that authority and power. Arguing that it is a part of that role, as a male Ted's Sect participant reported was done to female students in the way indicated below, is a misuse of power:

   The fact that you don't want to have sex with me is just your ego, not that you don't want to have sex, therefore you need to deal with your ego', you know, that sort of line. 'Don't you think a student should do what their teacher asks them to do?[295]

3. Taking advantage of vulnerability – The students had fewer resources and less power than the head teacher, and were therefore by definition vulnerable to him. Thus, to engage in sexual contact with a student was taking advantage of the student's

vulnerability and violated the mandate to protect the vulnerable from harm.

4. An absence of meaningful consent – Fortune states that 'Meaningful consent to sexual activity requires a context of not only choice but mutuality and equality; hence meaningful consent requires the absence of fear or the most subtle coercion'.[296] Previous sections in this chapter have indicated that there was a great imbalance of power in these groups and the presence of high levels of fear. The interview reports specifically relating to sexual abuse refer to the fear that they felt at the time of the sexual abuse and afterwards.

It is apparent that even had the women who were sexually abused in their groups been sexually attracted to Ted (participant interviews indicated that the opposite was the case), it was the leader's role to ensure that boundaries were not violated. A quote from one of the women sexually abused by Ted is given below:

> *The thought of him coming on to me never went through my head . . .*
> *He [Ted] started touching me up. My first thought was, 'get off me, you*
> *dirty old man'. Everything I had invested this energy and hope into. I*
> *couldn't grasp that he was a fake, and I wasn't strong enough at the*
> *time to cut off from that point on . . . I was trapped in this vice, where*
> *I thought somehow I was asking for it, deserved it and he was teach-*
> *ing me. I was always trying to find justification all the time. 'Is there*
> *something he's trying to tell me, like I'm a bad person?'.... When Ted*
> *started abusing me, I just felt really frightened. I was terrified, looking*
> *back on it. I was like a rabbit caught in a hedge.* [297]

An absence of meaningful consent

Victor Frankl[298] argues that in every circumstance, humans have choices – we are not just products of our environment. As a psychiatrist who spent three years in Auschwitz and other concentration camps, Victor Frankl suffered from hunger, cold and brutality. He expected to die as his father, mother, wife and brother died in concentration camps. He contends that the last of human freedoms is freedom of attitude. He argues that it is the last freedom because it cannot be taken away. Indeed Frankl's argument for this is convincing – to have choice in any environment is what makes an individual human. How does Frankl's theory regarding humans and choice fit with the concept of the sexual abuse of adults? Some might argue that these women 'choose' to have sexual relations with their leader (except in instances where physical force was involved); however, the environment was so overwhelming and the pressure so great they were actually sexually abused by the leader. Therefore, I would argue that, in these circumstances, the choice cannot be said to indicate meaningful consent and as such is not choice.

The law supports the view that, in certain circumstances, there can be an absence of meaningful consent in sexual relationships between adults. Specifically, the Sexual Offences Act 2003 states that 'a person consents if he agrees by choice and has the freedom and capacity to make that choice',[299] thus the law makes clear that submission is not consent. Further, Home Office Guidelines give the following example of a non-consensual sexual act: 'I said no and he tried to talk me into it. Then he started shouting and getting angry. In the end, I went along with it. I was too scared to say anything'.[300] The guidelines state that 'Giving consent is active not passive. It means freely choosing to say "yes".' The law support the view that choice must be meaningful and freely chosen.

The absence of meaningful consent has been covered in the section above. An additional reason for an absence of meaningful consent is that the group/leader had become the meaning of the victim's life. Victor Frankl[301] states that 'Man's search for meaning is a primary force in his life and not a "secondary rationalization" of instinctive drives.' For core members, the group and its leader appeared to have become perhaps the most important aspect of their 'meaning of life'. They had few relationships outside the group, and as one of the participants indicated:

> Everything I had invested this energy and hope into.[302]

THE EFFECTS OF SEXUAL ABUSE

Regardless of whether an individual accepts the arguments given above for some of the women in this group having been sexually abused, interview reports indicated the presence of harm in these women in the form of fear, terror and dissociative (altered state of consciousness) symptoms:

> It's almost like it didn't really happen or I can't really connect with what it was like. It was like I didn't really exist. I remember going home and seeing friends, and she would say, "What has happened to you? You used to be a bit of a laugh." I had been a jolly, outgoing girl, and I really did disappear. It's like 'Where did I go?' I was unhappy, unsure, I really didn't know who I was anymore and I was very lost. I didn't in a way have much freedom to really connect with my feelings . . . So when you ask me how I feel, I can look back and think, 'Yeah, I felt those things and I can see that I was, but I was unaware at the time of what was going on….. '. I began to dissociate, I didn't know how to deal with my feelings. I didn't know how to cope with what was going on, so I began to dissociate.[303]

As well as Ted's behaviour towards women, it also appeared common for other *dojo* leaders to have sexual relationships with female members of Ted's Sect while holding powerful positions in their *dojo*. This can be viewed as a gross misuse of their position of power and responsibility within the sect.

In considering the effects on the victim, Fortune states that one must bear in mind that such sexual abuse is first and foremost a betrayal of trust. Research looking at sexual abuse of adults by medical and mental health professionals and clergy has found the effects to include loss, emotional mistrust, depression and relationship difficulties. Intensification of the effects of abuse may also occur because of difficult complaints procedures.[304] Victims of exploitative sexual behaviour by practitioners generally suffer from post-traumatic stress disorder after the exploitation.[305] Experience of sexual abuse then is one of the factors that contribute to the harm found in former sect members. If adults in sects experience sexual abuse and this affects them in such deep ways, how much more are children (who have not yet developed fully in any way and therefore are in an even more vulnerable position and even less able to protect themselves) likely to find the effects of child sexual abuse devastating? Further, how does the abuse a parent experiences impact their ability to be an available parent who protects their own children from harm where necessary?

SPIRITUAL ABUSE

David Johnson and Jeff Van Vonderen, in their excellent book 'The Subtle Power of Spiritual Abuse', define the term 'spiritual abuse' broadly as 'the mistreatment of a person who is in need of help, support or greater spiritual empowerment with the result of weakening, undermining or decreasing that person's spiritual empowerment'.[306] After their definition, they explain that spiritual abuse can occur when a leader uses his or her spiritual position to control or dominate another person. Further, they state that when spirituality is used to make others live up to a spiritual standard, then spiritual abuse can occur. Within the context of a Bible-based sect, many of the standard practices within the group would fit into their definition. While the first generation also experienced spiritual abuse in the Bible-based sect, it was the second generation who, after leaving the sect, maintained or acquired a faith in God who most often mentioned that on leaving they had great difficulty in reading the Bible.

This is demonstrated by the following quote, talking about the leader:

> *And still I get times,… when I don't want to pick the Bible up…. It is a struggle, because everything we learnt really was through him, and… you can look up passages and it comes back, what he used to go on about, and I find that quite hard.*

What sort of stuff did he [the leader] used to go on about a lot?

> *Well, the Psalms, because he was doing all that work on the Psalms, and the way he used the Psalms against my mum like that. I find that really hard, so a lot of Psalms I can't look at.*[307]

Another second-generation former member recalled the following:

> *When *Jeremiah left . . . I remember Jason praying that his tongue would be pierced, and he would have lead weights hanging off his tongue and really awful things like that, in judgement, because he'd- what they called- 'betrayed' the leader.*[308] *(pseudonym)

Given that former members reported experiencing intense fear, and this event is talking about 'threatened serious injury', it might be the case that, during Harry's Sect meetings, individuals experience what might constitute a traumatic stressor as defined by the Fourth Diagnostic and Statistics Manual for mental illness.[309] This would then be another causal factor that might contribute to higher levels of post-traumatic stress disorder (PTSD). A study over time[310] of 69 assault survivors with and without post-traumatic stress disorder found that survivors showed enhanced priming for trauma-related words. These words act as a trigger for intrusive re-experiencing of traumatic events. Thus, where an event might be construed as a traumatic stressor and that event also involved the use of biblical words, it might be the case that words commonly associated with the Bible constitute trauma-related words and act as triggers for re-experiencing traumatic events. This might be an explanation as to why former members have difficulty in reading the Bible after sect membership or why they find it difficult to attend church.

Given the young age of second-generation former members while experiencing possible traumatic stressors, it might be worth noting that researchers observed that re-experiencing even includes 'affect without recollection,' that is, individuals with PTSD may re-experience sensations or emotions that were associated with the traumatic event without recollection of the event itself'.[311] Therefore second generation former members may find parts of the Bible trigger traumatic feelings and yet they may have no memories associated to that Bible passage and as such the experience may be particularly confusing and frightening.

The focus of this particular sect environment, the constant threat of damnation and the end of the world, coupled with other group practices such as public humiliation from the leader, appeared to result in some lives being lived on the edge of a precipice. In this context, any trauma experience is being reinforced and, as such, it might be expected that effects from such an environment might profoundly affect future faith and spirituality.

SPIRITUALITY AND ITS ABSENCE AFTER LEAVING A SECT AND RECOVERY FROM SPIRITUAL ABUSE

It was evident from the interview data that more of the first generation than the second generation maintained a faith in God.

Both the first and second generation reported confusion about their religious beliefs, spirituality and faith in God after leaving. Those who did not maintain a faith may understandably be alienated from any religion or religious belief, or they may be extremely confused about this. Psychological research has found that having a faith or religious belief is helpful for people,[312] therefore, as Steven Kent, a Canadian sociologist, says, 'used sensitively, religion can become a vehicle for healing the very scars that it may have helped cause'.[313]

Similar to the findings from a Bible-based sect, a Buddhist-based sect interviewee spoke of having done a course in Shiatsu (a healing system based on spiritual energies in the body) after leaving the sect and having a positive experience of it:

> *I ended up doing a Shiatsu course, which was a three- year course, which ended about a year ago . . . and that was superb.... It was a lot more structured and safe, and there were rules and regulations...., and the two guys were sound. They kept their own personal stuff out of the group.*[314]

Most of the literature examining spiritual abuse has been written regarding those who experience abuse in a Christian or pseudo-Christian context. However spiritual abuse within other religions is also relevant here. Those joining the Buddhist-type sect were introduced to what they thought was Buddhism (although it may be more accurate to call it a 'supermarket' approach to Buddhism, in that it was a bit of this and a bit of that taken from a number of spiritual paths). The Buddhist concept of the five elements of fire, water, ether, air and earth was taught and learnt. Like the second-generation interviewees who had been in the Bible-based sect, many of the interviewees did not continue with the Buddhist teaching after leaving their Buddhist-like sect.

For former members of both groups, issues of trust were sometimes paramount after leaving. Spiritual abuse is yet another area that may be influential in terms of post-sect harm, and specifically, it may influence the former members' move away from religion and spirituality or their difficulties with religion. However, these difficulties can be overcome, and for some, religion and spirituality may be part of their path to healing and recovery.

Witnessing the abuse of others

While discussing the area of abuse, it is important not to overlook the effects of witnessing the abuse of others. Interview reports indicated that some of the abuse occurring in Ted's Sect and Harry's Sect happened in the presence of other sect members. As one second-generation former member, when talking about public humiliation by the sect leader, put it:

So, but he never picked on me.

Did you think that he might?
Yeah, I was well scared. Every time he came I thought, 'today's the day'.[315]

Winfried Hempel stated the following about some of the events he witnessed in the group he was raised in:[316]

Imagine not being able to eat for a week sitting at a table with everyone else eating around you. And, if someone dared to hand him or her a crumb, they would be punished. So, in the end, everyone who ate was an accomplice and vice versa. In that way it encouraged the interaction of victims with victimisers. The one who was the victim acted as the victimiser in regards to the victim and so on. It was a perverse circle that went on and on.

In a paper looking at child abuse in the Hare Krishna movement, the researcher raises the issue of those who witness others being abused, and states that it represents a form of abuse in its own right.[317] The Fourth Diagnostic and Statistics Manual[318] for mental illness indicates that something might constitute a traumatic stressor simply by being witnessed or confronted rather than directly experienced. Thus witnessing, listening to or confronting other people being abused, maltreated or neglected is another factor that might contribute to harm found after sect membership.

JUSTIFICATION OF ABUSE: FOR THE MEMBERS' GOOD?

A disturbing aspect of the interviewees' reports was that, in a number of cases, they viewed the physical, spiritual, sexual, psychological maltreatment or psychological abuse either of themselves or others as being *for their own good*. Both first- and second-generation former members of both sects make such comments. The following example refers to a Ted's Sect member being hit:

> *But although I found it horrible to see, I kept willing Janet to defend herself, and my perspective of the situation was that Darren knows what he's doing, therefore Janet must deserve this (ego, etc) / be being taught something valuable, and somehow it must be okay and I just don't know enough yet to understand properly. I'd been told plenty of times not to worry, that I'll be told all I need to know.*[319]

When Harry humiliated people in meetings, they sometimes thanked him for doing this,[320] as they believed it was for their good. The following example is from a Harry's Sect publication:

> 'Knowing that the whole orb of the gospel is preached, including reproof and correction which is so necessary and yet never preached anywhere else for fear of man, or of being unpopular. Whom the Lord loveth, he chasteneth. What a great blessing

this is;… although the flesh shrinks from it. How thankful we are afterwards for it.'[321]

Researchers observing other sects have also found abuse being justified as for the members' good.[322] Other researchers[323] refer to victims' participating in their own abusive situations, with victims believing that apparently abusive events are either justified or not actually abusive. For example, an adult attending and not walking out of a sect meeting where they are being terrorised or humiliated.

EXPLAINING THE IMMORAL IN SUCH A WAY THAT IT APPEARS MORAL: DO CHILDREN BUY THIS?

Professor Albert Bandura's[324] social cognitive theory explains the cognitive processes (thoughts) that occur in individuals (in this case the sect leader) to make immoral actions seem unimportant or even moral. This moral restructuring not only reduces the likelihood of an individual stopping that behaviour, but actually becomes a source of viewing oneself in a positive light. The abuse and murder of children at Jonestown was carried out by adults. Understanding how reprehensible and immoral behaviour can be turned upside-down in the mind of a person goes some way to understanding the behaviour.

While children may have an innate sense of right and wrong, children also learn from others about moral judgement. Professor Albert Bandura[325] explains that adults, peers and symbolic models serve as the sources of most children's moral judgements and conduct. At a young age, this learning often includes physical sanctions, but as children grow older social verbal sanctions are given, and adults increasingly explain conduct and reasons for conduct. Bandura states that children do not just passively absorb these moral standards, but make generic standards for themselves based on what they learn from their role models. In addition, children may have an innate and strong sense of justice and right and wrong which is not learnt from the moral guidance or moral behaviour of role models. Bandura, however, asserts that acquiring moral principles does not mean that individuals always behave in a moral way. Rather, individuals can attribute blame to others or to circumstances, therefore allowing one's own actions to be excusable and even allowing oneself to feel self-righteous in the process. As Professor Albert Bandura explains:

> 'Because internalised controls can be selectively activated and disengaged, marked changes in moral conduct can be achieved without changing people's personality structures, moral principles or self-evaluative systems. It is shifting the blame from one self rather than character flaws that account for most inhumanities'.[326]

Research in support of this has been conducted. Specifically, researchers[327] psychometrically tested 438 males and 361 females with a mean age of 12 years, and found that seeing injurious behaviour as serving righteous purposes, not owning responsibility for harmful effects and devaluing those who are maltreated were the most widely used methods of alleviation from the blame of self-sanctions.

Moral restructuring might affect the parents' understanding of right and wrong.[328] In part, this might explain parents not protecting their children from Harry's maltreatment of them. An additional explanation for parents not protecting their children might have been their fear that if they had done so, they might be the next victim of psychological abuse, or that the psychological maltreatment of their child might be increased. Under 'normal' circumstances, a parent might remove both themselves and their child from such an environment rather than see their child suffer in this way.

In addition to an innate sense of justice and right and wrong for most children, the source of their moral standards, judgements and conduct also comes from adults and peers. In Harry's Sect this was mostly limited to parents, siblings, Harry and interactions that occurred at school. Sometimes in Harry's Sect, harmless and innocent behaviour was seen as morally wrong,[329] as has been observed by others looking at sects.[330] It was found in the study of Harry's Sect that parents placed a great deal of emphasis on what Harry said, as he appeared to act as the source of all matters of morality in the sect meetings. While it is common for there to be inconsistencies between what people practise and what they advocate, in Harry's Sect this was greater and Harry had a very different life to the one he expected his followers to adhere to.

WHY MIGHT CHILDREN IN SECTS BE MORE VULNERABLE TO MALTREATMENT, ABUSE AND NEGLECT THAN THOSE IN THE WIDER SOCIETY?

The very structure of sects seems to predispose them towards abuse and neglect of children, although it doesn't necessarily mean that child maltreatment, abuse or neglect is a consequence of family involvement in a sect.[331] Below is a list of reasons that children raised in sects might be vulnerable to child abuse[332], however, identified items are not relevant for all sects or for all children in any one sect:

- Parents' dependency on the leader or leadership, which means that the leaders' beliefs and ideas about child-rearing, no matter how bizarre and unusual, are high likely to influence the parents' child-rearing practices.[333]
- Primacy of ideology over biology. The teaching of the sect may include the abuse of children (e.g. lack of medical care resulting in the harm or even death of children from curable illnesses). In the Hare Krishnas, the ideology of the group 'became justifications used by the leadership to dismiss the *gurukula* [sic, those teaching the children], the children and their responsibility towards both.' Therefore, few resources were invested in the children, and the teachers had a severe lack of

training, while at the same time being solely responsible for huge numbers of children. At times, older boys were enlisted to physically abuse younger boys; they reported that had they not done so, they themselves would have been abused.[334]

- Previous authors[335] have noted that parents of those in sects tend to act like middle management, and this may especially affect the children when a parent's commitment to the leader is measured by their willingness to maltreat, abuse or neglect the children at the leader's request. Research, I did found support for parents acting as middle managers. Parents, who would usually be expected to protect children from this type of treatment, collaborated in the children's abuse, whether consciously or unconsciously, by continually taking the children to sect meetings. Therefore, those meant to protect the children from harm became complicit with the sect leader. Children rely on their parents (particularly children in sects such as Harry's Sect, who have so few other social contacts) for a basic sense of trust, security and emotional stability. This support was lacking when children attended the sect meetings. Some second-generation former members reported that, at times, parents served as protective factors for the second generation. They were a buffer against the sect leader, but this wasn't always the case.

- Parents who tend to work a lot for the sect or engage in sect activities may have little time for their families.[336] Studies of the Hare Krishnas found a lack of parental involvement with the children, who lived more or less separate lives from their parents in boarding houses.[337]

- A clinical social worker who specialises in trauma and spiritual or cultic abuse notes that parents may not be present emotionally for their children as they may themselves be dissociated (in an altered state of consciousness).[338] Dissociation of sect members has been previously noted by others, hence the Diagnostics and Statistics Manual of the American Psychological Association[339] includes states of dissociation in someone who has experienced 'thought reform' (i.e. someone who has been in a sect with a thought-reform environment) as an example of someone who might have a Dissociative Disorder Not Otherwise Specified (i.e. be experiencing an altered state of consciousness).

- Parents may come to believe that normal human feelings for their children are not 'spiritual' or appropriate.[340] This is likely to affect the parent–child bond negatively. Amy Siskind[341], in her study of 'The Sullivan Institute/Fourth Wall Community,' reports that children as young as three were sent to boarding schools. In this particular group, 'it was believed that, as long as a parent provided his or her children with good childcare, education, clothing, and enough money to buy or do anything they wished, it was preferable that they spend as little time with them as possible.'

- The unpredictability of sect parents' lives may mean that their behaviour towards their child may also be unpredictable in terms of support, neglect or anger, thus impeding the child's ability to develop a sense of safety in their environment.[342]

- Parents' experience of the sect may result in a large amount of suppressed anger, which may be vented along with their frustration onto their children. This may become physically abusive if the sect's doctrine emphasises harsh physical discipline.[343]

- We must also consider those who, having been raised in a sect, remain there to become parents themselves. If they have never seen positive parenting skills in action, and have been affected by their own sect involvement and remain in that environment with its potential for the maltreatment, abuse and or neglect of children, will they have the necessary resources to raise healthy children who know they are loved and have worth? It is likely that they will only have the negative model of their own experience to draw on. (Interestingly, I have spoken to a number of second-generation parents who left their sect after having children because they could not tolerate the thought that what happened to them as a child, would happen to their children). It is worth noting that, while generational abuse is well documented, research has found that the majority of abused children do not in fact grow up to become abusive adults.[344]

- One of the key issues separating sects from the wider society is the lack of external and internal balances and checks that serve to limit child abuse, such as child protection policies. While the presence of such checks and balances in the wider society does not rule out abuse, neglect or maltreatment, it does mean that there is greater protection for children and that child abuse is more likely to be detected and dealt with appropriately.[345]

- Some of those in sects may be dishonest or may withhold the truth, due to members being accustomed to leaders who frequently dishonour confidentiality or seriously encourage members to look good by using conformity pressures.[346] It is also important to be aware of research on impression management, which looks at how potentially discrediting information is not acquired by outsiders.[347] The members of a group work together as a team, and do not allow information that may destroy confidence in the group to be obtained by those outside the group. In one academic paper[348], the authors specifically mention that information from former members, as well as The Family's (a sect) own literature, reveals the existence of 'media homes', where everything looks as perfect as possible and members have been briefed prior to the arrival of researchers.[349]

I identify further reasons why research points to those raised in sects being more vulnerable or at risk of neglect, maltreatment and/or abuse than those in wider society:

- Control and dominance were found to lie at the heart of different forms of child abuse. The high level of control and dominance that were found to be present in the Harry's Sect and Ted's Sect suggested that the cultural context of these sects might be seen as conducive to child abuse.
- The negative view of self that members had and the cognitive distortions and lack of worth reflected to children by other members may mean that they are more likely to tolerate and accept maltreatment.
- The moral restructuring of maltreatment as 'for their own good' means that abuse might be justified or not recognised as maltreatment by parents who allow their children to be in situations where they might be maltreated, instead of protecting their children.
- Children in sects may be accustomed to living a double life in order to survive their environment. This involves keeping secrets. Perhaps the fact that those raised in sects are already accustomed to keeping secrets means they are less likely to inform others when maltreatment or abuse does take place. In fact, it is common even with children not raised in sects for them not to inform others when they are experiencing abuse.
- My research found that children in Harry's Sect appear to have a lack of various types of specific knowledge, and thus may have no awareness of the presence of agencies such as social services and Citizens Advice Bureaux, although those children brought into the sect in childhood as opposed to being born into the sect may have this knowledge.
- The lack of relationship with others experienced by children in Harry's Sect, and their general fear and anxiety levels, mean that the children may have had extremely limited opportunities to talk to others about maltreatment or abuse experienced, thus limiting the chances of it being detected and dealt with appropriately.

CONCLUSION

'In the broadest sense . . . child abuse is not to be given moral sanction because it is done under the cover of religious or ideological practice'.[350]

At the end of a chapter on children and sects, Langone and Eisenberg[351] contend that,

'The abuses to which children have been subjected can be horrendous. The degree to which cult leaders can escape accountability by hiding behind the First Amendment is troubling. And the lack of concern and action about this problem is shameful' Public opinion '. . . seems to favour protection of children over parental rights and freedom of religion," and it certainly should. The protection of powerless children must take priority over any other consideration.'[352]

Some of those raised in sects can be classified as third-culture kids, which refers to those raised in a culture different to their parents' culture, however the phrase 'third-culture adults' would be more appropriate when referring to adults. Third-culture kids may go through life seemingly with no conscious feeling of sadness.[353] They may be surprised when a small incident triggers off a huge reaction. Often they are aged 25–40 when this occurs. Usually it is associated with the birth of their own children, as it is at this time that the realisation and questions never before asked about their own childhood and how they were treated may come to the fore.

In Harry's Sect, individuals reported a fear of abusing their own children because of the abuse they themselves experienced in their childhood. This supports the view that having one's own children may trigger a renewed awareness of an individual's own childhood experiences. Those abused in childhood might benefit from realising that they were little children at the time of the abuse, and knowledge they now have about these matters cannot be applied retrospectively.

The film *Good Will Hunting* has a very moving piece where the main character Will speaks briefly about some of the physical abuse he endured in his childhood. His therapist responds:

'It's not your fault, it's not your fault, it's not your fault.'

The therapist repeats this over and over, and the scene finishes with Will sobbing in the arms of his therapist. The title of this chapter was taken from that film.

SUMMARY OF CHAPTER 4

Children in some sects may be extremely vulnerable, and sadly sect leaders are not held accountable for their actions, therefore children can, at times, become objects to be used and abused by the sect leader in the way in which his or his psychopathology demands.

All children everywhere have needs, and the neglect of those needs – whether they be nutritional, emotional, medical or indeed any other type of need, can have wide ranging and huge impacts on the child, even at times causing death. Neglect of children must not be underestimated as a cause of harm to children. There are heart-rending cases of children who have died premature and painful deaths due to medical neglect or physical victimisation. In some sects, it is only children in some families who experience physical victimisation, while in other sects, adults – including parents – are beaten up. The incident of a woman in Ted's Sect being beaten up by a number of men in Ted's Sect is recorded.

Psychological maltreatment occurred in Harry's Sect meetings, specifically in terms of the sect leaders treatment of both children and adults. Child sexual abuse has been found to be present in some sects, and has even been found to be integrated into the teachings of a few sects. Further, the sexual abuse of adults can also occur in sects when meaningful consent is absent. The effects of both child and adult sexual abuse are wide-ranging and severe and may include long-term effects that profoundly affect lives.

Spiritual abuse also occurs in sects, and witnessing the abuse of others is an abuse in its own right. Sadly abuse is sometimes justified as for members' good. There are a number of reasons why children in sects may be more vulnerable to maltreatment, abuse and neglect than children in the wider society. Further, these childhood experiences may resurface in adulthood and may become traumatic triggers.

What comes next in Chapter 5?

The next chapter looks at children and what their needs in childhood are. It addresses how their development might be curtailed in a sect environment. As Winfried Hempel stated:

It was incredible. I was standing on a street away from the colony, 20 years old, with a psychological mentality of an 8-year-old boy.[354]

CHAPTER 5

GETTING THROUGH CHILDHOOD!

'The children of the House of Judah have been reared
in a manner unacceptable to any and all standards....
Their intellectual capacities underdeveloped, minimal
decision-making and problem solving abilities have been
taught, the basic components of delayed gratification
under developed, feelings and their expressions
denied, trust misguided and nongeneralisable with
fear serving as the foundation of their way of lives.
Their ability to develop and maintain long-term
close interpersonal relationships is very limited.'
Dr Ray Helfer, Paediatrician and Educator, 1983: 261

INTRODUCTION

Appreciating how child development works and what happens to children in sects can shed light on why parts of their development may be stunted. This chapter discusses two important theories about child development and how they relate to children in sects in order to describe the gaps in development that children and adolescents in sects are likely to experience. It is particularly important for children, as they grow, to have strong bonds with adults, and it is to this we now turn.

THE IMPORTANCE OF CHILDREN'S ATTACHMENTS TO ADULTS

John Bowlby[355], a psychologist, observed children who were raised in institutions or hospitals, and noticed that many such children struggled intellectually and were unable to form close relationships with others. Bowlby concluded that children who do not have the opportunity to form a close bond with their mother or a mother figure in early childhood will go on to experience social, emotional or intellectual problems in later life. Subsequent research by psychologists indicates that while there is some evidence to support Bowlby's views, other factors need to be taken into consideration, such as family discord and bonding with fathers. Children who have multiple caregivers in early life or who live in total isolation may be the most damaged, resulting in an inability to form strong attachments. Children in some sects lack opportunity to form attachments to adults. Peer relationships can reduce some of the effects of paternal deprivation, but not all.[356]

In their excellent book, '*The Boy Who was Raised as a Dog,*' Dr Bruce Perry and Maia Szalavitz[357] detail what traumatised children can teach us about loss, love and healing, highlighting how the very early years of a child's life are absolutely vital for future well-being in both childhood and adulthood. If a child does not bond with another person in the first year or so of life, that may set a pattern for life. The disruption in the development of the brain through early childhood neglect may affect the areas of control, empathy and the ability to engage in healthy relationships. Neglect is often underrated as a hazard, but neglect in older childhood can also have very serious implications throughout a life. Being neglected as a child can have pervasive effects on one's sense of self and one's place in the world; adults neglected as children may struggle to live independently – for example, they may have trouble with achievement, or have overwhelming dependency needs.[358]

SEPARATING CHILDREN FROM THEIR PARENTS

Amy Siskind[359] describes her upbringing in a sect that was misguidedly called a 'therapeutic community'. True therapeutic communities are described as:

> '"psychologically informed planned environments" – they are places where the social relationships, structure of the day and different activities together are all deliberately designed to help people's health and well-being'[360].

The leaders of the sect in which Amy Siskind was raised required members who were parents to either hire full-time childcare workers and housekeepers, or send their children to boarding schools from as early as three years of age because they held erroneous beliefs that no parents should take care of a child full-time, and that mothers generally behave in an envious and hateful manner to their children. It was preferable that parents spend as little time as possible with their children as long as they provided good childcare, education, clothing and money.[361]

As researchers[362] who studied Centrepoint – another supposed therapeutic community – explained: 'One participant described how her sense of detachment from adults began at Centrepoint and then spilt over into her relationships with family members for many years after she had left.' Relationships with adults in this community were important, as parents themselves often spent little time with their children. Some children were able to find adults who acted as surrogate parents in the community, which was essential to their well-being.

Amanda Van Eck Duymaer van Twist[363] reports the following on children raised in ISKON (International Society for Krishna Consciousness, also known as Hare Krishnas) in the following way:

'Children needed to be trained in 'sense control', hence they were removed from parents from the age of 4 or 5, to avoid the 'ropes of affection' between parents and child. Children attend the *gugukula* on a year-round basis, residing in ashrams with other children of similar age and sex. Visits to their parents tended to be sporadic.'

HOW ARE CHILDREN IN SECTS AFFECTED BY BEING SEPARATED FROM THEIR PARENTS?

The School of Economic Science, a Hindu-based sect, taught that people should not be emotionally involved with their own children. Some children were sent to the sects' boarding schools in London. One child raised in this sect recounted:

It is impossible to convey the depth of loneliness and misery experienced by a child of 13 uprooted from all it knows and thrown unprepared into a strange country, strange company, huge cold old streets of tall grey buildings and endless rain. The hopeless, helpless vulnerability.. [364]

Winfried Hempel who grew up in a sect in Chile reported that:

It was a sad childhood. I remember that. I cried often. For example... even though I didn't know my father or mother I couldn't sleep at night because I felt so alone. [365]

The suffering of children in some sects is immense. The documentation of the experiences of children in some sects belies the magnitude of the suffering that an individual child in a sect can experience. The sense of estrangement from others, the confusion, loneliness, lack of opportunity, and ability to express themselves and describe what they are going through to the presence or absence of safe others, the fear, terror, rejection and difficulty that they have in getting through their childhood is hard to convey through words.

The abuse experienced by children, some as young as three years old, in Hare Krishna boarding schools, has been well documented, but even so, it still does not convey the full impact that this has on a child's life and how it feels to be a child going through the experience. The documented abuse included sexual physical and emotional abuse.[366]

In an international group called the Children of God (COG – which was then known as The Family), children were sent at young ages to other countries for what were called re-education programmes. COG children were often left behind in communal houses for months while parents were engaged elsewhere on COG business. There was a lack of protection and support for many of these children, and again, the abuse and neglect experienced by many of these children who were separated from their parents underlines the importance of the parent – child bond. Dr Steven Kent[367] reports that:

'The stories about the Children of God group's maltreatment of children warrant book-length studies on their own, but suffice it to say that many children rarely saw their parents, and when they did, their emotional bonding was strained, at best.'

Children separated from their parents and placed in very difficult circumstances, experience a profound sense of rejection and abandonment. The pain of loss of parents, coupled with the lack of positive adult input, alongside other forms of neglect and abuse, can be devastating for children. Kristina Jones, in her book written with two of her sisters described her experience at 10 years of age like this:

I had been a confident, outgoing child, but after Mum left I became quiet and withdrawn. I did not imagine things could get worse, but they did. It felt sometimes like I was suffocating with the weight of my suppressed emotions. I missed her desperately and talked to her all the time in my mind, wondering how she was and what she was doing. Was she sad without my brothers and me? They cried into their pillows at night, but I felt like stone inside and couldn't, as that would mean my acceptance of this frightening situation.

Eric Erikson's theory of human development

INTRODUCTION

Difficulties in forming attachments are not the only developmental setbacks children may experience as a result of sect involvement. Another psychologist, Erik Erikson, describes how issues of development pervade our lives. Eric Erikson's theory about child development helps us understand how parts of the development of children in sects may be stunted. The theory covers people's lives from childhood through to old age, and involves eight stages through which we all go. At each stage, there is a conflict of two opposing forces or alternative basic attitudes, and we need to achieve a positive outcome in order to develop a capacity or strength and move in a positive as opposed to a negative direction.[368]

As discussed in Chapter Three, children have basic needs such as for love, nurturance and physical touch. Erik Erikson's theory[369] goes into more depth about the needs of children, but he also makes clear that his theory was not formulated to be an absolute definition, but a tool through which to explore.

SUMMARY OF ERIK ERIKSON'S LIFE STAGES

Each of Erikson's stages follows on from the last. Erikson acknowledged that while each stage is most evident at one particular age range, these issues will appear in some form throughout life.[370] Table

5.1 provides a brief summary of each of the stages, which are covered in more depth afterwards.

Table 5.1: A summary of Erik Erikson's life stages (adapted from Piers Worth, 2000)

Stage	Approximate Age	Description
Stage 1: Basic trust vs. mistrust (Hope)	0–12/18 months approx. Infancy	This stage is influenced by and focused on providing/ gratifying the baby's needs for food and support from the mother (more recent research and writings[17] indicates that it does not have to be the mother or father; a devoted caregiver will suffice). It is to do with quantity and quality of care. If the 'balance of care is sympathetic and loving', basic trust will result. Erratic or harsh care leads to mistrust.[18]
Stage 2: Autonomy vs. shame and doubt (Will)	12–18 months to 3 years old approx. Early childhood	This stage is centred on whether parents will provide the child with guidance, yet allow choice. Too much autonomy (i.e. neglect) is where the child has no or overly wide boundaries, and can hurt itself because no one is protecting the child. The positive outcome occurs when the child is appropriately supported and allowed choice. If inadequately supported, the child is thought to feel forced or shamed into what he/she can or cannot do, and to question his/her own autonomy or self-control.[19]
Stage 3: Initiative vs. guilt (Purpose)	3–5 years old approx. Play age	As the child enters school, he/she must contend with restrictions and socialisations to their developing imagination and exploration. Guilt emerges when a sense of 'badness' is learnt – initiative is learnt when a child acquires a sense of purpose or direction.[20]
Stage 4: Industry vs. inferiority (Competence)	6–12 years old School age	This phase focuses on 'industry', which is associated with learning and developing 'competence at useful skills and tasks'. Inferiority is associated with failures in this area and a growing belief in the child that he/she may never be 'good at anything'. It occurs in the early stage of schooling, and alongside the learning of social and cultural norms.[21]

Table 5.1 continued: A summary of Erik Erikson's life stages (adapted from Piers Worth, 2000)

Stage	Approximate Age	Description
Stage 5: Identity vs. role confusion	13–18 years old	The child is experiencing the inadequacy of the childhood sense of self or identity and the need to reform it.[22] Identity is described as a 'stable sense of self confirmed by experience'.[23]
(Fidelity)	Adolescence	The outcome, it is argued, can be: a clear sense of identity achievement; a failure to commit to a sense of identity; 'foreclosure', where the child does not confront this issue, and takes on parental and cultural norms without questioning; or 'diffusion', where no sense of self or identity is reached.[24]
Stage 6: Intimacy vs. isolation	Approx. 19–20 to 40 years old	This stage centres on a young adult's thoughts and feelings about relating to and committing to an intimate partner. Some independence would be surrendered, and identity would be experienced in terms of two people. Erikson describes this as the 'ability to fuse your identity with someone else's without fear that you are going to lose something yourself'. He argues that this forms the security or basis on which the young adult proceeds safely into the world.[25] Failure to achieve this results, according to Erikson, in loneliness and self-absorption.
(Love)	Young adulthood	
Stage 7: Generativity vs. stagnation	40–60 to 65	Commitment and care are offered, and extended beyond the individual and family to that of a wider group, e.g. society. The focus at this time can be on people (the next generation) or creative products. The negative outcome of this stage is self-centredness and self-indulgence.[26]
(Care)	Adulthood	
Stage 8: Ego Integrity vs. despair	60–65 +	This stage involves coming to terms with one's life as it is, its 'inalterability'. Arriving at a sense of wholeness – the capacity to see life events as part of a larger whole. Responsibility is taken for the life lived.[27] Despair is described as a fear of death, often unconscious, and a wish, a search for another chance to experience life – accompanied by a recognition that the time remaining is short.
(Wisdom)	Old age	

STAGE ONE: TRUST VERSUS MISTRUST

The first stage Erik Erikson identifies is that of trust versus mistrust, meaning that children need to develop a basic sense of trust in the predictability of the world, for instance, that if he/she cries, someone will come. Those in sects are often taught throughout their childhood and on into adolescence and adulthood that they can only trust the group to which they belong; that the world outside is, as one former member was taught, *'a stronghold of Satan'*[371] or, as described in other groups, the 'devil's playground'[372].

In some sects, the child's confidence in his/her ability to affect the events around him/her and get his/her meets met would be marginal, and thus a basic sense of trust may be missing. Erikson expected that this strength should be developed at approximately ages 0–18 months, but also acknowledges that individual differences may occur. Some children in sects may develop more of a sense of basic trust dependent on their relationship with their mother/father at an early age. But membership in a sect may erode the trust. The sense of mistrust may continue after individuals leave the sect, and could explain the high levels of anxiety found in former members. According to Erikson, when mistrust wins over trust, the adult may be frustrated, withdrawn, suspicious and lacking in self-confidence. This sense of mistrust is, therefore, something that once the individual becomes aware of, they might hope or seek to overcome it in subsequent developmental experiences.

Significantly higher levels of post-traumatic stress disorder (PTSD) symptoms have been found in the second generation as compared to the first generation.[373] A research study that compared those with PTSD and those with other mental illness found that 'the distinguishing characteristic of PTSD is a pervasive feeling of interpersonal distrust even in the face of existing family and friend relationships'.[374]

STAGE TWO: AUTONOMY VERSUS SHAME AND DOUBT

Need for guidance and increased personal choice for the child
The second stage for a child is the need for guidance, yet there is also the need for increased individual choice from those who care for him/her. A positive outcome occurs for the child when supported in this area and allowed to make choices, leading to a sense of independence and autonomy. In the negative, the child feels forced or shamed about what he/she can or cannot do, and consequently questions his/her own autonomy or self-control.[375] If a child feels little sense of self-control or has no self-control as control is always externally imposed, then this may impact the area of delayed gratification and sense of personal control over situations.

Jayanti Tamm, in her book *Cartwheels in a Sari*, describes what it was like to grow up in and then leave Sri Chinmoy's sect. She states that: *All of my childhood memories involve trying to obey and please guru.*[376]

One Harry's Sect interviewee said the following:

> *I had no choice. It was either get out or, if you lived there, do what you were expected to do, and I was too young to get out. I didn't have any means.*[377]

Breaking the will of children is a repeated theme that occurs in a number of sects and was expanded on in the previous chapter, with a particular emphasis on physical abuse. A lack of choice can be evidenced in the requirement of control over emotions that is exercised in some groups, such as occurred in the School of Economic Science. As one individual explained:

> *I ran a small group of children from two and a half to five years old. They too were not allowed to cry, especially when their mothers left them. They were ordered to stop and if they persisted we had to smack*

them. When I asked Mrs Mavro if they could not be given a hug and distracted by being taken off to do something I was told for their own good they had to break the attachment to their mothers and must not cry when they left."[378]

A teacher attending the school reported that: 'Most of the children there looked and behaved like little old people. All their natural buoyancy was repressed and they were expected to conform to excessively rigid codes of conduct.'[379]

Too much choice can also be devastating for children. For example, they may have inadequate or no supervision, or they may have huge responsibilities that set them up to fail, i.e. a 12-year-old put in charge of a group of two-year-olds. Experiences like this, rather than leading to a sense of self-control and self-worth as is the ideal with this developmental stage, instead lead to a sense of shame and doubt about oneself.

Shaming experiences
As well as experiencing a lack of choice because of excessive control, children in sects may have additional hurdles in achieving a positive outcome at this stage because of shaming experiences. For example, in some sects, small children are expected to behave in adult ways, silent and un-childlike. This may be particularly evidenced in sect gatherings and meetings. A failure to do so results in 'shaming' responses from leaders and other adults. At other times, children in sects may experience shaming for reasons that they have no power over.

An individual below describes how the sect leader in Harry's Sect shamed and bullied children in group meetings:

Mostly he'd pick on people that'd been there – the kids if he picked on kids, mostly it was adults – but if he picked on kids, it'd be the kids that'd

*been there all their lives. Like once he said, 'You children not listening –
what did I just say?' Luckily I knew, but I thought phew ... he picked on
Chloe because her brothers and sisters had left basically, and he'd say,
"What, do you want to leave like your brothers and sisters?"*[380]

Stage Three: Initiative versus guilt

At this stage, the child must contend with restrictions and socialisa-
tions to their developing imagination and exploration. Guilt emerges
when a sense of 'badness' is learnt; initiative, when a child acquires a
sense of purpose or direction.[381] While some guilt is needed, as without it there would be no conscience or self-control, too much or guilt
over inappropriate matters can inhibit the child's creativity and free
interactions with others.[382]

Some sects induce a lot of guilt, as the following example of a sect
leader talking to a 14-year-old female child indicates:

> *Sometimes he would talk to me alone. On this occasion he was ex-
> pounding to me on the subject of women. 'All women always felt guilty,'
> he said. With much trepidation I ventured to argue. 'I don't under-
> stand,' I said. 'I don't feel guilty.' 'Oh yes you do,' he assured me. 'You
> just don't realise it yet because you're too young. All women feel guilty
> because of Eve's sin in taking the apple. And so they should. All women
> are guilty, and the only true aim of their lives must be to purge that
> guilt.*[383]

Thus, this sect leader may have given this young female adolescent a
sense of 'badness' just for being female, and hindered the strength of
initiative and the sense of purpose in life arising within her.

Degeneration of a particular gender happens in some sects. Common
to periods of history in various cultures, where women have been seen

as second-class or under par as compared to males, some sects also have a degenerative view of females, and may give females a sense of guilt and a feeling of being below men.

Child sexual and physical abuse and maltreatment occurs in some sects. It is common for children who have experienced abuse to blame themselves, particularly when they are in a situation where they are being blamed and held responsible for whatever is happening to them. These children may have a sense of badness, and feelings of guilt can be fostered by some sects – again, this will negatively impact on this developmental stage as well other stages.

Play and children in sects
Some sects inhibit play options for children. If children have the time and are given the freedom to do so, this can result in children being creative and lead to them developing their own play items from objects around them. However, if play is associated with a sense of badness, then guilt regarding initiative to play and wanting to play may be present. Some children in sects may have restricted or extensive limits in terms of time to play or peer relationships as compared to those not being raised in sects. Further, restrictions in the form of 'play' and life experiences, and lack of or limitations in the nature of schooling, (discussed further in the next chapter) that are considered acceptable suggest that stages three and four of the life cycle may result in negative outcomes for individuals raised in some sects.

However, not all sects restrict play options, and some second-generation adults report very positively on their play experiences as children. For example, in the *Lost Boy*, Brent Jeffs reports very positively on how the Fundamentalist Latter Day Saints (FLDS) diverged from the American obsession with safety by allowing the children to play in the great outdoors with their many siblings.

This made life in the FLDS much more fun when it came to things like playing with the trampoline. He describes the good part of his childhood as a child's version of heaven:

> *I had dozens of brothers and sisters to play with in a huge yard surrounded by mountains, with lots of trees, hidden vistas, streams, fresh air and places to explore.*

> *In the winter, we got an average of five hundred inches of snow. There was a whole side of an eleven-thousand –foot mountain behind a ski resort that was undeveloped. It was surrounded by white-capped green mountains on three sides, and we took full advantage of our frosty playground.*[384]

Sadly, at the end of 2011, news coverage indicated that the imprisoned leader of the FLDS, Warren Jeffs, has banned children's toys, including bicycles and trampolines.[385]

At Centrepoint, children appeared to have spent lots of time playing with other children, including tennis, playing in the sandpits, making tree huts and riding down the river on tyres when it rained.[386] The area of play also links into the area of industry versus inferiority, which comes next:

STAGE FOUR: INDUSTRY VERSUS INFERIORITY
It is at this stage that the child aged between six and 12 years old needs to develop the skill set, society requires. If these are developed, the child feels a sense of competence, but if they are not, the child feels a basic sense of inferiority.

> Skills that might be valued or necessary for a child in a sect may be very different to the skills a child or adolescent needs upon leaving a sect. Therefore, a child in a sect may attain the skill repertoire required in a sect, but if the child then leaves the sect, they may have a very large number of new skills they need to acquire.

In some sects this may be particularly difficult for females who have learn't to sew and be a home-maker, but have not had the opportunity for education or work skills and experience that their male counterparts have had. Even for males, their non-sect peers may have many skills that they learnt at a much younger age, and therefore a young person exiting a sect may feel a huge sense of inferiority compared to their peers. This may be especially the case with modern technology and all its advancements that those raised in sects may have no knowledge or experience of. The sense of culture shock, and the learning of new skills and behaviours on leaving a sect, is dealt with in more depth in later chapters. As sometimes Erik Erikson's stages fuse together, the section that follows on identity versus role confusion discusses schooling and employment and continues to address issues that come under the stage of industry versus inferiority.

STAGE FIVE: IDENTITY VERSUS ROLE CONFUSION
Factors that may significantly relate to psychological distress experienced on leaving sects relate to Erikson's stage of 'identity versus role or identity confusion', which occurs during adolescence. While all the prior developmental stages contribute to identity, in this stage it reaches a climax, and the task of adolescents is to integrate the various identifications from childhood into a more complete identity that reflects different parts of their life. Part of adolescents finding their identity involves making decisions about work and employment, and seeking an experience or indication of their true selves through social groups that give them the opportunity to try out new roles.

The experience of young people in most sects is likely to have been focused on beliefs, behaviours and lifestyles shaped by the sect's social culture. Therefore, they are likely to have to wait until after leaving the sect before they begin to work through this stage properly in ways more shaped by themselves and their own choices than sect constraints. Most individuals raised in sects have far fewer choices (or none, in some instances) regarding employment and education than their non-sect peers. Those raised in sects may have gaps in their childhood education, and full-time education may be forbidden past the legal requirements of a country, as may college or university entrance. In some sects, children receive very little education. This educational neglect can have far-reaching consequences, and places young adults as well as older adults at a massive disadvantage in the world outside their group, especially with regards to employment opportunities. This in turn affects their ability to earn money, and increases the chances of them raising their own children in poverty.[387]

Identity versus role confusion for children and young people in Harry's Sect
In Harry's Sect, further education was not seen as important, and second-generation members were expected to finish full-time education and begin working at 16. This clearly resulted in diminished work opportunities for them, which was exacerbated by pressure to attend sect meetings and a lack of travel opportunities. This experience would link into Erik Erikson's psychosocial stage of 'industry versus inferiority', which he describes as 'I am what I learn'.[388] He refers to children entering the larger world of knowledge and work, including schooling, as well as the learning of social and cultural norms.

Second-generation children in Harry's Sect attended schools, which may be an area where they can excel, have an equal experience to their peers and have a feeling of competence and mastery. However, they may have had little opportunity to learn of the social and cultural norms that prevail outside Harry's Sect (since these are learnt on the street, as well as at school, in friends' houses and at home, although probably only in a limited way in the home of a Harry's Sect member). This may bring a sense of inadequacy and inferiority, a feeling that one is a 'good-for-nothing'.[389]

Employment is likely to be limited to employment in the sect or a sect (which may or may not be paid), or to 'acceptable' jobs that do not interfere with sect meeting attendance or the sect's activities. Likewise, most young people in sects would not have had the opportunity to seek a more personally influenced identity through peer groups, clubs, political movements and so on. Consequently, when the second generation leave sects, they are likely to have had to work through this stage of identity again (or go through it properly for the first time), but at an older age than their peers.

The social impact of the environment and a feeling of separation
Erik Erikson's theories imply a 'healthy' identity resulting from coming in the balance between a push from within to explore/be a certain person, and the internalised constraints and social conventions of the family and broader social context. Therefore, his theories do not merely explain what is happening within a person, but also emphasise the social impact of the environment.

Based on Erikson's theories, I contend that where a child overwhelmingly receives the message from their social context (such as the sect) that what they are interested in, drawn towards, or want to express is frowned upon and negated, then that child may be left with the sense of not being 'normal', and of being separate from a wider social and human context. Therefore, their inner feeling may be that they cannot be 'normal' if what they are feeling and wanting is consistently communicated or experienced as 'wrong'.

Interestingly, the researchers who interviewed those who had exited Centrepoint recorded that:

'We also heard from participants who were invested heavily in appearing 'normal' in the aftermath of Centrepoint and there were a number of interviews that were littered with references to 'normality' as a desired state. One participant spoke about how she had quite consciously made her life appear as normal as possible once she had left Centrepoint yet was surprised to find how successful she had been in the process.'[390]

Those who experience neither an identity crisis nor a commitment to a chosen identity may have an identity that is 'diffused'. They are then easily influenced by others and change their beliefs often.[391]

Current second-generation Harry's Sect members and their possible identity
Changing one's beliefs often is unlikely to be the case for second-generation current sect members, given the steadfast cultures of sects. Those raised in sects who do not go on to leave the sect (approximately 20% of the second generation for some sects), and who do not attempt to lead a double life, might experience 'foreclosure' of their identity, i.e. they make a commitment without experiencing an identity crisis and may unquestioningly accept beliefs, attitudes and an occupation based on the views or values of others.

The lack of opportunity to commit to an identity
Perhaps the most likely identity crisis for an adolescent in a sect is that of the 'moratorium' person who is not yet able to make a commitment to an identity. Making a commitment one way or another in sects will likely have profound, lasting consequences for either a first- or second-generation member. It seems *unlikely* that some second-generation former sect members would be able to pass positively through Erikson's identity-formation stage until some years after leaving their sect, when they have had greater opportunity to explore who they are and who they choose to be. The most popular age for children raised in Harry's Sect to leave was 17, though many leave at an older age. (This is discussed further in Chapter Seven.) Leaving a sect makes a statement about who these individuals are *not*, but to find out who they *are* in terms of their sense of belonging to a group is not likely to occur for some time.

For some immediately after leaving their sect, their key tasks may be to hold down employment, find a safe environment in which to live, learn more social skills, etc. Therefore, even after leaving their sect, it may be some time before they are able to successfully work through earlier missed stages, and move on to explore and form a social identity that may reflect more of their own choice and expression. Those leading a double life within the sect – perhaps by having a 'secret friend' outside the sect – will be able to form an alternative social identity during group involvement, which will stand them in good stead after leaving.[392] They have had the opportunity to begin to process who they are or choose to be through relationships with peers. Those who do not develop coping mechanisms for the stigma they often experience at school, and who do not integrate with peers, are likely to have even less of a social identity or, particularly, a positively chosen personal identity.

STAGE SIX: INTIMACY VERSUS ISOLATION

This stage refers to the focus of forming one or more intimate relationships that go beyond adolescent love, and allow for a family group to be formed. Eric and his wife Joan Erikson[393] considered whether the stage of intimacy might precede the stage of identity for women because they found identity through relationship, i.e. relationship and intimacy first, then 'identity'. If this is the case, then being in a sect where one has to be very careful about what one says for fear of being reported, and where relationships may be actively discouraged, achieving intimacy may be a very important need. Otherwise, their lives may be void of the thing that can make life so meaningful and worthwhile: relationships with others. Difficulties with intimacy have been reported on by those raised in some sects.[394] This is discussed further in Chapter Six.

DEVELOPMENTAL STAGES AND THE IMPORTANCE OF RELATIONSHIPS

In fact, each of the developmental periods identified by Erikson are embedded in interpersonal relationships. Thus, development occurs within relationships and against a backdrop of prior development in relationships. Bruce Perry and Maia Szalavitz describe how psychologists in the past mistakenly thought that unless you love yourself, no-one else would love you. But in writing about trauma and children and what can be done, they state:

'The truth is, you cannot love yourself unless you have been loved and are loved.'[395]

In other words, we need social relationships! This is expanded on in the final chapter of this book.

Human development and the potential for 'harm' from the sect environment

Developmental or cumulative trauma occurring over time in the sect environment

Erikson's theory has been used here to show the potential impact for harm caused by time spent in a 'sect' environment. Potential 'developmental or cumulative trauma' may take place over time in the sect environment (or any other environment where life-stage development may repeatedly conclude in negative outcomes).

Erikson proposed that each stage of life involves a developmental challenge (a tension of opposite possibilities) that would be lived through on the basis or the context of the individual's experiences at the time. For on-going health and development to be achieved, Erikson implied that the tension of each opposite needed to be resolved, on balance, in the positive. If not, the theory implies that this becomes a disruption, and potentially a block to the developmental experiences for that life stage and to each subsequent stage.

DEVELOPMENTAL HARM TO THE HARRY'S SECT FIRST GENERATION, INCLUDING PARENTS

If, for example, first-generation members of a sect experienced 'harm' in the sixth and/or seventh phase of the life cycle, they could, potentially, have had positive outcomes in previous stages from which to develop their lives. A study reported in Chapter Three, which used the Family Experience Scale scored retrospectively, suggests that this was the case for many people joining sects. Previous stages become, potentially, a resource through which the individual may draw in future life experiences. Even where the first-generation members appeared to regress to earlier stages in their development, as expanded on in Chapter Two, the experience of having reached a positive outcome at an earlier life stage may enable the first generation to pass through the stage with a positive outcome for a second time. Nevertheless, first-generation former members still report being stunted in their development, as described by the following two individuals:

> *I do really think that the sort of system that prevails in Harry's meetings and meetings like it is such that personality and individuality can't develop in the way it should, and I think it would have happened in my case and it is still the case for those still in it. They can't really be what they are; you can't grow and develop as you would and should; and you can't be a useful person that you might otherwise be.*[396]

Another first-generation interviewee said the following:

> *I think my, probably, emotional development and so on would have been affected by years of being subject to a man who in fact was bad.*[397]

A relatively large number of older individuals remained single in Harry's Sect. This relates to Erikson's theory and his psychosocial stage of 'intimacy versus isolation', which occurs in young adulthood, and 'generativity versus stagnation and self-absorption', which occurs in middle adulthood. Generativity refers to the 'interest in establishing and guiding the next generation'.[398] This stage focuses on raising children and creative or productive endeavours.

In Harry's Sect, while those who did have children tended to have a fair few, there were a large number of single people who in mid and late adulthood had not married, and who had no children. Additionally, the research interviewees in the Harry's Sect sample showed limited evidence of them spending time with the children of others.

There appeared to be few opportunities for other creative or productive endeavours outside their working life. Harry's Sect members who had work where creative and productive endeavours were possible may have moved more successfully through this psychosocial stage, whereas those who did not may have experienced (according to Erikson) stagnation, self-absorption, boredom and a lack of psychological growth. My research supported this view, with former first-generation members describing their lack of psychological development while in Harry's Sect.

DEVELOPMENTAL HARM TO THE HARRY'S SECT SECOND GENERATION
For the second generation, however, interviews and psychological tests suggest that these individuals may have experienced the negative outcome from life phases perhaps as early as Stage One. In these circumstances, there is the potential, according to Erikson's theories, of several life stages resulting in negative outcomes for the second generation. I propose that this could be considered a form of cumulative or developmental trauma. My findings in two studies of post-sect psychological distress such as depression, anxiety, dissociation and PTSD symptoms in higher levels in the second generation than the first generation might be indicative of this 'developmental trauma' having occurred.

SUMMARY OF CHAPTER 5

In order to understand how and why children in sects are affected by their environment, it is important to understand more about child development in general, including children's attachments to adults. Children in some sects are separated from their parents, and this can be a devastating experience for them.

Eric Erickson's theory of human development across the course of a lifetime is a useful tool to further understand the experiences of those raised in sects and how they might be affected by that experience. The first stage refers to trust and its opposite mistrust, and is particularly pertinent as sect membership may often erode trust, resulting in frustration, withdrawal a lack of self-confidence and suspicion.

The second stage discusses the child's need for guidance, and yet also the need to be allowed and supported with increased personal choices which can lead to a sense of autonomy, although if personal choice is not allowed, it can impact individuals in terms of high levels of shame and doubt. This may be magnified in groups that major in shaming children and adults alike. Breaking the will of children, which is taught in some groups, is another tool, which again may have a debilitating effect on children's development.

The third stage, if not gone through adequately may result in excessive guilt and a sense of badness, as it has to do with imagination and exploration, and a positive outcome results in a sense of purpose and direction. Play is an important part of childhood and adulthood, and therefore it is discussed at length, including both restrictions and/or opportunities for play being present for children in some sects.

The fourth stage is concerned with industry and a sense of competence as opposed to a sense of inferiority. As the skills needed in a sect may be different to those needed outside the sect, this is an important area, which is also discussed in later chapters.

Identity and its opposite: role confusion is important in terms of both children in sects and young people who leave sects. Particularly relevant here is whether there is or has been opportunities for being part of social groups outside of the sect and hence social identities. Those children and young people in sects who have these opportunities may find the transition out of a sect easier than those who have not had opportunities to belong to other social groupings, and hence form identities outside of the sect environment.

The sixth of Erik Erikson's stages is intimacy versus isolation, which very much links into relationships, and is vital at each stage of development. Each developmental period is embedded in relationships and each builds on the previous stage. In a sect and other environments there is the potential for developmental or cumulative trauma occurring over the course of time spent in a sect and other environments, which results in on-going negative outcomes in life stage development. Effectively, an individual may end up with developmental gaps which they seek to overcome when they leave the sect environment.

The developmental harm is not limited to the second-generation – rather there were also reports of first-generation members, including parents, being stunted in their development in such a way that their personality and individuality did not develop in the way it could have.

What comes next in Chapter 6?

Learning from the people around you is another important aspect of child development. The next chapter looks at why those raised in sects might have gaps in their social learning. It will analyse how the lack of relationships with those either in or outside Harry's Sect, as well as how a lack of media and socialisation experiences can be present, and may affect children and adolescents in sects. Even children surrounded by people can experience intense loneliness. To have no-one know what it is like to be you, or to be unable or not have the opportunity to express your own thoughts and/or feelings, can be incredibly isolating even when there are numerous other people present. Perhaps this is part of the reason why the second generation often have such a strong bonding with each other.

The following quote demonstrates the extent to which one leader can go in attempting to control and rule the lives of others:

Even laughter was forbidden, as it allowed the spirit of God to escape.[399]

CHAPTER 6

WHY DO PEOPLE STARE AT ME?

BELIEVE ME, I don't choose to wear these clothes!

I was out on Saturday, I went to do a first-aid course actu-
ally, and I'd just come back from it, and I was wearing my
trousers ... well, I put my trousers on because I thought 'How
can you do first aid in a skirt? Shame!' So I changed into my
trousers in the bus station toilet. That was embarrassing, 'cos
you go in with a skirt and come out with trousers, and you
think everyone's looking at you, thinking what's she changing
for? Feel like a right weirdo, one of those weirdos that hang
around the bus station[400]

OVERVIEW

This chapter will look at why children in sects may not learn the cultural
norms of the world outside the sect, leaving them unprepared for state
schooling and life outside the sect, and increasing their vulnerability
on leaving. Cultural norms refer to behaviour patterns and attitudes
that are socially learnt – for example, what types of things to say when
engaged in small talk in social settings; or what to do when entering a
coffee shop; when going on a date; or attitude and expression of that
attitude towards someone of a different religion or sexual orientation.

In some sects, the clothes worn by members are distinctly different
from those in the wider society. How we dress sends a powerful message

about the groups to which we belong. Children who wear clothes that are different from others may experience stigmatisation when they are interacting with or seen by those in the wider population. This can impact some children in sects in the way of fewer opportunities for positive relationships with those not in the sect, and therefore they have less opportunities to learn cultural norms. This chapter expands on the coping mechanisms children, and particularly teenagers, use to deal with stigma.

RELATING TO OTHERS IN SOCIAL SITUATIONS – ALBERT BANDURA'S SOCIAL LEARNING THEORY

INTRODUCTION

Albert Bandura, in his social learning theory,[401] describes how children learn by observing others. The theory can help us understand why children raised in sects might have gaps in their social learning ('social learning' refers to learning from other people, which includes actual flesh-and-blood people, or via people in books, TV or other media). Children raised in sects who then leave the sect have learned about a different culture ('culture' here refers to socially transmitted behaviour patterns and attitudes) from the culture they enter when they leave. Bandura's social learning theory[402] deals with different types of socialisation, and also takes into account how people think about what they observe. The theory gives us a lens to see how the society around us affects children's (and adults') behaviour, knowledge, belief systems and thinking.

DIFFERENT TYPES OF LEARNING

Below is a list developed from Albert Bandura's work to aid the reader's understanding of how we learn from others.

- Socially guided learning: This involves imparting important knowledge, as well as teaching children what and how they think about different matters. Those who serve as 'social guides' include parents, teachers and other important figures who educate and mentor children.

- Informal learning: Socially guided learning promotes informal learning by providing children with the tools needed to gain new knowledge and deal with situations encountered on a daily basis.

- Observational learning: Observing from that which we see and hear, but which does not have direct experiential consequences (vicarious experiences, e.g. the media). Bandura argues strongly for the increasingly powerful role that advanced technology and, hence, observational modelling has in people's lives.

- Live learning: Observing the actual behaviour of others and the consequences of their behaviour. Live learning occurs through direct contact with other people in the environment. It is learnt through important figures in children's lives, including family, school, friends and people at social clubs or activities.

HOW WE LEARN

How learning actually occurs may or may not be socially guided and can occur through observational or live learning. It may happen deliberately or inadvertently. To learn, you must observe behaviour and pay attention to it. Behaviour is then remembered by forming it into rules, judgements and concepts (our ability to make sense of what we saw and therefore remember it), and therefore we store the relevant knowledge, which is known as domain-relevant knowledge. We may or may not be able to observe the consequences of behaviour. Whether we behave in certain ways will be impacted by how motivated we are, which is in part motivated by the consequences of behaviour. There are different types of motivation including: self-produced, direct and vicarious motivation.

Learning occurs inadvertently as well as deliberately. Learning takes place through what we pay attention to and how we interpret and generalise from what we see. We restructure information into rules and concepts. Environments differ, but generally parents, teachers and others, children come into contact with, guide children in their learning experience by being sources of knowledge. They convey the abstract rules of reasoning to children that promote thinking,[403] therefore enabling children to develop the tools to engage in successful informal learning.

AN EXAMPLE OF INFORMAL LEARNING OCCURRING IN A SECT

Children in a sect may witness others being humiliated by the leader or leaders, as the following quote from a first-generation former member interviewee some years after leaving the sect shows. Usually children will extract something from what they observe, as children were part of these meetings:

> *There was a lot of bullying in the meetings, a lot of bullying. We'd have a little bullying theme sometimes at our meeting. If you noticed two sisters choosing to sit at the back and he picked on them for that, he said that's where sinners sit. And that was his theme for the meeting, needling them.*[404]

The children in this example learnt that they shouldn't sit at the back in the meeting. From this acquired knowledge, children develop what they consider to be appropriate courses of action. Whether an individual engages in behaviour, or not, is based, according to Professor Albert Bandura, on their motivation to do or not to do so. In the example above, the child is likely to be motivated to listen as they would fear being picked on. Therefore, children who observe negative consequences to behaviours of others are less likely to perform similar behaviours than if they see positive consequences.

Informal learning might involve either observational or live learning. Live learning refers to children actually meeting and seeing the behaviour of actual people they meet, where the children have the opportunity to observe the consequences of that behaviour as in the example of Harry's Sect above.

OBSERVATIONAL LEARNING

Observational learning refers to indirect or vicarious experiences through what people see and hear (e.g. through DVDs and other new technologies). For example, a child might come to know of the existence of organisations to help children such as Child Line and the National Society for the Prevention of Cruelty to Children (NSPCC) through watching TV or through the Internet. Bandura[405] comments that most psychological theories were invented before the advent of enormous advances in technology. Therefore, they give insufficient attention to the increasingly powerful role that multimedia plays in present-day human lives.

One young woman gave the following description of some of the changes that occurred when her parents and therefore she joined a sect as a child:

> We moved up and the TV disappeared, and you know the videos and the tapes and all that kind of stuff, … well, soon as I moved here, I wasn't allowed to like go out and stuff … oh, and music and girly magazines that you get into when you're about 13, and then you start to worry about things like your moustache and stuff, and you're not allowed to peel it off. Oh yeah, and I'd already had my ears pierced, but I wasn't allowed to wear earrings now anymore, and Mum had to take off her wedding ring.[406]

The extent to which a child pays attention to, remembers, is motivated to imitate and is physically able to adopt the behaviour of another is likely to be related to the child's age.[107] Professor Albert Bandura argues that change occurs over time in children because of maturation and experience. He looks at not only what is happening to the child in their environment, but also how the child responds to incoming information. The lack of access to media, computers, phones and socialisation experiences that exclude relationships with those outside the sect is likely to affect children and adolescents, particularly in terms of their social abilities, knowledge about the world and sense of identity. In those sects where children have access to appropriate books, they may achieve some symbolic learning through reading. The problems that children might experience when having had very little opportunity for multimedia learning, including via computers and the internet, are evident in some children in sects, as the following quotes show:

> *I found school difficult because I didn't have the experiences of … my peers, and so if they would talk about television I felt left out, and I was often. They attempted to bully me because I was different, and fortunately I was in one way able to stand up for myself, but it was obviously quite trying.*[408]

For some children in sects (such as those in Harry's Sect), part of the difficulty in socialising was connected to the fact that mainstream children (not in sects) utilise Bandura's observational learning objects (e.g. the TV, such as soaps and sport, media games, music and magazines) in their conversations, referring to characters and situations unknown to children in sects. These references may be culturally specific, such as a popular film, TV series or reality TV show.

LIVE LEARNING AND CHILDREN IN HARRY'S SECT

Professor Albert Bandura's social learning theory also addresses live learning and again there were fewer opportunities for this for those raised in Harry's Sect than for children raised in the mainstream society, whom we might expect to visit the homes of other children, attend

preschool nursery, go out and socialise with other children, and attend clubs, etc., as the example below shows:

> *I think the biggest thing I noticed was the lack of social interaction.*
> *OK. For example, when I was invited to go round to parties, I wouldn't*
> *be able to go – therefore lacking being able to interact in that way....*[409]

One sense in which diminished social skills did appear to be evidenced in those second-generation former members of Harry's Sect
was in terms of difficulties they had with peers at school and a lack of
confidence after sect membership, which might also be related to a
poor, sect-implanted self-image. A former member who was born and
raised in a sect reported many years after he left that:

> *I still think that I lack self-confidence, although I have made tremen-*
> *dous strides in that realm.*[410]

SEPARATION FROM AND LACK OF RELATIONSHIP WITH THOSE NOT IN THE SECT

In some communal groups, there may be virtually no contact with
people outside the sect. For adults in both Ted's Sect and Harry's Sect,
there was little contact with those outside of the sect, outside of relationships and acquaintances with colleagues and people whom they
briefly interacted with, such as other mothers at the school gates or
those working in the supermarket. A study of Ted's Sect found that
members spent more and more time on Ted's Sect activities, with
the result that they were exhausted and saw little of outside friends.
Friends who were not involved in Ted's Sect were not allowed to visit
those who shared homes with other Ted's Sect members, because it
was thought that they were building something precious and that visiting outsiders would suck away all the energy. Having friend's external
to the sect was actively discouraged.

Lack of time also meant that external relationships with family members tended to deteriorate or diminish. Furthermore, part of the teaching of Ted's Sect centred on the fact that one's parents were to blame for one's ego or selfishness. Those who left Ted's Sect were generally ostracised by remaining members, as was also the case in Harry's Sect.

In Harry's Sect, relationships with those not involved in the sect were also very limited. As most individuals who joined the sect moved geographically, this meant that they moved away from their friends and family. Members were expected to attend all the sect meetings, and there was little time available to travel to see family. Additionally, individuals were encouraged to be separate from those not in Harry's Sect. Some individuals were encouraged to cut off all relationships with their families. Children were not allowed to see peers outside school hours. There was an 'us and them' attitude, with some members becoming intolerant of anyone who did not think the way they did, as in the example below:

> *I think probably from an early age that kind of 'us and them' attitude –*
> *you know that we're all right and they're all wrong – basically that, but*
> *that didn't help you to mix with your peers at school and had a kind of*
> *unhelpful attitude towards the world, how you related to other kids. You*
> *put it* [in the] *back in your mind, but it raises subconscious barriers of*
> *what's right and what's wrong.*[411]

CLOTHES, STIGMATISATION AND IDENTITY

DRESS CODES
Dress codes in sects emphasise and increase separation and isolation from the outside world. The dress code in some sects links into Goffman's[112] work on impression management; 'When the body

diverges from the norm in any way, whether in terms of proportion, movement or symmetry, it becomes a "traitor" to social rules and moral order'.[413]

The individual who does not conform in terms of dress, will be responded to differently, and will be judged and compared with the way the majority dresses. A research study[414] has found that people are so sensitive to being left out that they even feel hurt after rejection by a computer; those experiencing this reported lower self-esteem, less sense of belonging and a reduced sense of meaningful existence compared to those not rejected by a computer.

THE DRESS CODE OF TED'S SECT

In Ted's Sect, members 'dressed down', thus maintaining an impression of frugality and austerity (apart from special occasions, where women were supposed to dress up), which may have affected members' self-esteem. During training, Ted's Sect members wore traditional karate clothes.

Demonstrated in the quote below, where a former Ted's Sect member describes another member leaving the Ted's Sect, is the strong sense of identity and clothing – shown in this case by a karate belt:

> *He waited until Pete* [the dojo leader] *had gone away for the weekend ... and then got the removal van, moved everything out without saying goodbye to anybody, moved everything out, and he just symbolically left his ... belt, his karate belt in his room.*[415]

THE DRESS CODES OF HARRY'S SECT

In Harry's Sect, men and women wore quite different styles of dress. Men dressed formally with short haircuts, while the women dressed in relatively old-fashioned clothes, and wore no jewellery or make-up. Membership of Harry's Sect was characterised by dress, which, like other groups – particularly in previous centuries – could be described as 'anti-fashion'. Indeed, Harry's Sect could be compared to Utopian movements, which, up until the 18th Century, were often character-ised by the wearing of uniforms that marked them out as different from those not in the group, and acted as a powerful indicator of shared values and community boundaries.[416] In the case of Harry's Sect, the style of clothing was out dated and had basically remained the same over many years – women were only allowed to wear skirts or dresses as opposed to trousers, while men and boys wore quite formal clothes and no jeans, as the following quote shows:

> *Another aspect of the meetings was what you had to wear. I remember having to wear, well, I think for us kids it was school uniform, because that was the only smart clothes we had. But I remember having to dress up even when I was a tiny little kid, having to wear a shirt and tie and stuff ... I remember, talking about dress, that things like jeans weren't allowed to be worn, even though I was a boy. I always wore proper trousers instead of jeans and that was like, people outside wore jeans, and so there was that big division outside and inside.[417]*

Therefore, clothes seem to have contributed to the 'us and them' mentality in Harry's Sect. Clothes served to enhance the group identity and reduce individual uniqueness within the group.[418] For example, some Utopian groups have advocated the wearing of simi-lar or even identical clothes by men and women to encourage equal-ity of sexes.[419]

Perhaps one of the reasons for Harry's insistence on the differentia-tion of men's and women's clothing was to support his teaching on the differentiation of the sexes and women's lower status in Harry's Sect. In Ted's Sect, however, where women were not viewed as having lower status, there was not the same insistence on the differentiation between female and male clothing.

DRESS CODES, CONTROL AND FRUGALITY

Clothes can serve as instruments of control, and perhaps make those who leave sects uncomfortable in mainstream clothing. One former member of Transcendental Meditation (TM) described buying a pair of jeans after she left, but feeling unable to wear them for three years as she had been indoctrinated that trousers on women were immoral[420].

In communal sects, children often do not have their own clothes, rather, they share clothes. For example, at Centrepoint, children shared clothes.[421]

The cost of fashionable clothes may encourage frugality for those not wanting to part with cash.[422] In Harry's Sect, the anti-fashion and anti-jewellery emphasis may have also been linked to the cost of these items (which would have meant less money left for members to give to Harry and Harry's Sect). In Ted's Sect, dressing scruffily would have helped members to live on their low wages.

Previous research supports the view (also evident in Harry's Sect) that dress codes are a powerful weapon of control and dominance. Historically, the conquered Scots were forbidden to wear a particular item of clothing, by their English conquerors, because the item of clothing was 'seen as a potent symbol of Celtic identity, as virtually a call to rebellion'.[423]

STATE SCHOOLING AND STIGMATISATION

ADAPTION STRATEGIES FOR SCHOOL

Some second-generation former members reported difficulties socialising at school. Burke Rochford explored the lives of Hare Krishna children in state schools through interviews with them, and found that in order to cope with an unfamiliar and even hostile world, they tended to be shy and act as loners. This strategy of social adaptation was for some a temporary adaptation. For others, this became a stable social role, and they did not integrate with their peers.[424] The quote below indicates an example of an adolescent who used this temporary adaptation:

> I was shy and extremely self-conscious. I found that going to school with these 'strangers' made me very uncomfortable. Dealing with girls was difficult and the most embarrassing aspect... But I adjusted after a while and learned to relate to this new "species" of human.[425]

Brent Jeffs[426], in his autobiography, *Lost Boy*, explains how rejected he felt by the different groups of children and how difficult school was. However, he found friends in 'the stoners', who accepted everyone, and he was happy to join in with their extracurricular activities doing what they liked best – smoking pot.

STIGMA CONCEALMENT AS A COPING MECHANISM

> I was scared. I didn't know how to deal with my fellow classmates. I was very uptight. I thought I was so different from them because we had been raised to believe they were bad people. Mainly, I was terrified that everyone knew how I was raised.[427]

Individuals employ numerous strategies and adaptations to cope with stigma, such as concealing the part of themselves that causes stigma and living a 'double' or 'dual' life.[428] This response to stigma may not be as easily available to those who were born into Harry's Sect as for those who joined Harry's Sect in childhood, as they may not have enough knowledge about the world to conceal the felt stigma of Harry's Sect membership. Stigma concealment, which was particularly connected to changing the way they looked, was successfully employed by some children in Harry's Sect. The research interviews showed that clothes were very important to the second generation, as clothing can make group members particularly identifiable and visible.[429]

STIGMA CONCEALMENT AND THE STRESS AND FEAR OF DISCOVERY

The Harry's Sect data is supportive of Goffman's[430] work on impression management, and the second generation appeared aware that if they could change how they dressed, they could be in control of changing how they were perceived by others, as shown below:

> . . . I used to get headaches as well, 'cos I was really stressed, 'cos I was lying. I was leading a double life, because at home I was good Kate with my hair in a bun . . . and then I went to school, and my skirt was rolled up, my hair was out, my earrings were on show. I had my shirt untucked, and everyone, no one at school knew about anything, they didn't even know I went to church on Sundays. I actually did sneak out a few times in the evening . . . it was quite stressful, it was a double life. Don't know how anyone would do that willingly. It was really stressful.[431]

This individual demonstrates well that every coping response exacts a cost on the stigmatised person and must be weighed against its likely value in reducing stigma-related stress. 'Stigmatised people who conceal their stigmatising condition face the constant risk of discovery. Avoiding discovery may require vigilance to avoid giving the secret away. This can create a host of problems, including intrusive thoughts about the stigma and reduced resistance to physical ills'.[432]

The indication is that, since this research interviewee was prepared to pay a high cost in stress by concealing her stigma and living a double life, the original perceived or actual stress occurring as a result of the stigma must have been very high. Perhaps this is due to fear, since she is going out among the 'bad' people; perhaps also guilt plays a part, as she is violating the sect's clothing code, and perhaps it is due to the experience of 'shame' to which members were sensitised, bearing in mind the shaming practices that occurred in Harry's Sect meetings.[433] Shame is a sense or feeling that one is a mistake. Guilt is related to how we sometimes feel about what we have *done*; shame is a feeling about who we are, and it can be crippling.

Interestingly, even those who had begun working full-time and therefore must have been at least 16 years old also reported living a double life, as the following quote shows:

> *We had to walk down there again feeling a bit idiotic because we were carrying black bibles and wearing suits which didn't fit in with the neighbourhood. ... Yes, well, one of the things that I remember was the feeling that complete, well, I suppose the word 'dork', but I can't think of another word at the moment, because you weren't allowed to wear fashionable things. I can remember in the 70s when flares and things were all in fashion and I came home with these flares because I used to work then and I could buy my own clothes and you know, I got into an awful lot of flak for wearing flares, and then I had platform shoes as well, and I got into trouble for those, and again your hair ... but I was almost forced into a double life for my own sanity, really.[434]*

POSITIVE EXPERIENCES OF SCHOOL

The values and beliefs of sect children are likely to be quite different from those not in the sect, although the extent to which those beliefs are brought to school obviously differs from child to child. For example, one interviewee who was involved in Harry's Sect towards its beginning explained how they viewed school as a place t͏ ͏ ͏ould escape from Harry's Sect:

I loved school. I thought it was an escape and I was good at it. . . . So no, I enjoyed school. I didn't go out and try to convert people, ever.[435]

Another interviewee spoke of their enjoyment of school like this:

It was embarrassing sometimes because we couldn't talk about television and music or anything, but I made some good friends, and they seem to have accepted that, that people could be different without being weird. So no, I enjoyed school.[436]

For children in sects, school can have both positive and negative aspects. In his autobiography, Tim Guest writes the following about children from Bhagwan Rhajneesh's group who attended state schools:

Two of the older kids went to outside schools, where they occasionally got beaten up – but they also had Saturdays off.[437]

THE IMPORTANCE OF STATE SCHOOLING FOR CHILDREN RAISED IN SECTS

While state schools may have their drawbacks, some second-generation former members report that they would have been delighted to attend a state-run school. Brent Jeffs[438] reports the following advantage:

Going to public kindergarten gave me something that most other kids in the FLDS didn't have: an implicit knowledge that outsiders weren't all that different or bad. In fact, some were, contrary to what we had been taught, kind and good. Like my father's experience in the army, it planted a seed and made me just that little bit less fearful when I would venture again into the outside world as a teenager. That early experience also gave me some hope as I later faced the great evil that lurked inside our church leadership.

146

INTERACTING WITH OR AVOIDING OTHER CHILDREN IN THE SECT AT SCHOOL

Some of those raised in Harry's Sect reported that they did not really enjoy school as they felt different from the other children, experienced stigmatisation and, in some cases, were bullied. However, in some school situations there are others who are also in the sect attending the same school. People who are potentially highly stigmatised individuals may choose to stick together. They may selectively affiliate with members of their group and therefore gain social support from other stigmatised people. This allows them to compare themselves with their group and gain self-esteem through this social comparison.[439]

However, social support and validation provided by affiliation may not occur. At school, if their strategy for coping and adapting to stigmatisation was stigma concealment, it was unlikely that they would want to associate themselves with the other children in the sect attending the same school. Indeed, doing so would put them at risk of being discovered and reported on by other children in the sect.[440] The quote below is from someone raised in Harry's Sect who reportedly acted out in an attempt to cope with the stigmatisation at school and the restrictive lifestyle at home, he would be unlikely to want to affiliate with others from the sect:

> *I over-reacted because of the restriction at home. I kind of behaved in a . . . silly way, but I was trying to be one of the lads all the time. I was trying to, you know, compensate really for the fact that . . . I had a very restricted and religious upbringing, and therefore I almost wanted to show that I was irreligious and to compensate for the restrictions in my home life and went a bit wild at school, I think.*[441]

THE IMPORTANCE OF ACCEPTANCE BY PEERS

Children's social skills often influence their acceptance by peers. Those who are accepted by their peers have been found to have richer friendships, and to show better school adjustment.[442] Therefore, the lack of social acceptance and the experience of stigmatisation at school reported by some children in sects suggest that they may have had deficient social skills, been less well-adjusted at school, and may have had poor-quality peer friendships. Indeed, they may have adopted a 'loner' strategy permanently or temporarily while they learnt the rules and developed knowledge of the mainstream culture.

Brent Jeffs describes his first day at school in the following way:

> *And I felt everyone's eyes on me. I knew they were thinking, 'Who is this weird kid?' I felt they could see through me and knew where I'd come from, and judged me for it. It took all my strength not to run out the door and never go back.*[443]

In summary, most children in sects, who are also in state schools, have experienced stigmatisation, being different, at the same time they have been deprived of opportunities to learn in differing social contexts. Therefore, on leaving a sect, they may relate to or remember earlier experiences of stigmatisation and struggle to break into or break through to a social group. It is important to remember that state schools can also impact children in sects in a positive way.

SECT SCHOOLS AND HOME-SCHOOLING

In the UK, parents often send their children to preschool classes, but for children in some sects, this is unlikely to be the case. Sects differ in the way they school their children, with some being home-schooled, some attending sect schools (sometimes these are boarding schools), and some being sent to state schools where they mix with those not in sects.

Some children, who otherwise have no contact with a sect, may be sent to a sect school by parents who may be unaware that they have placed their child in a sect school. Historically, this criticism was lodged against the SES (A group called the School of Economic Science) where parents who were not members of the sect sent their children to SES schools without knowing of the link between the day schools they sent their children to and the SES sect.[444] Other sect children may have had very little input in terms of traditional or, for that matter, non-traditional education, having spent much of their childhood labouring and working. For example, they may have been fundraising or caring for other children in the sect.[445] Therefore, the schooling received by those in sects varies tremendously, but a significant proportion of those raised in sects will have educational gaps as compared to their mainstream peers. Schooling outside of legal requirements may be unheard of for children in some sects.

Some sects have their own schools. Standards of education can differ from group to group, country to country, and school to school. For those who are home-schooled or in a sect school, there may be limited or no access to the range of reading material and resources that might be available to children in state schools. Having said that, Amanda Van Eck Duymaer van Twist, in her PhD thesis,[446] records an instance of a second-generation former member of the Bruderhof describing a large and well stocked library. Some spend considerable time reading sect literature as opposed to curricular topics. Others might excel in some areas such as art, but be sorely lacking in other areas. Some children and young people may have no or non-recognised qualifications,[447] and children in some sects actually receive very little in the way of schooling or education. This is likely to have a massive impact for an individual when they leave the sect and attempt to enter the world of work.

They may have to accept low paid work and they may struggle to find employment.

THE UN CONVENTION ON THE RIGHTS OF THE CHILD

Matters such as children receiving no or minimal education in childhood are in fact children's rights issues. In 1989 the UN Convention on the Rights of the Child was adopted by the UN. It has now been ratified by 193 countries meaning they have agreed to do everything they can to make the rights a reality for children around the world. However, there is a gap between the ideal expressed in the document and the reality in many of the signatory nations. Below is part of the preamble of the document as well as the first article:

"Recalling that, in the Universal Declaration of Human Rights, the United Nations has proclaimed that childhood is entitled to special care and assistance,

Convinced that the family, as the fundamental group of society and the natural environment for the growth and well-being of all its members and particularly children, should be afforded the necessary protection and assistance so that it can fully assume its responsibilities within the community,

Recognizing that the child, for the full and harmonious development of his or her personality, should grow up in a family environment, in an atmosphere of happiness, love and understanding,

Considering that the child should be fully prepared to live an individual life in society, and brought up in the spirit of the ideals proclaimed in the Charter of the United Nations, and in particular in the spirit of peace, dignity, tolerance, freedom, equality and solidarity,...

PART I

Article 1

For the purposes of the present Convention, a child means every human being below the age of eighteen years unless under the law applicable to the child, majority is attained earlier.

Article 2

1. States Parties shall respect and ensure the rights set forth in the present Convention to each child within their jurisdiction without discrimination of any kind, irrespective of the child's or his or her parent's or legal guardian's race, colour, sex, language, religion, political or other opinion, national, ethnic or social origin, property, disability, birth or other status.

2. States Parties shall take all appropriate measures to ensure that the child is protected against all forms of discrimination or punishment on the basis of the status, activities, expressed opinions, or beliefs of the child's parents, legal guardians, or family members."[148]

The convention on the Rights of the Child is widely available on the Internet and should also be viewable in public libraries. Rather than include the whole of it here, I have instead written a poem about parts of it which has been linked into children in sects:

Children's Rights Charter

In adulthood when I read that charter
My heart beat even faster
My eyes went wide with the shock
The sects were in the dock

Behind freedom of belief they cannot hide
For the charter has been ratified
Somalia and the US may lag behind
For them it's such a bind

But for every child there are rights
Regardless of the sects might

The right to privacy
So I could have written a diary
But, no, instead
They tried to crawl in my head

The right to expression
Open your mouth
Say what you think
Thinking doesn't stink

The right to be heard
While eating lemon curd
No silence restriction here
No need to shed a tear

The right to information
Without risking subducation
To read books from a store
On religion and subjects galore

To have an innocuous thought in your head
No shivering on your bed
No guilt, no need to confess
No need to report, you couldn't care less

The right to freedom of belief
Would have been such a relief
Freedom of conscience
Like a soothing ointment

To freely participate in cultural life
Instead of taking so much strife
The right to enjoy the arts
And so heal our hearts

Then, I had another shock
It's not just the sects in the dock
The governments are there too
There are things that they must do

They must do everything they can
Yes, do everything they can

Protect children everywhere
So that they know we care
Giving them a sense of safety
Despite sect leader crazy

For children who have been used
Neglected and abused
Even after they leave
There is no reprieve

Governments have a duty of care
Specialist help must be there
That they would know they are accepted
Definitely not rejected

Know that they belong,
Know freedom like a song
That love would flood their hearts
Bringing healing to the deep parts

This poem could be long
It could go on and on
I could have written much more
There are articles - fifty four

I've just given a taster
Don't think I am a waster
Much more could be said
But I care about your head

Child labour, working for the sect

As well as attending sect functions or meetings, in some sects some or most members work full-time for the group, for which they may receive very little or no financial reward. Further, children may also have to work. Children may work long hours in sects for no pay, so effectively, in some sects children are forced into slave labour. This is particularly evident when the hours of work are long and this therefore interferes with a child's life preventing them engaging in school work, play and socialisation. For example, they could be on the streets fundraising or they may be caring for younger children.[449] This is exploitative of the children, and when they work to the extent that they don't receive schooling, it is educationally neglectful. As in the case of the dignity colony started by Paul Schafaer, described by the second-generation former member Winfried Hempel and journalist Faris Kermani in a documentary:[450]

Faris Kermani: *By the late 60s the colony was highly efficient, making money for Schaefer and his inner circle. The workers only had one rest day a year and never received a penny.*

Faris Kermani: *The colony was effectively a state within a state where the laws of Chile did not apply.*

Winfried Hempel: *At times when the punishments were very tough and the work was hard, I thought of running away knowing that I wouldn't get far, but that maybe I could rest for a while or at least take a walk without someone monitoring me all the time.*

Childhood should be a time when children are able to be children, to be able to play with others, receive appropriate care and input from adult caregivers, develop themselves in terms of their interests and discover their gifts. Those children who do not have these opportunities upon reaching adulthood may experience a great feeling of a missed or lost childhood. Further, these children may miss out on quality time with their parents who themselves may work many hours for the sect and/or attend numerous sect meetings.

EXPECTED MEETING ATTENDANCE IN HARRY'S SECT

In Harry's Sect, as of 2003, members generally held outside jobs, adults and children from around 12 years of age attended in general six meetings a week:

Sunday – Three meetings: morning, afternoon, evening; these meetings are for everyone.

Monday – evening men's prayer meeting, only for male converted members.

Tuesday – evening meeting for everyone.

Thursday – evening meeting for everyone.

Friday – evening women's prayer meeting and cleaning of the meeting place, only for converted female members.

Saturday – evening meeting for everyone.

One second-generation former member described the family's involvement not only in meetings, but in doing work for the sect leader, as follows:

I think, totally, I think it's the whole family life revolved around meetings... in my case, my father was always around Harry's house doing maintenance and stuff because Harry never did it himself – he always expected my father and others in the group to maintain his house for him, maintain the chapel, and in the summer holidays we were often dragged down to help out. I dreaded it because I'm not a practical person. I dreaded it. I didn't fit in at all with that system.[451]

WHAT DID HARRY'S SECT AND TED'S SECT MEMBERS DO WITH THEIR TIME

In Harry's Sect, children invariably ceased full-time education at age 16, at which time they were expected to work full-time. In some sects, while members may give many hours to sect activities, some or most members also have full time jobs outside the sect. In both Harry's Sect and Ted's Sect, members did little with their time apart from sect-related activities and employment. One Harry's Sect former-member interviewee recalled a conversation that he had had with another Harry's Sect member while he was still involved in Harry's Sect. Although this was not reported as the way all current Harry's Sect members behaved at work, this does show why those in Harry's Sect could be unlikely to have friends even in their workplace:

He told us how at work he went to lunch, he'd buy a newspaper and hold it up there while he had his meal, to protect him, shield him from other people.[452]

In Ted's Sect, time not used for Ted's Sect was considered wasted time. Members described life as revolving around classes. Those in Ted's Sect generally described themselves as having a very intense experience and being physically and mentally exhausted as a result. At the Gashaku, particularly, the leaders controlled time usage and members got very little sleep.

By contrast, Harry's Sect second-generation members described themselves as bored, among other experiences. They attended school and spent most of their other time in sect-related activities and doing homework. At age 16, they left full-time education and went to work. After moving to the main Harry's Sect location, Harry's Sect members attended many meetings, went to work, read books authored by Harry and maybe did some gardening.

Some Harry's Sect members were involved with working for Harry (e.g. doing his gardening) or selling books written by Harry. For a time, when Harry preached at a hired hall, individuals travelled around the country on Saturdays, free evenings and during their holidays to help publicise these meetings.

Work in Ted's Sect was viewed as a means to an end. The object of employment was to earn money, which was used to live on and pay the small fees that being a part of Ted's Sect required. Individuals generally took low-paying jobs, which they could maintain while devoting many hours to training and spending time joining in Ted's Sect-type activities such as Buddhist discussions. Their activities in Ted's Sect sometimes affected their work because of exhaustion. Most Harry's Sect first-generation members had professional jobs that would not be considered low-paid, although there were some limits on the work that individuals took because of meetings.

Relationships with others in the sect

Children in some sects may have found that their sect peers were their only or their main support. This is clearly demonstrated in the research on Centrepoint, where relationships between peers were described as 'bonded'. Kids were siblings, just from different blood, a tribe of children, or a close group of children who relied on one another for support.[453]

However, some sects have very few children,[454] and in Harry's Sect, while there were lots of children, members, including the children, had limited relationships with one another. This was partly because members were not permitted to speak to each other while in the meeting hall. Even at the end of sect meetings, communication between individuals was discouraged on the grounds that it would detract from what they had heard in the meeting. Additionally, Harry interfered with relationships between members by informing individuals about whom they should and should not be friends with. Therefore, he exerted great influence over members' friendships.[455] Here is how one former Harry's Sect member described it:

> There was a security, and there was a pal-ly-ness [sic] and a friendship, like, you know, you'd have that if you belonged to the army or any club or any group, you have that, and that's about the only compensation you do get, because you are very close because it's a small community.

In what way are you close?

> Well, you're all fighting for the same supposed cause, which is a fallacy, but you're all fighting for it. You're never very close, you weren't allowed to be that close, because he stopped you getting close, and he stopped me getting [close]. If he saw me getting close to someone my own age, you know, like the other mothers, that kind of thing, you know, he'd say,

158

*'well, you should keep at home, get off to your work, you lazy woman'
and all this sort of thing.*[456]

Some Harry's Sect members also reported that they did not trust other members because they were scared. There are similarities here to what Osherow[457] reported in his analysis of Jonestown, where there was a diminishment of solidarity and loyalty that individuals felt towards families and friends. Expressing doubt or criticisms about Jones even to a friend, partner or child became risky for the individual. Jim Jones publicly ridiculed and discouraged members whose sexual partnerships and activities were not under his direction and control.

Harry had influence in the area of dating between Harry's Sect members. In Harry's Sect, there was a particular lack of contact with the opposite sex. Where it did occur, it sometimes led to marriage if Harry advised this for the couple. An interviewee explained the increasing limitations as the group continued:

*You know, as we got older it became more restrictive because we weren't
allowed to go out or have boyfriends/girlfriends, and it was very much
a lifestyle that was restricted, I think.*[458]

By contrast, relationships between children at Centrepoint involved sanctioned sexual contact between children. Encouraging sexual promiscuity is a way of discouraging the intimacy that might grow in a more committed relationship. Upon reaching adulthood, intimacy is an area that some of those raised in sects can find especially difficult. Of the 23 research participants, 13 who had spent time at Centrepoint as teenagers described 'voluntary' teenage under-age sex.[459] Opposite-sex contact between adults in Ted's Sect was frequent and much dating occurred, although some intervention from the leadership seemed evident. On the surface, it appeared that much more interaction occurred between members in Ted's Sect than in

Harry's Sect. However, although 'togetherness' was reported – e.g., they trained together and spent a lot of time together – participants recounted that they did not seem to talk to each other about problems that they observed in Ted's Sect.

EFFECT OF LACK OF RELATIONSHIPS

LACK OF SOCIAL SUPPORT FOR PARENTS IN HARRY'S SECT

The children of those who were married when they were in Harry's Sect may have been affected specifically in terms of the social support that their parents received. Social support, both physical and emotional, has been found to be important for parents as it enables them to respond to their children with more warmth and consistency.[460] Children whose grandparents are not in the sect may have no contact or limited contact with them. Grandparents have been found to be a major source of informal support for families: their support has been found to contribute to the mother's psychological well-being and perceived adjustment.[461] This particular support is also therefore likely to be missing for many families in sects. However, for third-generation members who have grandparents and parents still in the sect, their parents may receive this type of support.

LACK OF RELATIONSHIP OPPORTUNITIES FOR THE SECOND
GENERATION IN HARRY'S SECT

For both the second generation and those who remained single in Harry's Sect, the isolation experienced was likely to be detrimental. Erikson's theory - discussed in the previous chapter – highlights the importance of achieving psychological intimacy with opposite-sex relationships and also same-sex friendships that help form the personality, and give the individual access to intimate feelings, as well as allowing them to move away from the dependence on parents towards the independence of adolescence and young adulthood.

'If a youth's attempts at intimacy fail, she retreats into isolation. In this case social relationships are stereotyped, cold and empty.'[462] The lack of social opportunities and friendships for the second generation was likely to be a factor in psychological adjustment, specifically their level of depression.[463] The lack of relationship opportunities for children in Harry's Sect was likely to be detrimental to them in terms of their socialisation, which in turn was likely to impact their psychological distress levels after leaving Harry's Sect by contributing to the degree of culture shock and anxiety they felt on leaving the sect.

Summary of Chapter 6

Bandura's social learning theory assists us in understanding both different types of learning and how children learn, including informally by observing others, and via the TV and other media. This is helpful in terms of understanding what children in sects do and don't learn. Children in sects may have few if any relationships with people outside of a sect. A former member explained that there was an 'us and them' attitude, which was unhelpful in terms of children's attitude towards the outside world and relating to children not in the sect.

The dress codes present in both Ted's Sect and Harry's Sect may relate to control, frugality, sex differentiation and stigma. The adaption strategies used by children at school to deal with stigma included being a loner, finding friends amongst other subgroups such as 'the stoners' and stigma concealment. However, stigma concealment was a stressful coping response as those children using it live with the risk of being found out, of people discovering that they are in fact part of a sect and not who they have portrayed themselves to be. Some second-generation former members reported positive experiences of the state schools they attended and where they felt accepted by the other children despite being different to them.

However, not all children in sects have the opportunity for state schooling – some may be home-schooled, attend a school run by the sect, or they may have limited or non-existent education, especially where for example they work long hours for the sect for no pay. Forced labour, very frequent meeting attendance, lack of play opportunities and other factors can mean that on reaching adulthood, individuals may have a great sense of loss for the childhood that might have been. Outside of their working life, members of both Harry's Sect and Ted's Sect spent a lot of time on sect-related activities. Parents in Harry's Sect had a lack of social support.

Children in sects may see each other as their key source of support, and they may bond closely with each other. But not all sects have lots of children, in addition to which in some sects such as Harry's Sect there may be few opportunities for the children to get to know each other. It may be that the sect leader interferes with relationships and exerts a great deal of influence including stopping individuals in a group interacting with each other. While some groups might strictly separate men and women as well as boys and girls in a few sects there has been sanctioned sexual contact between children. This may affect individuals into adulthood, particularly in the area of intimacy.

WHAT COMES NEXT IN CHAPTER 7?

Another aspect of the lack of relationship inside and outside the sect is the resulting shortage of social identities. Most individuals identify with a number of social groups, but membership of Harry's Sect or Ted's Sect precluded most of these. This could contribute to trauma found after sect membership when the loss of the key previous social identity occurs, as well as contributing to difficulties in leaving the sect as the following quote indicates and which is looked at in depth in the next chapter.

'When you've grown up in the group, when you've grown up afraid to have friends who aren't followers – forbidden to have such close contact with people; forbidden to be like them, even down to dress code and ways of behaviour and styles and interests and hobbies; when the whole world is cut off from you and all the significant people in your life are Harryians, at least as far as you can tell, even if they're harbouring secret alienation, they don't dare show it, because of this kind of paranoid fear that if you reveal to the world that you live inside that somebody will report you, when you try to leave, what are you leaving to? Where are you going? Are you going to your Mum and Dad? No, they're still in. Are you going to your brother or sister? No, they're still in. Are you going to your friends? What friends? All your friends are inside. Well, you can go to your secret friends. "Well, I don't know if I know them well enough to take that chance". …

In practice, people raised in the group had someone that they could at least make tentative contact with, for the most part … but it's hard. There's always that question in the back of the mind, it seems, that says, yes, but what if this person turns out to be bad for you, isn't as safe as they seem? What if you're being tricked? What if everything that Harry said is true?'[464]

CHAPTER 7

WHY DIDN'T ANYBODY TELL ME?

THANKS AND ACKNOWLEDGEMENTS to Dr Trevor Hussey, Emeritus Professor of Philosophy, Buckinghamshire Chilterns University College, High Wycombe, England for his lecture notes and input for the fallacies of logic section in this chapter.

I think basically, I was young, and I thought my life was in front of me, do I want to stay in a situation where I don't experience life around me. I felt there was so many things I wanted to learn, find out and do, it was all exploding in my head as it were and I couldn't do these things, so psychologically I was, I wanted to leave.... It took me longer perhaps than other people to come to the position where I felt that I just couldn't go on.

Once I began to entertain the thought of leaving, it seemed to grow in you until you had to do it. It was like if you had never entertained that thought, if you had kept it out, if you had kept it at bay, it would not have got into you and followed you until it came to a point where you had to act on it, and this is really what happened to me.

One evening I remember sitting in one of these meetings and an overwhelming certainty that I had to leave, as if I had made the decision at that point and there was no going back, and because of the sort of secretive and the fear and the secretive nature of the group, because if you do anything, most things that you did outside the prescribed boundaries obviously you did in secret, so you know there was an element of fear and hiding and secrecy about. A second-generation former member of Harry's Sect.[465]

Overview

This chapter will look at why it is difficult to leave, including the fallacies of logic that cloud one's thinking, which leaders might use to keep their members in a sect. It will go on to look at what percentage of the second generation leaves sects; at what age; and for what reason. It will address issues of culture shock, what it is, and how long it lasts. Some of those raised in sects may actually be what have been termed 'third culture-kids'. This refers to children who spend all or part of their childhood in a country which is native to neither of their parents. The chapter will further discuss the stages of adjustment to a new culture. It will address feelings of not being 'normal'.

Errors of logic used to keep individuals in sects

Cognitive distortions

Chapters 1 and 2 showed how social influence processes might induce people to join and stay in a sect. False logic, cognitive distortions (thoughts we have in our minds that are not true or are exaggerated) further contribute to the confusion that sect leaders and their followers are generally immersed in. Cognitive distortions can lead to mental health problems, specifically anxiety and depression[466], because they create conflict between thoughts, feelings and behaviours.

'Human beings have the capacity to formulate logic and consequently the capacity to misformulate it. Hence the possibility of logical error'.[467] When individuals argue or debate, they sometimes employ, either knowingly or unknowingly, various devices and tricks that aim at winning the argument by any means rather than arriving at the truth. Logicians and philosophers have identified many of these tricks. Hence it is possible to objectively pick out fallacies of logic and, by so doing, show how these are used to overcome opposition or dissent, even when dissent and opposition are justified.

Black-and-white thinking

During sect membership, leaders use rhetorical devices that may be categorised as examples of twisted logic. The resulting distorted cognitions, such as black-and-white thinking (excluding other options such that the shades of grey in between two extremes are not considered), may continue after sect membership has ceased. Previous work[468] identified 10 types of distortions in thinking[469] that may occur during sect membership. One researcher[470] found that individuals scoring their group in the abusive range for the Group Psychological Abuse Scale (discussed at the end of Chapter 1) also scored high on cognitive impairment. The use of 'twisted logic' and resulting cognitive distortions may contribute to personal distress experienced, and may become a form of habitual thinking that members take with them on departing the sect and which they subsequently have to change.

It is ironic that many errors of logic do, in fact, occur in these groups, considering they often think or teach that they have the most logical beliefs. It may be that once someone has accepted a thoroughly off-the-wall premise that an individual is God or has direct contact with God, then everything else that follows is in fact quite logical.

Don't think and don't speak

Some members of sects may have been encouraged to be 'logical' with slogans like, 'Don't trust your emotions, just follow your logic', or its opposite 'Don't think, just feel!'. In addition, in many sects it is not okay to ask questions, as in 'Revolutionaries don't ask questions'. Or those of us raised in certain sects might have experienced blatant condemnations of children speaking, as in the 15th Century, which was also popular in the Victorian era, that 'Children should be seen and not heard.'[471] This may be because children are naturally curious, open and liable to ask awkward questions.

In some groups, children have been put on silence restriction, i.e. they were not allowed to speak. Lord Chief Justice Ward recorded in a court judgement in 1995 that in The Family: 'Putting the children on silence was used as a means of punishment, and even after making all due allowances, I am still satisfied that they were kept on periods of silence which were both prolonged and abusive.' If it is not okay to ask questions or speak, sorting out fallacies of logic by discussing these with others is unlikely to occur, further it decreases the likelihood of finding others with questions.

TRUISMS

Another type of cognitive distortion is a truism which is when something that is true, is in fact an irrelevant argument. E.g., 'Many people in the world are lonely. Therefore, you should stay in the group or you will be lonely.' (While many people in the world are lonely, there are many who are not lonely and, you may be very lonely in the group.)

FALSE ALTERNATIVES

Interviews of former members revealed that sect leaders used cognitive distortions as a tool to maintain the sense of group/sect identity, to enforce cohesion (unity) and to limit perceptions of the leaders and the group, or alleviate doubts in otherwise difficult or confrontational situations. A false mode of argument particularly evident in Ted's Sect was the device of offering 'false alternatives', which forces the other person into having to accept either of two unacceptable positions. For example, someone might say 'either you are for us or against us' therefore all other alternatives are excluded. Alternatives that do not allow for other possibilities produce all-or-nothing (black-and-white, or polarised) thinking. This encourages individuals to view a situation in terms of two clearly opposing categories instead of recognising a continuum of possibilities.

INCORRECT IDENTITY-LEVEL BELIEFS

Another cognitive distortion, which became evident from interviews with former members of Ted's Sect, was that individuals, after conversations with their leaders, came to believe that their former perceptions of their personal strengths were incorrect. For instance, those who were clearly very intelligent, including those with higher degrees, came to believe that they were stupid. This is likely to affect individuals' sense of identity and lower their self-esteem, which in turn contributes to psychological distress, as does the confusion that such radically contradictory beliefs about oneself would cause. If one comes to believe that one doesn't have any strengths, then one is left only with weaknesses.

Double binds
Another type of cognitive distortion evident in Ted's Sect was 'double binds'. This occurred as a result of teaching about one's ego. For example:

> *One of the things was kind of, a double-bind thing. Like you could always get it wrong. Like there was one bit where this girl said, suggested, that she might teach a yoga class. Now if you didn't say that, it'd be "Why are you being so selfish and irresponsible about passing on the knowledge that you've got? You know, why are you being so selfish?" If you do suggest it, "How can you possibly be so arrogant as to think you're in a position to teach other people? How arrogant are you?"....[472]*

Questioning and disagreeing – one and the same?
In order to fully understand the magnitude and comprehensiveness of the control by leaders of a sect, it is important for the reader to be aware that in a sect there is often no distinction between 'questioning', as in, 'Can you explain why you decided this?,' and 'disagreeing,' as in, 'I don't think this is the right thing to do.' Further, for the child in the sect, a question will likely not only be a disagreement, but will also be a demand or command for information and might also be accusatory, there is no option about whether or not the child answers the question. The option of responding to a question with another question, or with 'I don't want to share that' is not acceptable. This may impact a child

in terms of increasing their ability to lie proficiently. The ability to pause before responding to questions, as well as the ability to deflect questions, not answer questions and to be aware that often someone asking a question is simply inquiring with the best interests of the one questioned at heart, are understanding and responses that second-generation former members may need to learn upon leaving a sect.

ERRORS OF LOGIC IN TED'S SECT: AN IN-DEPTH ANALYSIS

Errors of logic are another part of what makes it very hard to leave sects. In Ted's Sect, the leaders got together and thought about the possible reasons that members of the group might give for wanting to leave the group, one of which was that they 'Don't agree with what they are being taught'. What follows is an analysis of some of the answers suggested by the leadership in response to a member saying they don't agree with what they are being taught. Increasing the pressure for individuals is that these words were said to them by, authority figures. In addition, we have the advantage of seeing the arguments written out, whereas these individuals would have been confronted with them in conversation without the benefit of time to think before responding to what had been said to them. The leaders' prepared responses to a member who wanted to leave Ted's Sect because she did not agree with what she was being taught include the following:

What do you think that you're being taught?

What is it that you're being taught?

These sentences do not argue the case. These questions don't address the member's disagreement. An appropriate question would have been: What do you disagree with in what you are being taught? However, the leaders' suggested response hints that the individual has misunderstood, implying that they are the ones with the problem, as opposed to there being anything wrong with what they are taught.

You don't understand what you're being taught, so listen, be patient and then you'll understand.

Again, this does not address the problem. The individual has said that they disagree, not that they don't understand. This states more directly what the previous two responses alluded to: that the teaching is fine and the problem lies with the individual member. It implies that to disagree is to not understand. This is what philosophers refer to as an 'error in the truth of the premise', and is a form of begging the question, i.e. assuming that disagreement is lack of understanding. It is a false assumption to say that the individual does not understand what they are being taught. There is also an *ad hominem* element, that is to say, the practice of making a verbal attack upon the person rather than answering his or her arguments, since it implies that the person is lacking in important qualities such as understanding and patience.[473]

If you don't agree with it, then leave if you're not willing to be taught.

The above statement basically states that to disagree is to be unwilling to be taught. Again this is a truth error: not agreeing is not the same as not being willing to be taught.

This is what we do in Chinese Yoga: if you want to learn this, then this is what you have to do. This is the way we teach it here. If you don't agree with it, then go somewhere else. Go away and go train with someone else then!

This answer is very similar to the previous one – it gives no reason to believe that what is being taught is correct. Rather, it implies that it does not matter whether the individual disagrees or not. It also states that if you disagree, you should leave rather than have an intelligent discussion regarding the issue at hand with the possibility that what is being taught is not right.

You are not even in a position to begin to understand that which you are being taught.

Similarly, this is a claim that is left unjustified and is a false alternative. It implies that the student knows nothing and the teacher knows it all.

Shut up you.

This is an abusive technique. It uses emotive words rather than relying on a good argument. It implies that to question is to disagree, and to disagree is wrong, and that members should not vocalize when they disagree with what has been taught.

Just do as you're told.

This again implies that to question or disagree is wrong; that members are to be obedient rather than think:

What makes you think that your way of doing things is best? If you really know what's best for you, then why bother going to any teacher (of anything) in the first place?

This is an argument that does not address the member's concerns. It implies that to question or disagree with what is being taught is to think that you know best. This is untrue, as an individual might know something is wrong but not know what is best. Alternatively, they might know what is good for themselves, which may be to seek education. Therefore, this response is invalid. The second part of the sentence does not follow from the first part of the sentence. It contains a false alternative: to be entitled to criticise, you must know everything. The result is an argument that has neither truth nor validity.[171]

Then you don't agree with yourself! (Because you are studying this with that person, you agree that they are your teacher. Since you agree that he has something to teach you, you contradict yourself.)

The initial part of this response is both confrontational and states that the individual is being illogical. If the individual wants to leave, then obviously he is in agreement with himself, having changed his mind about the teaching in question.

The invalidity lies in denying this obvious truth. The individual does not want this particular teacher any more, however much of the teaching may be true.

Then you don't agree with yourself! (Because since you are your greatest teacher, and the job of the teacher is merely to show you yourself, if you disagree with the teacher then you disagree with yourself). [Parenthesis included in original]

This is an irrelevant argument. The student is rejecting what their teacher is teaching. The fact that they may also teach themselves (and even be their greatest teacher) is irrelevant because they are not rejecting their own teaching; indeed, that may have led to their complaint.

If you don't agree with what you are being taught, you must know then what you should be taught. You cannot learn if you already know. Do you know everything there is to learn? No? Then be willing to be taught.

This argument is a false alternative: either you know everything or you do not know enough to question what we have to teach.

In that case, it sounds like you've missed the point about what you are being taught. Your teacher has more experience than you and knows more than you do; that is why they are the teacher. It is wise to respect this and to acknowledge that there are people who are much wiser than you are who can see things more clearly. Don't make hasty judgements – put your question aside until you can see things more clearly.

This is an appeal to authority, i.e. claiming that something must be true or right because of the prestige, power, reputation or status of the source. It does not rely on supporting evidence or arguments and again it is attempting to get the individual not to ask questions.[475]

Humility is needed in order to learn.

If you really know so much, why don't you teach the class then?

If you are such an expert, why don't you go away and form your own school of yoga then?

What makes you such a know-it-all?

If you're such an expert then, why don't you set up your own class?

The individual is not claiming to be an expert; they are merely stating their disagreement. It is an *ad hominem* argument, which refers to an irrelevant attack on an opponent's character for the purpose of undermining their argument. It avoids addressing the question by accusing the individual of conceit, over-confidence, and of being a 'know-it-all'. This means that if they disagree in the future, they may again risk being put down. All of these responses by the leaders are in fact put downs and when a child experiences this, it is likely to leave a child thinking that it is okay to let others put you down, when in fact, in life, it is not okay. The second generation, upon leaving their sect, may need to learn how to stand up for themselves in an appropriate manner when and if others put them down.

Twisted thinking like this not only squashes disagreement and dissent, but can have the additional effect of locking an individual into a sect in their mind, which makes it very difficult for them to leave. When an individual is enmeshed in the sect thinking, then thoughts of leaving a sect are likely to be met with resistance within one's mind, which can make leaving very difficult. Even after leaving, cognitive distortions may contribute to the confusion present in the mind of a former member, and at some point, cognitive distortions may need to be worked through. Difficulties with leaving will now be looked at in more depth.

Difficulties associated with leaving and reasons for staying in a sect

Individuals have a need to belong, a sense of being at home somewhere, of being known and knowing others. Groups may provide us with a sense of belonging and therefore leaving any group to which you feel a sense of belonging can be difficult. For a child raised in a sect, even where they feel at odds with the sect, it is still their home.

Special language

In addition to the fallacies of logic discussed above, there are a myriad of reasons as to why it can be especially hard to leave a sect. Part of the difficulty with leaving is the problems with communication with those outside of the sect, particularly in terms of spirituality. Sects often redefine words and may also make up words. This makes it difficult to communicate with those who don't know the special language. Alternatively, words may be used which have vague but very negative meanings in the group, which effectively means they can be used to describe practically anything negatively.

In the group (Harry's Sect) to which I belonged, it seemed that everything the leader disapproved of was considered 'worldly', whatever that meant.

SOCIAL INFLUENCE: RECIPROCITY

As is also the case in many other sects,[176] it was emotionally very difficult to leave either Ted's Sect or Harry's Sect. As well as the followers' dependency on their leaders, 'reciprocity' was another social influence mechanism at work to get people to stay. Reciprocity was identified by Robert Cialdini,[177] a psychologist, in his book *Influence: The Psychology of Persuasion*. This mechanism is present in all cultures, and refers to the fact that when we have been given something, we try to give something back in return.

In Harry's Sect and Ted's Sect, members saw the leaders as giving them the only 'real truth' for their spiritual path. In this case, reciprocity does not refer to money or gifts. In the members' eyes, the spiritual path was far more important than gifts or money, and involved the leaders' giving of their time and knowledge. The members, in turn, gave, for example, their time, obedience and loyalty. In many groups, members give significant or very significant sums of money[178]. This type of reciprocity may not be in operation for all of the second generation who did not like to go to meetings and reported being particularly scared when Harry attended the meeting. However, those in the first and second generation for whom this influence process is at work may feel a great indebtedness to the group and/or leader of the group.

SOCIAL INFLUENCE: SOCIAL PROOF

'Social proof', as also identified by Robert Cialdini, involves individuals trying to find out what other people think. Cialdini states that 'Social proof is especially applied to the way we decide what constitutes correct behaviour. We view a behaviour as more correct in a given situation to the degree that we see others performing it. Whether the question is . . . how to eat the chicken at a dinner party, the actions of those around us will be important in defining the answer'.[179] This was particularly evident in Ted's Sect and Harry's Sect. In Ted's Sect and Harry's Sect, however, interview reports suggested that members' most important social proof was what their leaders thought. Realising that leaders do not know another person completely and that leaders are not endowed with the capacity to judge all behaviour correctly, may assist former members with not caring what leaders think. However, knowing in one's head at some level can be different to having a deep intrinsic heart-felt knowing that it does not matter what a leader or someone else thinks.

For the second generation, because all significant others appear to hold to the group view, social proof is likely to be in operation. This is particularly significant when second generation think about the spiritual ramifications of leaving and their eternal destiny as taught in the group. For example, reasons given for remaining in Harry's Sect included spiritual reasons as, in their minds, to leave was to go to hell for eternity.[480] The reasons for staying in Ted's Sect were more diverse.

SOCIAL INFLUENCE: SCARCITY

This links into another social influence process highlighted by Cialdini, which he calls 'scarcity'. This refers to the fact that, when something is going to be available for a limited period and we would like that thing, we fear that if we do not have it right now, we will not have it at all. Harry's Sect members claimed that their sect was the only place where 'the truth' was. Ted's Sect members thought of themselves as the only people who really did martial arts properly. Therefore, what the group offered was considered a scarce resource. Research reports indicated that members thought that to leave the group would be to lose the scarce resource, with the result that they would either never be satisfied or would lose their salvation. In some sects, members fully expect they will die if they leave.[481] This supports Robert Cialdini's[482] finding that individuals are more motivated if they understand what they will lose than if they understand what they will gain.

LEAVING IN AN UNSEEN WAY

Both sects usually exerted considerable pressure on individuals to remain once they were involved, although there were occasions when the leader told members to leave. It appeared that the leaders were bluffing in some instances, hoping that the individual would stay. In both Harry's Sect and Ted's Sect, members were likely to be verbally abused if the leaders suspected they were thinking of leaving. It was probably for this reason that individuals (particularly the second generation) tended to pack their bags when nobody else was around and leave quietly.

This 'unseen' way of behaving seemed to produce guilt feelings in some former members. Sometimes this was evident even years after leaving. If more second-generation former members were aware that one research interviewee, as an adolescent, informed her parents of her decision to leave and was physically held against her will in the family home, they would perhaps feel less guilty about leaving in an 'unseen' way. Additionally, acknowledgement and remembrance of physical abuse and psychological maltreatment might explain the fear of behaving in a 'seen' way.

SECOND GENERATION LEAVING DESPITE THEIR FAMILIES' CONTINUED INVOLVEMENT

One of the reasons for staying, and a key difficulty and obstacle to leaving, was the knowledge that one might never see family members again (in some cases, involving children, grandchildren or parents and siblings), and therefore the second generation who left would effectively become 'orphans'. A demographic study of Harry's Sect showed that whether an individual was still involved or had left Harry's Sect was significantly related to whether one had family members involved in the sect. It is less likely that an individual will leave a sect if their family is still involved. Nevertheless, this research showed that a significant proportion (at least 70%) of the second generation do leave, despite continuing family involvement. The pie chart below shows current family involvement for first-generation former members of Harry's Sect.

Figure 7.1: Pie chart showing family involved for first-generation former members

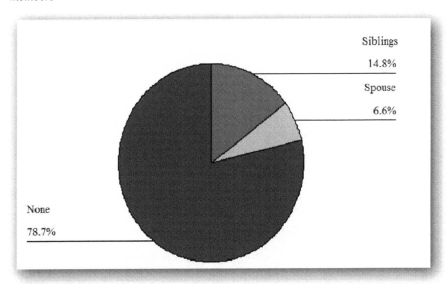

Figure 7.2 is a pie chart which shows family involvement for second-generation former members of Harry's Sect. Of the former second-generation members, 54% had parents and, in some cases, siblings, who remained in the sect. In this sect, if an individual is raised in it, parents and other family members who remain in it are unlikely to have contact with them after they leave. This happens in many, though not all, sects.

Figure 7.2: Pie chart showing family involved for second-generation former members

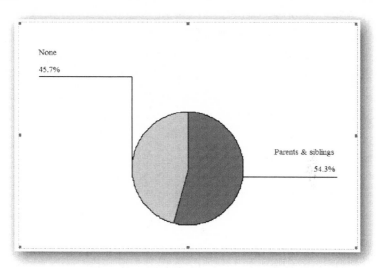

SECOND GENERATION LEAVING WHEN THEIR PARENTS LEAVE

Some second-generation members leave sects because one or both parents leave, and they leave with them, although some stay despite their parents leaving. The quotes that follow are from a second-generation former member whose parents left with others.

How did you come to leave the meeting?

Well, that was when my parents decided to leave, … So I left it then.

What do you remember about that?

Well, I was about eight at the time, and I think I remember it was a really big deal. I remember my parents being very stressed and worried, talking a lot about it, people coming around late at night without him knowing, and chatting about it for ages and ages. I remember seeing adults crying and that kind of thing … I remember all about the families, a whole group of people who had to leave, being terrified by the situation, thinking that Harry was going to do something really violent, because I think he'd just come back from where he'd been before to try and sort out the fact that people were leaving, and I remember being frightened by that, thinking he was going to do something horrible, because we heard he had guns. And so we all went away, a whole group of people went away in several cars and eventually just came back, so I think I remember my Dad saying that it was really stupid, but he was scared he was going to do something. So I remember that. I remember being sort of scared and stressed.[483]

NO CHOICE ABOUT LEAVING

For some of those raised in Harry's Sect, their reason for remaining was that, as they grew older, they felt they had no choice but to attend the sect meetings and therefore remain in the sect.[484] Interviewee reports indicated that for the second generation whose parents were in the sect, the only way to leave Harry's Sect was to leave the family home,[485] but they reported that they were so young that they lacked the means to leave.[486] Others reported feeling that they grew up in a loving home and just accepted the sect meetings and did not have a great desire to leave, at least not when they were very young.

CRITICISED AND INSULTED AFTER LEAVING

For those sect members who have witnessed and listened to people being slandered and spoken negatively about after leaving, the fear of this (especially when it's their own family members) is yet another factor that may contribute to it being difficult to leave a sect and to negative psychological consequences after leaving. Most people want to be liked, and unless we have a strong positive identity it can be hard to deal with harsh negative comments about oneself.

Despite the reasons for staying in the sect and the difficulties associated with leaving, many sect members leave, including those raised in sects. Occasionally, a sect disbands or a group of people leave the sect. This phenomenon is addressed in the next section.

Disbanding of Ted's Sect and a large group of Harry's Sect members leaving and leaving alone

Comparisons can be drawn between Ted's Sect disbanding and the events that led to a group of those in Harry's Sect leaving around 20 years ago. Both involved a female recounting acts of sexual misconduct by the leader of the sect while he was also in a relationship with another woman. In the case of Ted's Sect, it involved sexual abuse by Ted and a written statement by the female member concerned, which was circulated to other members by one of the leaders of the sect, who appeared to realise that the group was going under and that he could look like a saviour by doing this.

In the case of Harry's Sect, a current member disclosed to some core male members that she had had an affair with Harry and, again, this was written down. In Ted's Sect, all members got to hear of the incident. However, the *dojo* (a *dojo* is a place designated for training) leader had informed members of problems with the head teacher in the months preceding the circulation of this letter. Therefore, when the letter came, there may have already been doubt about the group and it was after the letter came that the group disbanded. In Harry's Sect, only a few selected individuals heard, and women were not included in this group. A group of people who left Harry's Sect at the time of the sexual misconduct being revealed indicated that their reasons for leaving was their doubts having been affirmed by other sect members and their having heard first-hand about Harry's lifestyle.

Leaving with others or leaving alone

While research on Harry's Sect showed that the second generation did not, on the whole, list doctrinal reasons as their reasons for leaving, Jill Mytton's research on those raised in the Exclusive Brethren[187] found that 54% of the sample left the Exclusive Brethren because of changes in doctrine. Many left in a group. It could be that there is a difference between those who leave individually and those who leave as a group, with those leaving as a group being more unhappy with some aspect of doctrine.

Many individuals, including the second generation, leave sects on their own. A demographic study[488] of Harry's Sect found that 46% of the sample left Harry's Sect alone. Another UK study[489] looking at numerous groups found that of the second-generation sample, 57% left their sect alone. Of the second generation, 39% had fathers still involved and 65% had mothers still involved in the sect at the time of participating in the research (which was on average over 13 years after leaving the sect).

Jill Mytton's study[490] had a similar result. Looking at those who have left the Exclusive Brethren, she found that, of her sample of second-generation former members, 3% had children, 45% siblings, 36% their mother and 37% had their father still involved in the sect on average 27 years after leaving the sect. This concurs with the work of others[491] who, when speaking of those raised in sects, state that the second generation sometimes leave sects alone, leaving behind friends and relatives, which can cause feelings of isolation and desolation after leaving.

The loss of parents who are still alive, yet with whom there is no contact, can be particularly difficult for the second generation as it is for those who have not been raised in sects. Charles Dickens, who had a deep insight into people, in one of his books *Dombey and Son*, writes about a man's daughter, Florence, who was neglected by her father because she was not male. Dickens wrote the following about Florence: 'For not an orphan in the wide world can be so deserted as the child who is an outcast from a living parent's love.'[492]

LEAVING THE SECT

Some of the former Ted's Sect interviewees left before the sect disbanded. Their reasons for leaving included the strange behaviour of one of the dojo (a dojo is a place designated for training) leaders, interaction with dojo members in another location, which enabled them to challenge their dojo leader after which he recorded that:

I was kind of removed from the group by the fact that he then took all the other people in the group to one side and said, 'Don't listen to him, don't trust him' and that was it. I was suddenly living in no man's land, living in a house with people that were either shouting at me or ignoring me, and that was quite a painful bit.[493]

Another former member left because of the influence of work colleagues, who helped one individual move to a job in another location and a different, less-abusive *dojo*. One Ted's Sect member was told to leave.

Many of those in Harry's Sect reported that they had niggling doubts, which increased as time went on. Those doubts usually focused around Harry's lifestyle and character. One individual who was only involved on the fringe of the sect revealed that what drew him away from the sect was that the teaching was not helping him live his life in the way he thought he should. The reasons for the second generation leaving the sect included: not being able to handle the restrictive lifestyle; wanting to learn more; wanting to have new experiences; and feeling unable to carry on in the sect, as the following quote from a second-generation former member shows:

I couldn't cope with just going to church and living a life that someone else told me how to live, without any chance to learn anything new or different, 'cos he'd lived a life already. ... So I told him that I would like to leave home and live in a place of my own, and I was locked in my room for a number of days.

Really?

Mm, and then on the Sunday I was babysitting for Kimberly, and my father knew I was going to go. I just literally packed a carrier bag and ran around the corner to someone I knew and got a lift.

And where did you go?

I went to a friend in [location] *and he came around that night to get me. I wouldn't go to the door. And that was the last I heard of him.*[494]

AGE OF LEAVING SECT

Table 7.1: Showing average and most common age of leaving sects across studies

Study	Average age of leaving	Most common ages for leaving
Second generation, UK study, multiple sects*	24 years	19 (by which age 38% of the second generation had left)
First generation, UK study, multiple sects*	32 years	
Demographic Harry's Sect UK study, second generation*	15 years (21 years for those leaving alone).	17 (of the second generation who left, 74% left the sect at or below the age of 19)
Demographic Harry's Sect UK study, first generation*	41 years	
Wellspring US study, first-generation multiple sects*	32 years	22, 26 and 30. By age 30, 51% of the sample of first former first-generation members had left their sect
Wellspring US study, second-generation multiple sects*	21 years	15, 18 and 30. Of this sample of second-generation former members, 50% left at or below the age of 19
Exclusive Brethren study, second generation✹	Age of leaving clustered between 15 and 21 years of age.	In her study, 35% of 201 former second-generation members left between the ages of 11 and 20

*Lois Kendall, 2006: ✹Jill Mytton, 1993

Combined, these studies indicate that the most common age to leave a sect is in the teenage years; between 35% and 74% of the second generation leave before reaching their 20th birthday[495]. Research has found that the second generation may want to leave their sect as young teenagers, but are unable to do so[496]. Once these individuals reach their later teenage years, they may then be in a position to leave and will then do so.

Some second generation sect members are forced out in their teenage years. Other reasons for the second generation leaving at this age may include a growing intolerance of the restrictive lifestyle that occurs in sects. This may become particularly prominent for the second generation as their non-sect peers may have an increasing amount of freedom and autonomy at this age. Figure 7.3 shows the frequency for age of leaving for the second generation leaving Harry's Sect on their own.

Figure 7.3: Bar chart showing second-generation age of leaving for those who left Harry's Sect alone

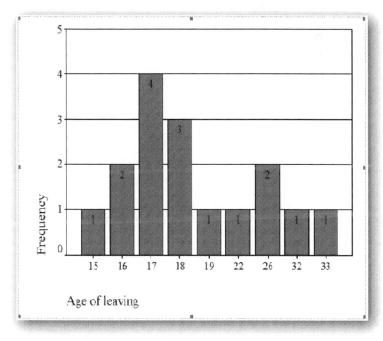

A researcher found that adolescents in religious groups that are not sects question their faith, and this reaches a peak at age 16.[497] Other researchers found that this takes place at a younger age for children who are more intelligent.[498] This may also be the case for children in sects, who may not outwardly be able to question their faith, but may have unspoken doubts and questions. It could also be that reasons for the second generation leaving a sect may differ depending on the child-rearing practices they experience while growing up in the sect. Or the country of residence might affect the age at which they can legally work full-time to support themselves, which is likely to have a knock on impact to their age of leaving.

THE METHOD OF LEAVING A SECT AND FORMER MEMBERS' ACCOUNTS OF THEIR EXPERIENCES

There are a number of different ways of leaving a sect. Table 7.2 shows the results of a number of studies, and demonstrates that the majority of individuals walk away from their sect.

Table 7.2: Method of leaving a sect – comparison of different studies

Study	Walked Away	Forced out by Sect	Other	Group Disbanded	Exit counseled	Deprogra mmed
Second generation UK study*	87%	9%	4%	–	–	–
First generation UK study*	54%	9%	7%	30%	–	–
First generation Wellspring US study *	66%	9%	4%	2%	16%	3%
Second generation Wellspring US study*	87%	4%	9%	–	–	–
Second generation UK study✻		6%				

*Lois Kendall, 2006: ✻Jill Mytton, 1993

FORCED OUT OF THE SECT

Table 7.2 shows that between 4% – 9% of the second generation are forced out by their sect. However, in some sects, this number can be much higher. For example young-second generation males in the Fundamentalist Latter Day Saints (FLDS) are often forced to leave the sect so that the older men can take multiple wives. There are between

400 – 1000 boys and young men who have either left themselves or been thrown out of the sect who are referred to as the 'Lost Boys'. It has been reported that:

> 'Many of these "Lost Boys", some as young as 13, have simply been dumped on the side of the road in Arizona and Utah, by the leaders of the Fundamentalist Church of Jesus Christ of Latter-day Saints (FLDS), and told they will never see their families again or go to heaven.'[499]

EXIT COUNSELLING AND DEPROGRAMMING

Exit counseling is a voluntary process whereby an expert on a sect meets with an individual sect member and presents them with information that potentially allows them to reassess their involvement in the sect. Deprogramming is a similar process, but, unlike exit counseling, the individual does not voluntarily, participate in and is not free to leave the process at any time, and it is unethical and as such is illegal in most countries.

Only small minorities of sect members are exit-counseled[500] or deprogrammed from their sect, and the vast majority of exit counsellings that do take place are arranged by the parents of first-generation members. This is supported by the UK research reported in Table 7.2, which showed that none of the former members reported being exit-counseled or deprogrammed. The US sample comprised those seeking help at Wellspring Retreat and Resource Centre. As some exit counsellors refer their clients there, it is unsurprising that the figures are high: 16% exit-counselled and 3% deprogrammed.

BELIEVING THE FIRST-HAND ACCOUNTS OF FORMER MEMBERS' SECT EXPERIENCE

Some have argued that exit counselling and deprogramming might result in individuals retrospectively colouring accounts of their sect experience, such as by exaggerating abuse. Thomas Robbins and Dick Anthony[501] argue that a 'deprogrammed ex-sectarian may, conceivably, honestly exaggerate the degree to which he was "brainwashed," regimented, or involved in spectacularly bizarre and depraved scenes prior to being once again "saved" by deprogramming.' They then discuss how a first-generation former member might wish to see themselves as a 'a passive victim of manipulation who has no responsibility for his or her prior actions and statements.' They then go onto state that 'None of the above considerations are really adequate to "explain away" the negative accounts of apostates from authoritarian sects; indeed much of what is said about the deception, manipulation and regimentation in "cults" is probably true.'

Some researchers have criticised those who work in the field for believing the accounts of those who leave sects or for not also studying current members of sects. This is argued despite the fact that sects have high defection rates. Most members of sects do eventually leave.[502] The previous section of this chapter included a discussion of studies that indicate that the most common age for the second generation to leave a sect is in the teenage years, and between 35% and 74% of the second generation leave before their teenage years have ended. In addition, those born into sects may never actually become members of sects as such.

NEGATIVE LABELLING OF FORMER MEMBERS BY ACADEMICS
In some instances, academics have labelled former sect members as 'apostates' or claimed that their negative accounts of membership are 'atrocity tales' and the harm that they report should be discounted.[503] Sociologists James Lewis and David Bromley[504] state that negative testimony from former members does not represent sociologically useful material. I consider these exclusions to be too sweeping and generalised and I agree with Benjamin Zablocki,[505] a research sociologist who states that labelling former members as apostates denies a voice

to a whole class of people, just because that voice is not positive or neutral. In fact, those not engaged in a group may give a more objective picture than those currently involved. Benjamin Zablocki comments that we should take the claims of former sect members as seriously as we take the claims of a wife who has been abused by a spouse.

IS THE METHOD OF LEAVING RELATED TO PSYCHOLOGICAL DISTRESS AFTER LEAVING?

Some studies have found that those who leave sects have significantly higher levels of psychological distress than the general population. James Lewis and David Bromley[506] argue that we cannot assume this occurs because of sect membership. They provide survey evidence to show that psychological distress post-membership is related to the exit process. They gave questionnaires to 154 former members of controversial groups. The questionnaire identified three methods of leaving the sect, namely, no exit counselling (N = 89), voluntary exit counselling (N = 29) and involuntary exit counselling (N = 36). They found a strong link between the method of leaving and psychological symptoms of distress, with those who had no exit counselling reporting the least distress. However, research by Ron Burks[507] on a similar but larger sample, using standardised measures, found the opposite to be true. His research found that those who had walked away from their group reported greater psychological distress than those who had been exit-counselled from their group.

Regardless of the method of leaving, it may be the case that the pressures inherent in leaving a sect affect individuals. Some even go so far as to say that this alone may precipitate a psychotic breakdown.[508]

CULTURE SHOCK

Upon leaving a sect, many former members experience a sense of alienation and confusion resulting from culture shock, the loss of previously valued norms, ideals or goals. For example, one second-generation former member reported the following about what to do on a Sunday, which was viewed in Harry's Sect as a day of rest when people attended three meetings:

> *It felt really weird waking up on Sunday and thinking 'I don't have to go to three meetings'. Like the day is all mine. That was really weird. 'You can sleep in for as long as you want and stuff.' It was quite disturbing.*[509]

While this could also relate to first-generation former members, this may be particularly relevant to those second-generation former members who often have had no prior experience of mainstream culture, which they enter after sect membership, as Winfried Hempel[510] explains below:

> *I had never heard a radio. I had never read a newspaper, except for some clippings that they would show us very briefly, and I had never seen a television except for some taped news videos that they showed the community about Pinochet in order to indoctrinate us.*

> *It was incredible. I was standing on a street away from the colony, 20 years old, with a psychological mentality of an eight-year-old boy.*

> *I was in front of an automatic door that opened by itself. Something I had never seen in my life. I saw traffic lights and saw how traffic worked for the first time at the age of 20. I was like Mowgli (Tarzan) leaving the jungle for the first time. And it's incredible that something like this could happen in the 20th century.*

UNIVERSAL ASPECTS OF HUMAN NATURE AND NEEDS

Many of the research samples in the area of sects (including in this book) report on samples drawn mainly from the UK and the US. Both the US and UK are English-speaking societies that are industrialised and relatively secular, with a predominantly Christian heritage. Critics point out that much psychological research ignores issues of cultural differences and focuses too much on individuals rather than cultures or societies. However, recent research and theorists claim that amid considerable surface diversity in cultural goals and values, certain universal aspects of human nature in the form of basic developmental tendencies and psychological needs still exist.[511]

One theory[512] proposes that, regardless of their culture, individuals have basic psychological needs: autonomy, inner choice regarding one's action and lifestyle,[513] competence and the need to relate to others. Well-being is enhanced when these needs are supported in the culture in which one finds oneself and the individual can fulfil these needs. The way in which needs are fulfilled and the expression of these needs varies greatly across cultural and social contexts. But the theory supposes that these needs are important across variations in cultures.

The need for autonomy has been confused with 'individualism' and 'independence' by a number of writers in the field, and has therefore produced controversy. A study conducted within varied cultures showed that the concept of autonomy can be distinguished from the concepts of individualism and collectivism (in an individualist culture, attitudes are more important than norms, whereas in a collectivist culture, cultural norms are given more weight than attitudes[514]). The study supported the concept that autonomy is a basic human concern.[515]

In light of this theory, the research findings in this book should not be dismissed as simply culturally bound. However, culture is still an important variant. Those who leave sects may experience culture shock in different ways, depending on the culture in which they find themselves. Therefore the results of research based on UK and US

participants may not apply to cultures that are not similarly industrialised societies.

The commonest age for second-generation members to leave Harry's
Sect was 17. By British standards, they are still classified as children.
On leaving the sect (unless they left with their parents), these children had a host of immediate practical details they needed to address. As it was not possible to leave Harry's Sect and stay in the
family home, these children/young people needed to find accommodation for themselves.[516] They also had other issues to contend
with, perhaps for the first time in their lives, such as what to wear,
eat and do.

Second-generation members leaving Harry's Sect were usually educated up to age 16, and most would have already taken up employment
at the time of leaving, hence they had an income (unless they were
working full-time for Harry's Publishers). Second-generation former
members exiting some sects (particularly communal ones) may leave
their sects with very little or no money, with no employment, or with
few, none or non-recognised qualifications.[517] Additionally, second-
generation former members need to learn a mass of knowledge and
skills. Bruce Perry, speaking of the Davidian children he assisted, recounts that:

'As I got to know the Davidian children, I saw similar contrasts
again and again: islands of talent, knowledge and connection
surrounded by vast empty spaces of neglect. For example, they
could read well for their ages, as they had to study the Bible
regularly. But they knew virtually no math. The talents were
linked to brain regions that had been exercised and behaviours that had been rewarded. The lacunae resulted from lack
of opportunities for development, in Michael's case, lack of opportunities to make choices for himself, lack of exposure to

the basic choices that most children get to make as they begin to discover what they like and who they are.'[518]

A CROSS-CULTURAL MOVE

Leaving a sect and entering mainstream culture can be viewed as a cross-cultural move. Research on those moving cultures has found that adjustment to the new culture over time follows a curve, as shown in Diagram 7.4:[519]

Diagram 7.4: Cultural adjustments over time

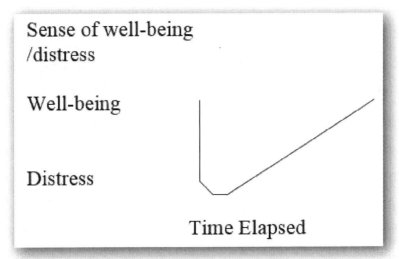

Initially, some individuals feel enthusiastic and fascinated by the new experience. As time goes on, they feel a sense of isolation, anxiety and frustration. Still later, they feel better again. Research has also shown a strong connection between acculturation and mental health, with lowered mental health often evident in terms of anxiety, depression, identity confusion, feelings of marginality and alienation,[520] which stem from feelings of frustration, isolation and anxiety in a new culture.

Newcomers to a culture may have problems because they lack social skills and are unfamiliar or not at ease with the social norms and conventions of the culture.[521] Some of the Harry's Sect former member accounts support this theory of culture shock, although an initial period of enthusiasm and fascination on entering their new culture may be lacking. Additionally, a feeling of relief at having left the previous culture was present for some, often followed by guilt and fear due to them feeling like traitors. The following quote illustrates this:

> *After I left, my first reaction was a tremendous feeling of relief. It's happened. I've done it. It's over. I can remember about a couple of days later, I can remember sort of a black depression falling upon me. Sort of a guilt feeling. . . you know, I've done some awful crime, some unforgivable crime, and it was basically a sort of black depression, a feeling of total guilt and fear and everything else. But it took some time to work through, and I don't think I've got much of that left now because I've worked through it, but at that time it took me several years before I could actually get through that.[522]*

MOVING ACROSS CULTURES: THIRD-CULTURE KIDS

Ruth Useem coined the term 'third-culture kid' (hereafter referred to as TCK) in the 1950s to refer to those children brought up in different countries whose parents formed a lifestyle that is different from both the home culture and the host culture. With the increase in globalisation and immigration, the body of knowledge on TCKs will continue to increase.[523] A number of definitions of TCK exist, including, 'a person who has spent a significant part of his or her developmental years outside the parents *culture.*' The TCK builds relationships to all of the cultures, while not having full ownership in any. Although elements from each culture are absorbed into the TCK's life experience, the sense of belonging is in relationship to others of similar background.[524]

The concept of a TCK might be criticised on the basis that, with the fast advancement of technology, the environment (and hence culture) in which any individual is raised might differ significantly from their parents. For example, being brought up by English parents in the 1950s might have been very different to having been raised by English parents in the 1980s. This criticism may be valid. However, this might be true for the vast majority of children in that culture. The concept of a TCK is that they relate to those with a similar life experience rather than to those raised in their parents' culture.

A number of those raised in sects would fit the definition of a TCK. Even though they may not have travelled abroad, they may find the experience of being in a sect so different from the culture in which they reside that their experience parallels that of TCKs. David Pollock and Ruth Van Reken have identified a number of issues that TCKs are likely to encounter, particularly once they reach adulthood. These include issues like practical skills, developmental issues, relational patterns and unresolved grief, as well as beneficial aspects of the experience. For example[525], they may have cross cultural skills such as a high acceptance level of differences. They may see other cultures as different, but not necessarily better or worse than their own and they may have the ability to incorporate the best characteristics of the cultures they have experienced. They may also not be in the same developmental stage as their peers and may, for example, engage in adolescent rebellion during their early 20s and leave career decisions to a later time as compared to their mono-culture peers.

HOW INDIVIDUALS REPORTED FEELING AFTER LEAVING THE SECT

In both Ted's Sect and Harry's Sect, individuals reported feeling relief, liberation and freedom[526] on leaving.[527] Ted's Sect former members reported needing a lot of space,[528] and being really excited upon realising that they did not have to live their lives according to the sect's way anymore.[529] Some Ted's Sect former members also described how they found it quite frightening because being in Ted's Sect had actually been their security for years. However, they also reported enjoyment of the rediscovery of the joys of everyday life.[530] Harry's Sect former members reported feeling insecurity,[531] confusion, vulnerability, distress, devastation, deep shock and fear.[532] Those who left in a group were afraid of what the leader Harry might do.[533] Second-generation former Harry's Sect members reported a sense of fear about meeting current members.[534]

Quite a number of former Harry's Sect members had a sense of frustration as they wanted to help others in the meeting but were unable to do so.[535] A second-generation former member mentioned that when they originally left the sect they felt proud of themselves for having left, but they also found it a struggle.[536] Another former member felt that they were not overly troubled after leaving Harry's Sect.[537]

While a number of former Ted's Sect and Harry's Sect members reported that they found the period after leaving very difficult for various reasons, not all reported this. Some said that they felt okay.[538] Former Ted's Sect members seemed more likely to report extremely negative consequences of being in Ted's Sect as well as a wide range of positive benefits – for example, fitness, self-confidence, useful life skills and an expanded vocabulary.

SUMMARY OF CHAPTER 7

Distortions in thinking may be experienced by those in sects, and these distortions may negatively impact an individual in terms of their mental health, creating a conflict between thoughts, feelings and behaviour and keeping a person locked into a situation or place making it difficult to leave. Black-and-white thinking, false alternatives, incorrect identity-level beliefs (e.g. I am ugly, when in fact the truth is you are beautiful) and condemnation of thinking and at times speaking, may be present in the sect context. Questions and disagreeing may become locked together in the sect environment, resulting in former members being sensitive to questions. Numerous cognitive distortions were present in Ted's Sect as evidenced by a document that the leadership produced for themselves to persuade people who were thinking of leaving not to leave the group.

The fallacies of logic and distortions in our thinking are just one of the reasons why it can be difficult to leave a sect. Other reasons such as the changing of language can make it hard to communicate well with those outside the group, especially with regards to spiritual matters. A number of social-influence processes identified by Robert Cialdini were found to be present in some sects, such as how we decide what constitutes correct and appropriate behaviour in a given situation.

To leave a sect may involve leaving behind one's family and not being allowed contact, consequently avoiding loss of family may be one of the reasons that some remain in sects. However, statistics are presented from a demographic study of Harry's Sect which show that despite many individuals leaving alone and leaving family behind, at least 70% of the second generation do in fact leave Harry's Sect.

The disbanding of Ted's Sect and a group of members leaving Harry's Sect involved a female member disclosing sexual misconduct by the leader while he was also in a relationship with another woman. For Harry's Sect members, hearing first-hand about the leader's actual lifestyle resulted in doubts about the sect leader being affirmed.

Statistics on the second generation from a number of research studies indicate that the most common age for the second generation to leave a sect is in the teenage years. Between 4% – 9% of the second generation were forced out of the sect, but by far the greatest number, 87%

(two studies one from the US and one from the UK) walked away from their sects. Some academics have negatively labelled former members, and criticised researchers who believe the accounts of former members. I agree with Benjamin Zablocki that negatively labelling former members denies a voice to a whole group of people, just because that voice is not necessarily positive or neutral.

The cultural move from a sect to mainstream culture may be so great that culture shock is experienced, and cultural adjustment over time occurs where the learning of cultural rules and acquisition of knowledge happens, leading to a feeling of less distress and greater well-being. A number of second-generation former members are actually also third culture kids, or at least may relate to their experiences, including the opportunities and challenges that entails.

Individuals reported differently on how they felt on leaving, including that they had felt a great sense of relief, liberation and freedom, the need for space, fear, frustration, struggle and pride.

WHAT COMES NEXT IN CHAPTER 8?

The chapter that follows looks in more detail at the losses and other psychological effects experienced by those leaving sects. It also points out the reported benefits of sect involvement as the quote below from a former second-generation Harry's Sect member shows:

> *Positive effects may have been disciplined use of time and whatever, learning how to cope without too much money, therefore getting some true perspective on what is important in life and what's not. And similarly, the lack of television is quite good in making good use of time and not getting pre-empted in that way, but then the con side to that was the lack of any television, full stop, is not good.*[539]

CHAPTER 8

Nobody Understands!

*So why do I share all that, despite the fact that I realize
the overall picture is less than flattering to me personally?
Clearly, my personal issues and struggles are of an entirely
different nature than those of a young second generation
trying to overcome a traumatic and abusive upbringing. I'm
not trying to say I can even begin to understand how any one
of them must feel. (Although through close personal experience I have had to learn a little about the interior landscape
of trauma victims.) But I say all of that simply to lay out for
any second generation reader that your struggles affect me
deeply. As a first generation former member I feel deep shame
about your experience. I am deeply, deeply sorry for how we
as a generation, and myself as a parent, simply failed.* Ray
Connolly – First-generation former member of the
Family International (Children of God)[540]

Overview

WHEN ADOLESCENTS AND young adults leave a sect, they inevitably experience multiple losses that can be very painful. This chapter will show why
there may be multiple losses that impact people and may result in complicated grief and mourning. It will also look at the types of dangers and
risks to which those raised in sects might be vulnerable after leaving, such
as drug addiction and one-on-one abusive relationships. The chapter will

discuss the major emotional and psychological difficulties as well as some of the benefits that those raised in sects might uncover after leaving.

WHO AM I?

Our sense of who we are is, in major part, linked to our social identity; who we are in relationship to others and to groups of people. For example, I might identify myself as a mother, sister, daughter, granddaughter and friend. Outside of my family, my social identities might, for example, include, being part of a football team, artists or writing group, religious group, school, college and/or workplace.

For most sect members, their primary group, and therefore their primary social identity, is the sect to which they belong and for the second generation in some, though not all, sects – it may also be their flesh-and-blood family. They may have few or very limited social identities other than this. Some children in sects may have had the ability and opportunity to form relationships with peers at school. They may have lived a 'double life' at school while also being in the sect, and this may help them to have another social identity on leaving the sect. Those who leave sects with no social identity outside the group (apart from perhaps their work identity, or a limited social group identity that they have managed to form through a double life) are likely to leave behind their strongest and, in some cases, their only social identity.

Our social identity[541] is very important[542] to us. No individual is an island – rather, we tend to define a major part of who we are in terms of our relationship to others, our social identity. Therefore, leaving behind one's social identity, may be a large loss. It may in fact be a traumatic loss for those raised in sects, and may evidence itself in psychological problems. A sense of not knowing who one is may follow such an experience. After leaving the sect it is the time to both develop and settle into a new identity. This can be a mammoth task particularly given some of the other necessary tasks, such as loss and mourning, and it is to this we now turn.

Loss, complicated grief and mourning

There are often very high levels of loss experienced after leaving the sect environment, this section will look at the theories of stages of grief developed by Kübler-Ross,[543] as well as the more recent theoretical developments in the area of complicated loss and mourning by Therese Rando.[544]

Those leaving sects may lose their homes, their jobs and their belongings, and be cut off from other members, including family members.[545] Where this occurs, there is a loss for both the former member as well as the sect member. For example, younger siblings still in a sect may feel a great sense of loss when older siblings leave a sect, as would parents who leave children or grandchildren behind them in the sect. Further, current-second and third-generation members whose parents/grandparents leave a sect and whose group then forbids or constrains contact may also have a sense of grief for the loss of their parents. Current members in a sect may have little opportunity to grieve openly for the loss of loved ones who leave. They may not be allowed any contact with loved ones who have left, or they only have very limited contact. An additional cause for a sense of rejection occurs when parents are the ones who actually force their children to leave the sect, although they may only be following the orders of senior sect members.

Brent W Jeffs records the following about the 'lost boys' who were kicked out of or left the Fundamentalist Latter Day Saints:

Parents weren't completely heartless... Many moms cried as they drove their sons out of town[546]

Although no-one has physically died, and therefore the loss is not at the level of 'death' as discussed by Kübler-Ross[547] and Rando[548], still people who leave sects may experience losses that amount almost, but not completely, to a death: valued connections, a large part of their social world and even their families. Many second-generation former members of Harry's Sect have hidden losses due to ostracisation by all sect members, including their family.

The poem below details some of my feelings of loss about my sister who was still in the sect when I left the group. The poem illustrates both the sense of grief for the loss and the sense of false responsibility and false guilt that those raised in sects who leave may carry for family members and at times other children in the sect.

THE SMOULDERING AND FABRICATION ABOUT THOSE LEFT BEHIND

I wish I could have taken you with me
You were five
And though twelve years younger
You were a sister not a daughter

I agonised
Should I stay?
Wait for you to become of age?
I could not
I couldn't do the time
Eleven years – eternity. No

And so I left
And the loss and guilt about those left behind
Plunged the depths of my heart
It burned deep red, in the recess of my heart
Smouldering grief
Fabricated guilt – ridiculous but present

I put you in a photo frame
And took you with me
The kibbutz, Egypt, the mushav, then Turkey
Finally, hitch hiked home: Istanbul to England
For five months I carried you in that little photo frame
Ten years later
When our parents left
You were free
Oh happy day

It brought relief
But complication: smouldering and fabrication, continued in
that deep place
The secret compartment in my heart
The lost years 5 – 15
Irreplaceable

But now, as I understand better
The roots of false responsibility
And I am looking at the dress
That I trawled racks and racks for
That I chose, because I didn't look quite so chunky
A dress for my sisters wedding
I am wondering if I look too old
And should I buy another?

And, as I look at you my sister
Adult to adult
Sister to sister
And despite our having other sisters still in the group
I know we are the lucky ones
What of those who have had no loved ones appear
Whose escape we await

Even those who, after having left a sect, are initially not 'let go' of by loved ones and others in the sect and experience pressure to return, they too may also feel a sense of loss for those left behind. The sense of loss and resulting grief does not only involve the loss of loved ones through death or lack of contact, it can encompass many other experiences. For example, the second generation may have lost treasured possessions.

The sense of loss may also attach itself to experiences of which the second generation has been deprived as a result of group membership (e.g. certain activities of childhood). Some second-generation former members may look back on their younger years and because of their experiences in the sect and their lack of opportunity such as for play, schooling and socialising with peers may feel as if they have had a loss of or completely missed out on aspects of their childhood, particularly if they compare their childhood to other people not raised in sects in the country of their nationality.

Hidden losses

The sense of having been robbed of something precious may extend into adulthood, as because of the lack of proper developmental building blocks, adult life as well may be affected. For example, by missed opportunities, because of the sect upbringing impacting an adult's life such as through being past the age of being able to give birth to children[549]. These missed opportunities may be hidden and not obvious to others. The problem is that with hidden 'losses no one actually died or was divorced, nothing was physically stolen. Contrary to obvious losses, there are no markers, no rites of passage recognising them as they occur – no recognised way to mourn.'[550]

Yet each hidden loss relates to the major human need to belong and feel significant to others and to feel understood' Often these hidden losses, can cause disenfranchised grief, in other words grief that is not properly acknowledged. This may be because one is supposed to be happy to be out of the sect and living in freedom, but one also grieves for loved ones left behind and these losses are often non-acknowl-edged and can be so devastating. I would like to take the opportunity here to acknowledge just some of those losses for those readers who are second generation former members and indeed for other readers who are not second-generation former members, but who have experienced these losses. Not all of these may apply to you.

I am so sorry that your mum was not there at your graduation, your wedding, that she was absent from major events in your life.

I am so sorry that your dad has not been there for you. The absence of a father, your father, is huge. I am especially sorry that you have not heard your father say to you 'I am proud of you'.

I am so sorry that your needs were not met as a child. The on-going effects into adult hood can be devastating.

I am so sorry for your lost childhood.

I am so sorry for any and all abuse that you both experienced and witnessed, especially that which happened to your sisters or brothers.

I am so sorry that any of your brothers and sisters are still in a sect.

These are huge losses. I know there are many more losses that are not covered above but for those too I am so sorry. I am also sorry that you have felt and feel so much pain. My hope is that you are able to find someone whom you can trust to whom you can express these hidden losses and that they will be able to acknowledge the loss that you have experienced in your life that your grief may no longer be disenfranchised.

THE WORK OF ELISABETH KÜBLER-ROSS ON LOSS AND GRIEF

Although each person responds to loss in an individual way, Elisabeth Kübler-Ross[551] found from working with those who were dying, as well as their friends and family, that most individuals experience stages of grief. These stages are summarised in bullet points below:

- Denial and isolation - a sense of numbness or shock. This acts as a buffer after unexpectedly shocking news or happenings. It is usually a temporary stage.
- Anger - The question 'Why me?' is often asked at this stage. Involves rage and resentment, and may be evident in nightmares, fears and disruptive behaviour. Anger may be displaced and projected onto the environment. Those in this stage of loss require respect and understanding.
- Bargaining - Individual makes an agreement whose purpose is to regain what has been lost or postpone the loss. Such bargaining often includes a promise to do something in the hope of getting something in return, and is usually made with God and kept secret. Expression may come in the form of threats, tantrums or demands, angelic behaviour or perfectionist tendencies.
- Depression - A feeling of being overwhelmed by the anguish, pain and hurt of loss may be evident when an individual realises that anger and bargaining do not work, and they start to recognise that the loss will be permanent. Allowing expression of the sorrow as opposed to encouragement to cheer up the individual facilitates movement towards the stage of acceptance.
- Acceptance - With enough time and, for many, enough support, people reach a stage where they are no longer depressed or angry about their fate. This stage involves a period of calm after a release of emotions. At this point, the sadness has lifted and individuals are more willing to face the future, or the acceptance could also involve a transformation from the enervating sadness of depression to a continuing sense of loss that no longer gets in the way of one's present and future living. Acceptance should not be confused with hopelessness, resignation, a sense of giving up or a happy stage.

Elisabeth Kübler-Ross expands on how individuals maintain hope when faced with loss: 'It is the feeling that all this must have some meaning, will pay off eventually if they can only endure it for a little while longer'.[552] She expands on this further by saying 'no matter what we call it, we found that all our patients maintained a little bit of it and were nourished by it in especially difficult times.' While experiencing loss, people do not go from one stage to the next in a predictable order. They mix between the two and some would argue that from some losses, such as the loss of a child, people never fully recover and continue to grieve.

Harry's Sect and loss

In Harry's Sect most of the second generation leave the group without telling anyone or leaving a note. Not having had the chance to say goodbye properly may make grieving more difficult. Those still in the sect could not openly grieve those who left. Rather, those who left may never be spoken of again, or may have extremely harsh words spoken about them or, in some instances, curses prayed against them. Consequently, second-generation current and former members may have grief issues remaining from their time in Harry's Sect, particularly if siblings or parents left Harry's Sect before them. This is supportive of Kübler-Ross's stage of depression where she states that it is important for individuals to be able to express their sorrow, as opposed to receiving encouragement to 'cheer up' or being told to 'move on'.

Additionally, if, on leaving, those around the Harry's Sect second generation (such as colleagues at work) view them as rebellious for leaving the group, they are unlikely to comfort them regarding their recent losses. Again, this will hinder the grieving process, as will a lack of time to process the grief due to issues such as dealing with culture shock and sorting out the practicalities of where to live in their lives at the time.[553]

This is consistent with Elisabeth Kübler-Ross's work on loss, which states that there will be individual differences dependent on the nature of the loss, our individual personalities, our experiences, including what we have learned about loss from others throughout our lives, as well as the support we have in helping us grieve our losses.

COMPLICATED GRIEF AND MOURNING

The work of Kübler-Ross on grief was ground breaking in its time (1969). Since then researchers have recognised a 'syndrome' (which carries a slightly different name dependent on the researcher) of 'complicated grief and mourning', whereby loss becomes more problematic when it occurs under traumatic circumstances. Therese Rando is a world leader in this field. She theorises that loss under traumatic circumstances, can profoundly impact an individual's identity and life structure.[554] I propose that the 'loss' of a family that occurs to an individual on leaving a sect (that often results in rejection of contact from that point on, or only contact with a view to recruitment back into the sect) might for some former members constitute an experience similar to the complicated grief and mourning usually occurring from death and bereavement that Rando has identified.

According to Therese Rando, recovery from complicated grief and mourning takes place when the individual moves on from the experience, forming a new identity in the light of the loss, and reinvests positively in a changed life and life structure. Change can though be stressful, even when it is change for the better. In one sense, by simply leaving the sect a former member has a changed life and life structure, and thus Rando's definition of recovery from complicated grief and mourning might not seem to apply. But, I propose that some former members might experience being emotionally 'frozen' following such loses. For example, they might live day to day life doing the things that others in their culture also do, but rather than experiencing the joy and pain of life, they feel nothing, they are in effect, shutdown emotionally.

This is likely to impact a former member's ability to form satisfactory family relationships and also impact their experience of work. Rando's research identifies a wide range of symptoms, syndromes, mental disorders and even death that might result from complicated grief and mourning.

PROBLEMS WITH DECISION-MAKING, FEAR AND ANXIETY FOLLOWING SECT MEMBERSHIP

POSSIBLE DIFFICULTIES WITH DECISION-MAKING

The losses that the second generation experience and why they might be more traumatic than under other circumstances become clearer when we consider the position of the second generation after sect membership. After experiencing domination and control in the sect, simple decisions for those raised in some sects might often be difficult at first. This is because they may have come from a sect environment where, unless they were in leadership or being groomed for leadership, they were dependent and not expected to make decisions about things that involve their lives, their choices and therefore their decision making was very much curtailed.

FEAR AND ANXIETY

In addition to the difficulty in decision making some former sect members report experiencing a great deal of fear[555], not only of current sect members,[556] but also of people in general although this subsided after a time.[557] The quote that follows indicates the interviewee's fear of seeing current sect members:

> When I first left home I used to be so frightened of seeing people. I remember seeing, what's his name, Mr Gorden ... at a petrol station somewhere, and ducking down under the dashboard until he'd filled his car up and gone. But that was a long, long time ago.[558]

Former members of some sects fear that their death is imminent[559], or they fear the wrath of God or both. This is because of what they have heard said in the sect which they have just exited. Such is their anxiety that these second-generation former-members may initially be quite reclusive. Again, this may mean it is difficult for them to form new social identities.

Living a childhood fast-forward and stigmatisation

Some former second-generation members speak of living a childhood fast-forward, being a bit rebellious and wild after leaving.[560] For example, this could include drugs, promiscuity or excessive partying. This may be linked to their past markedly different life experience for which they were now making up, and a search for identity, which may for them be a developmental stage occurring at a time when they don't have anyone to support them. Or it could be connected to experiences of abuse or neglect, or a manifestation of unresolved grief, or some combination of the above.

Social support is important for those working through grief, but it may not be forthcoming. Seeking different life experiences after leaving Harry's Sect may have been healthy for this population, as it may have helped them to form an identity and experience life, thus resulting in less naivety. However, others, who don't understand the experience of having been raised in a sect, may view this exploration of life as rebellion. The view that the second generation are being rebellious may be confirmed in the minds of others when they learn that the second-generation former members' parents have little or no contact with the former member and they assume that this is as a result of the second- generation member as opposed to realising that it is as a result of sect teaching.

This stigmatisation and assumption of rebellion is not limited to young people leaving sects. Merely being a teenager may involve being stigmatised and teenagers from all walks of life have been branded as delinquent and trouble-prone.[561] This is unfortunate because social support is so important for everyone, including teenagers who may lack social support because of negative stigma.

LENGTH OF TIME SPENT IN SECT

We may assume that the length of time someone spends in a sect is important when considering how someone is affected by the sect experience and how they may feel afterwards. The table below gives the length of time spent in a sect for both first and second generation former members from a number of studies.

Table 8.1: Time spent in sect for first-and second-generation former members

Study	Mean time spent in sect	
	First generation	**Second generation**
UK study multiple sects*	7 years	19 years
Demographic Harry's Sect UK study*	7 years	13 years (second generation leaving alone, 19 years)
Wellspring US study (help-seeking sample) multiple sects*	7 years	18 years
*Lois Kendall, 2006		

The table shows that the mean time spent in a sect was consistently longer for second-generation than for first-generation former members.[562]

Sometimes research can be contradictory, an older study of 400 former first-generation sect members from 48 different groups[563] found that as the time that members spent per week in ritual and indoctrination increased, so the rehabilitation time needed increased with length of membership, levelling off after three to six months in the sect. The average age of respondents in this study was 21 years, with an average period in the sect of 34 months. The study of first generation former members found that over one in five reported suicidal or self-destructive tendencies. Interestingly, more research of both first- and second-generation former members has found no significant correlations between the length of time spent in a sect and the degree of distress experienced after leaving.[564] Researchers have speculated that those most harmed by sects may leave,[565] but as already discussed, this option isn't available for most children in sects.

Harm and groups

Few would argue with the proposition that 'Some groups under some conditions harm some people some times'.[566] This is evidently true when considering sects such as Jonestown (where nearly 1,000 people, including 260 children, died[567]), Solar Temple[568] and Aum Shinrikyo.[569] Hundreds of members of the Movement for the Restoration of the Ten Commandments died in Kampala.[570] Michael Langone[571] argues that it is more important to study the harm resulting from sects than from other groups because:

- Evidence points to harm being more prevalent and/or more serious in sects than in other types of groups (e.g. mainstream religious groups).

- The types of harm found in mainstream groups are more reflective of individual pathology than of harm resulting from an abusive social structure.
- Mainstream religions and other groups are more likely to have built in accountability mechanisms that, while not perfect, offer some protection to society.

Post-sect effects on first-generation former members

WHAT HARRY'S SECT AND TED'S SECT FORMER MEMBERS REPORTED

The issue of the potential effects of former sect membership upon the first generation is important to the second generation, especially when we consider that some of them are the parents of the second generation. Some first-generation parents leave taking some or all of their children with them, or they may leave a sect before or after their children have left.

Former members of Harry's Sect reported a wide range of different emotions and feelings[572], including anger.[573] They reported a loss of their sense of morality, and described problems with judgementalism.[574] Harry's Sect former members also reported having difficulty with decision-making and being judgemental towards other people and groups after leaving.[575] Some Ted's Sect former members identified feeling anxiety, fear, depression and not being able to stand to be around other people because of not feeling that they could interact with them at all.[576]

HARM SUFFERED BY FORMER MEMBERS

Evidence shows individuals in sects may suffer from psychological, physical, social and financial harm.[577] For some, problems were present prior to sect membership, but the group exacerbated these problems. In others, no psychological disturbances seemed present prior to their joining and exiting the sect.[578] Individuals may suffer lasting effects in terms of their spirituality, they may experience great confusion and difficulties in this area.[579] Below is a summary of the psychological symptoms that clinicians have found present in former sect members:[580]

- dissociation (a mental process that produces a lack of connection in a person's thoughts, memories, feelings, actions or sense of identity, explained in more depth later in the chapter) atypical dissociative disorders (a dissociative disorder which doesn't fit any of the dissociative disorder categories);
- cognitive deficiencies such as simplistic black/white thinking;
- difficulties in making decisions;
- depression;
- anxiety and relaxation-induced anxiety (anxiety caused by a relaxation technique, such as meditation);
- psychotic symptoms, though found less frequently;
- post-traumatic stress disorder (PTSD);
- anhedonia (inability to enjoy anything); and
- apathy (absence or suppression of emotion, feeling, concern or passion. Additionally, apathy is an indifference to things generally found to be exciting or moving).

Due to difficulties in accessing current sect members, research involving former sect members is more extensive, than that involving current sect members.[581] A summary of the research indicates that:

- Some former sect members showed no problems on emerging from sect membership.
- There was evidence for a range of potentially serious symptoms or conditions of mental ill-health (e.g. depression, PTSD, cognitive impairment, psychiatric symptomatology, burnout

and acute stress, dependent personality disorder, anxiety disorder, suicidal tendencies and psychiatric hospitalisation).[582]

- It is possible that some (specifically those who had experienced sexual or physical abuse in their childhood), although by no means all, experienced some of these problems prior to their sect membership. Sect membership could have worsened or exacerbated prior problems.[583]

- Symptoms diminished following treatment or over time (a number of years).[584]

Psychiatric hospitalisation in the UK

A study by a UK psychiatrist, Elizabeth Tylden,[585] examined 152 cases of first generation former sect members. Of the 104 individuals from religious sects, 37.5% needed in-patient treatment in a psychiatric hospital for psychosis. Of the 48 individuals involved in what she called a self-improvement sect (i.e., therapy/training, political sects), 23% needed in-patient treatment. Of those involved in a religious sect, 46% needed outpatient treatment because of dissociative states compared to 71% of those involved in a self-improvement sect.

Finally, 17% from the religious sects required no psychiatric treatment, compared to 6% from the self-improvement sects. Tylden also observed 'people in my series of cases who had been involved in drugs before they became involved in cults had a worse prognosis, medically speaking, than those who came to the cults *per se*'.[586] She also found many similarities between the symptoms shown by former sect members and those present in people who have taken drugs such as LSD and cannabis.

Former members who don't participate in research

Elizabeth Tylden's work looked at the first generation. Research such as this has not yet been conducted on the second generation. My research and other work such as that conducted at Centrepoint did not include those most harmed and distressed by their sect involvement, as the research in and of itself might have been too distressing for them to participate in. The table below lists the reasons that former sect members gave for not wanting to participate in my research in the UK. To give a comparison point, below are reasons for non-participation from former members of mainstream groups not considered to be sects.

Table 8.2: Reasons given for non-participation in one research study (Lois Kendall, 2006)

Reasons given for non-participation in research	Ex-sect	Comparison (those who had been in mainstream groups as opposed to sects)
Not viewing themselves as former members		✓
Still members of same denomination		✓
Too busy – lack of time	✓	✓
Uncomfortable with one or two questions	✓	✓
Poor health	✓	✓
Spiritual reasons	✓	✓
Dyslexic	✓	✓
Difficulty in reading and writing in English	✓	✓
Embarrassment	✓	
Fear of being sued, harassed, or having character assassinated	✓	
Fear for family members still in group	✓	
Negative view of psychiatry and psychology because of former group membership	✓	
Have moved on from sect experience	✓	
Questionnaire too upsetting	✓	
Questionnaire asks too personal questions	✓	
Makes them feel like a traitor	✓	

It is important to include the work of psychiatrists and others in discussions of research of this kind. Otherwise a skewed picture emerges which will not include those most harmed by sects. Therefore, unless psychiatric diagnoses of former members are considered, sociological research alone may result in an overly optimistic picture.

Post-sect effects for those raised in sects

Since the early 1980s mental health experts and others started to have extensive contact with those raised in sects.

Clinician's work with the second generation

Margaret Singer,[587] a psychologist from the University of California, worked with children raised in these groups. She states that, because of the nature of sects:

> 'anxious-dependent personality traits can be built into the cult children's developing character . . . after the cult . . . some children emerge flat, melancholic and phobic, whereas those raised in militant, confrontational groups may be more defiant and assertive . . . [They have] restricted learning, fewer skills and below average socialisation . . . it can be difficult for them to form opinions, express themselves and sort out conflicts between cult beliefs and new post cult experiences . . . Children raised in some cults will have learned ideas and practices that the broader society may regard as bizarre, bigoted and antisocial, and casually expressing these ideas can lead children to be ostracised . . . Many cults are anti-career and induce members to accept low-level jobs in order to keep members available to work for the leader. Higher education or sometimes any education is devalued. Afterwards, it is difficult for teenagers to fathom out what to do.'[588]

The anxious dependency present in adults in sects goes beyond dependency in terms of physical needs, and includes both spiritual and psychological needs. It is similar to the bond between a parent and infant. The child is dependent upon the very person that he or she is anxious about.[589] For children in sects, this is concerning, as children usually grow towards maturity and independence, but in sects this is often not encouraged. Rather, the sect fosters dependency in both adults and children.

For example, both Ted and Harry were reported as keeping people at arm's length, particularly anyone who wanted to get close to them. This type of behaviour has been found previously to be dysfunctional, as it is a way of relating that utilises rejection to keep people dependent. Again, this would be an indication of the leaders trying (perhaps unconsciously) to ensure that members continue to be dependent on them.

> *Ted was a character who would keep people at an arm's length, and the more they wanted to be his student, the more he'd keep them away. That's how he kept people interested, and not asking too many question. He kept quite an air around him.*[590]

It was evident from participants that they were considerably attached to the leaders in Harry's Sect and Ted's Sect who (according to interview descriptions) behaved in an abusive manner towards them. Members, particularly core members, were dependent on the leadership, were scared of them, had high anxiety about them and tried to please them.

Therapists who have worked with former members of sects, including children raised in such groups, conclude that parents in sects act as middle managers, for the sect leader, following policies and carrying out instructions from above, rather than exercising their own discretion when making decisions about their children. Children who have been raised in these groups but then leave have big adjustment problems focused on issues relating to acculturation (adopting the beliefs and behaviours of the new culture which they enter), lack of self-control, decision-making, boredom, living in a non-sect family, distrust of others, clashing loyalties, developmental arrest, lagging social development, lack of self-esteem and parental input.[591]

Two therapists[592] who have worked with former members of sects state that growing up in a sect can be likened to growing up in traumatic circumstances. For some children in sects, this is undoubtedly true, especially when we consider some of the items discussed in the chapter on child abuse and families in sects in this book. Imagine, for a moment, growing up in an isolated group where rules change according to the whim of a leader, where everything you do or say is considered wrong, where you have no freedom of expression, where those above you who do have freedom of expression and movement invade your boundaries and violate your sense of self, where your family, (who, one might think would protect you), are more part of the problem than the solution, where due to statements of the leader, you believe that you will soon die if you leave the group.

Therapists[593] state that the traumatic symptoms of this upbringing include terror and rage. This rage may be turned inwards and include behaviour such as self-harm. Individuals may take an inactive stance in the face of repeated victimisation. Alternatively, victims may identify with their aggressors and bully or act out in abusive or even criminal ways. The victim stance may be the more likely identification, but those who do identify with the leaders are likely to become leaders themselves.[594] These two alternative types of reactions to growing up in a sect are very similar to those identified by Margaret Singer, i.e. they either identify with the leader's power and dominance or become passive, dependent, obedient, and often emotionally subdued and flattened.

While some of those raised in sects who have left might fit one or other of these categories, it could also be that some might demonstrate both these effects, which might be interchangeable depending on the specific environment in which the second-generation former members find themselves.

People may do what they know how to do. Some of those who have learned that it's 'bully or be bullied' may upon initially exiting a sect lack other means of response. Others may be very sensitive to the feelings of others and may go to great lengths to ensure that their interpersonal communications do not hurt the feelings of others, they may apologise excessively[595], which is something they will need to address at some point.

STATISTICAL STUDIES ON LEVELS OF DISTRESS IN SECOND-GENERATION FORMER MEMBERS

I analysed information on levels of distress[596] found in those raised in sects when they entered Wellspring Retreat and Resource Centre in the US for assistance. Out of a total of 23 individuals, I found the following percentages in terms of levels of distress and different symptoms:

65% Depression[597],
70% Trait anxiety [598] (a general tendency for extremely frequent and severe anxiety)
22% Trait anger[599] (a general tendency for extremely frequent and severe anger)
44% Dissociation[600]

The high levels of dissociation are closely linked to traumatic experiences,[601] as are high levels of avoidance and intrusion symptoms, indicative of Post-Traumatic Stress Disorder (PTSD),[602] 52% of the second-generation former members showed such symptoms, compared to 41% of the first-generation former members. This is considerably higher than the estimated 10.4% of American women, and 5.4% of American men that at some point in their lives experience PTSD.[603] This finding may be linked to individuals having found leaving the sect traumatic, and/or they may have had traumatic experiences in and/or since leaving the sect.

A further study[604], this time in the UK, found that 36% of 25 second-generation former members had high levels of avoidance and intrusion symptoms[605]. Full details of the levels of clinically significant distress for first-and second-generation former members, as well as a comparison group who had not been in sects, are recorded[606]. The second generation shows consistently higher scores than the other groups[607]. The study[608] supports the view that those raised in sects have a higher risk factor for developing psychological distress in later life.[609]

A study[610] with a different sample in New Zealand found that two thirds of their research participants had psychological problems after leaving their sect. The majority of the participants had fairly significant psychological problems including post-traumatic reactions and experiences of psychosis.

Combined, these findings indicate that former sect membership for these participants may result in psychological distress even years after leaving the sect, specifically in the areas of depression, anxiety, anger and dissociation.

REASONS FOR PSYCHOLOGICAL DISTRESS EXPERIENCED BY SECOND-GENERATION FORMER MEMBERS

The reasons for psychological distress experienced by second generation former members are most likely numerous, they could include loss experiences, developmental gaps, lack of social support, abuse, neglect, maltreatment, lack of attachment opportunities with adults or needs not being met in early childhood, and a vast array of other items which are likely to interact in a complex fashion.

A key area that may link into psychological distress is former members self concept which may link to the groups teachings. A person's set of beliefs interlinks with their cognitive processes and hence with their psychological health. On the face of it, the beliefs and teaching of the Harry's Sect and Ted's Sect sects would be very different, as one purports to be Christian and the other Buddhist. Further examination of the teaching and its effects revealed similarities on some items, such as individuals' view of self. Partly as a result of the teaching in both sects, it appears individuals were led to think of themselves as terribly bad people. In Harry's Sect they were taught that they were 'sinners' and that it was appropriate to have 'the meanest and lowest view' of themselves. In Ted's Sect, they thought they were bad people because of selfishness and large ego problems.

However, in both sects there may have been instances when speaking negatively about themselves had more to do with social convention than a genuine view of themselves. In general, interviewed members of both sects reported a negative view of themselves and this is likely to be one of the key factors that linked into psychological distress found in this sample after sect membership. This negative self-view was exacerbated not only by the teaching but by the maltreatment and abuse some suffered as well as the lack of worth that was reflected to them both by other members (though not all and there were exceptions in both sects) and particularly by the main leaders of the sects.

Repeated maltreatment in childhood, such as rejecting, degrading, terrorising, isolating, mis-socialising exploiting, lack of stimulation and responsiveness, withholding sleep and applying developmentally inappropriate expectations[611] may contribute to depression and anxiety and also result in trauma symptoms in adulthood.

Psychological maltreatment in childhood would go some way to explaining the empirical findings of high levels of trauma symptoms[612], dissociation, anxiety, depression, etc. in the second-generation adult participants of this research. However, as the first generation also received this type of treatment in the sects, and as a study I did covarying[613] out child maltreatment and physical child victimisation still found some significant differences, it could be hypothesised that the sect environment is more damaging for children because they are still developing. They cannot leave the group and are the least powerful members of the group and consequently have the least amount of control in what may sometimes be an otherwise terrifying environment, which they nonetheless have been taught is a safe environment and the world outside is terrifying. This supports findings[614] that trauma sustained in childhood is more difficult to recover from as an adult than trauma suffered when an adult.

DEPRESSION AND SUICIDAL THOUGHTS

Depression is a frequent reaction after exiting a sect. While everyone may feel low at times, the type of depression referred to here is what psychologists call clinical depression, which can be completely debilitating and affect a person's life in a profound way. For example, for most or all of the time people may experience a very dark cloud over their lives; they may struggle to find meaning in anything and feel a great sense of hopelessness.

While some may hold down employment despite being in the depths of despair, others may have great difficulty in motivating themselves to do even the simplest tasks, such as getting dressed. They may enjoy no part of their life and find interpersonal relationships so difficult that they would rather be left alone. Individuals suffering from depression may consider suicide or have thoughts of harming themselves. Despite this type of suffering, some individuals may appear cheerful, which is why they may occasionally be referred to as the 'smiling depressed', when their depression becomes known.

Depression can result in a lack of interest in sex, disturbed sleep and unexplained aches and pains. Feeling a constant feeling of sadness and finding it difficult to be positive about the future is wearing. If these types of symptoms persist, assistance is needed.

Symptoms can come on gradually. Some second-generation members may have spent most of their lives being depressed, without having re-alised that they are depressed as it is their norm. It may be important for those close to former members to gently suggest that they may be experiencing depression and encourage them to seek support.

For those coming out of groups where all psychological or health care assistance is seen as sinful or a lack of faith, receiving support from caring friends and from professionals familiar with sects may be par-ticularly helpful. What that support may look like in a practical sense will differ from person to person. For one, it may entail a listening, non-judgemental accepting ear, allowing the second-generation for-mer member to begin to express themselves. For another it might be assistance with basic household chores or simply shopping for food and then cooking meals together.[615] As well as talking therapies, which are discussed further in chapter nine, some people who are depressed find that prescription drugs can be helpful in alleviating symptoms, at least while the drug is being taken and sometimes beyond that time period.[616]

I recently heard of a guy who had planned how he was going to com-mit suicide but was really helped when someone sat with him and asked him to make 100 positive statements about himself, which the supportive person then wrote down. The man feeling suicidal came up with things like: 'I am good at …' ' My little brother looks up to me,' 'Something I said to someone two years ago really assisted in them changing the course of their life in a positive way', etc.

He took the 100 positive statements about himself away with him and read them at times when he felt he needed to. This really helped the individual, and years later he introduced his wife and son to the supportive person and handed back the list of 100 positive points saying that he didn't need them anymore as he knew them through and through.

SUICIDAL THOUGHTS

Suicidal thoughts are far more common than people realise, and they occur not just in people who are depressed, although they do indicate that an individual is emotionally distressed. After leaving a sect, individuals often grapple with big questions such as, what is the point of life?

Research surveys differ in the estimated percentage of the general population who have had suicidal thoughts at some point in their lives. However, one study[617] found quite wide differences across nine countries for suicidal thoughts across the life time, ranging from 2% to 19% of the samples. The authors concluded that the differences between countries are probably due to cultural features that we do not yet understand. I would like to, at this point, say thank you to all those reading this who have occasionally or often thought about suicide, and yet are still alive. Thank you for being alive.

FEAR AND ANXIETY

The research I have reported on in this chapter shows that some second-generation former members have debilitating levels of anxiety and fear. It may be that second-generation former members have never actually felt safe.

Maia Szalavitz and Bruce Perry, in their book *'Born For Love'*[618], as well as elsewhere[619], describe how when we feel a threat and start feeling fear, our stress response is activated and our adrenalin levels rise, and chemical changes appear in our brain. We get ready to flee, hide or fight back, our heart rate is elevated and our blood pressure increases. When this stress response is activated in small and moderate doses, that is a good thing. However, when this is activated in an extreme way or is constantly aroused, this affects individuals long after they have left an unsafe environment. For example, they may be hyper vigilant to threat, perceiving even the tiniest hint of aggression in someone's face, voice or manner. Therefore these changes in our brains may underlie the fear and anxiety experienced in adulthood, and this despite now being in a safe environment.

Children who have been traumatised need predictability, routine, a sense of control and stable relationships with supportive people[620]. However, in some environments, including sects, children may have had to somehow find a sense of safety in what was a fundamentally unsafe environment. Confusingly, they may well have also been told that their environment was safe and the outside world unsafe. In order to survive, their sense of safety may have had to be in people or things that were actually unsafe. Coming out into a world they know little about, but may have been told very negative things about (including being told that it is unsafe), can be a fearful thing. Couple this with negative pronouncements discussed already in this book, and we might expect a significant proportion of second-generation former members to be fearful when they exit their sect.

They may have specific fears such as fears about the end of the world or about events in the news, or about being punished for their wickedness in leaving, or they may have a fear of seeing certain people and what might happen if they do. (Those fears may be entirely justified.) They may additionally have more generalised fears. If adults joining sects report fear when in the sect and on leaving the sect as adults, then it is no surprise that those with even less power because of their physical size and developmental maturity in the sect might find that experience fearful.

Coming out, often alone, into an adult world for which they have not been prepared, it is no surprise that fear and anxiety levels in second-generation former members might be high when they exit the sect. As I mention elsewhere, finding an environment of relative safety and security is of paramount importance for second-generation former members. Again, as in instances of depressive symptoms, some former members might find therapeutic care and support and prescription drugs helpful in alleviating symptoms of anxiety and fear.

POST-TRAUMATIC STRESS DISORDER (PTSD)

What is PTSD?
The question 'Who am I?' is asked, not just by adolescents, but also by those who have been traumatised. Trauma means a severe emotional shock that can result in substantial psychological damage.

A person who experiences or witnesses a traumatic event may, weeks, months or even years later[621], develop PTSD. While the majority of people don't develop PTSD after experiencing a threat, PTSD nevertheless is described by many psychologists as a normal emotional reaction to an abnormal situation, a threat, a deeply shocking and disturbing experience. The individual's response to the traumatic event or events involves intense fear, helplessness or horror.

PTSD[622] includes symptoms such as:[623] vivid flashbacks (feeling that the trauma is happening all over again), keeping busy, being unable to express affection, feeling there's no point in planning for the future, disturbed sleep, extreme alertness and being easily startled. For many, symptoms such as these and others not listed will disappear after a while, however if they endure for longer than a month, then a diagnosis of PTSD may be given by someone qualified to give such a diagnosis.

Traumatic events of an interpersonal nature

Trauma inflicted by a supposed caring relative or friend is more difficult to recover from than fires or floods,[624] which goes some way to explain the finding of psychological distress in former sect members. Research on 75 women[625] in abusive relationships found support for the effect of relationship dynamic factors, such as extremity of intermittent maltreatment and power differentials, on long-term felt attachment for a former partner. Their research showed evidence of effects on self-esteem. Trauma symptoms were still present six months after separating from the abusive partner. This tied in with the findings of my research studies[626], where those exiting sects were found to have trauma symptoms that may be partially explained by the abuse experienced from leaders and the power differential between the members and leaders.

Previous research has found that shame is a predictor of PTSD symptoms among survivors of sexual or physical assault.[627] Where the traumatic event is of an interpersonal nature (which involves being hurt by other people), it may be particularly harmful to the individual and result in additional symptoms including shame and the destruction of trust in others.[628] PTSD with this particular combination of symptoms has been put together under the heading of 'complex PTSD' and refined further by van der Kolk[629] 'under the umbrella of DESNOS (Disorders of Extreme Stress Not Otherwise Specified). In part, the rationale for this has been that in many cases, adult survivors of child abuse may indeed be suffering from PTSD', but what is currently most debilitating is not so much their memories but their inability to relate to others, and DESNOS highlights this.

Judith Herman[630] refers to 'complex traumatic stress disorder' as the effect of recurring prolonged trauma. She expands on the impact of traumatic experiences, especially repeated ones, and scrutinises them from the perspective of growing up within a traumatic environment.

Self-blame and trauma

A UK charity called Mind, which supports individuals with their mental health,[631] reports that: 'Sometimes survivors of trauma feel guilty, as though they were responsible for the event, or could have done more to save themselves or others. One study showed that those who blamed themselves in some way for the outcome of the disaster were more at risk of severe and long-term distress.'

Risk factors for PTSD

While individuals can react differently to traumatic events, nevertheless all things being equal (which they invariably are not), the more severe the traumatic stressor, the greater the likelihood of an individual developing PTSD.[632] However, in most research studies of those exposed to a traumatic stressor, the majority will <u>not</u> then go onto develop PTSD.[633]

Research often acknowledges that 'traumatic stress' is the main cause of PTSD,[634] and yet the research also seeks to identify other risk factors for developing PTSD. For example, a range of adverse experiences, such as parental divorce and failing a grade at school, can be risk factors and that along with the severity of trauma such as witnessing violence, contributes to individual differences in the development of PTSD.[635] Other risk factors which might make one more vulnerable to the development of PTSD after a traumatic stress include being single; having low levels of social support;[636] being of a minority race; having depressive symptoms; anger; and perceived social support.[637] This is discussed further in the section on dissociation.

Recovery from PTSD

PTSD can start quickly, or it can have a delayed onset and then remit or persist as a chronic form, which in turn may resolve, recur, or fluctuate in intensity.[638] The good news, however, for those who suffer from PTSD is that it is treatable and specialist treatment is available. BBC health[639] reports that:

'You will know you're on the road to recovery when you:

- Think about it without becoming distressed.
- Don't feel constantly under threat.
- Don't think about it at inappropriate times.'

Dissociation and dissociative disorders

What is dissociation, and what are dissociative disorders?

Dissociation refers to a mental process that disconnects a person's thoughts, memories, feelings, actions or sense of identity from the reality.[640] One individual described their experience after the sect in the following way:

> *Losing limbs, it was like suddenly I don't have this specific aspect of my personality that I used to have, which makes it so that you can judge whether you like somebody or not, that was incredibly disorientating.[641]*

Dissociative symptoms and disorders are closely linked to traumatic experiences.[642] Severe trauma in childhood is regarded as a major cause of dissociative disorders. Most clinicians believe that dissociation exists on a continuum of severity.[643] At one end are mild dissociative experiences common to most people, such as daydreaming, highway hypnosis, or 'getting lost' in a book or movie, all of which involve 'losing touch' with conscious awareness of one's immediate surroundings. At the other extreme is complex, chronic dissociation, which may result in serious impairment or inability to function.

An example of a dissociative disorder is dissociative amnesia – the inability to remember significant personal information or particular periods of time, which can't be explained by ordinary forgetfulness. People may also experience mild to moderate depersonalisation (a sense of being outside looking in), derealisation and identity-confusion, which occurs when people feel dissociated from their environment. Those who suffer from depersonalisation or derealisation most often describe feeling as if life is a dream, sometimes it is experiencing life and the world as if through a fog, with the world appearing meaningless and hazy. Sometimes people feel detached from their own body. Paul David[644] writes that:

'Another symptom of this condition can be the constant worrying or strange thoughts that people find hard to switch off.

People often say that no matter how hard they try, they don't feel like they can interact with the world around them. They feel a sense of detachment from their surroundings, finding it hard to talk and connect with others. Also they feel no love for the people closest to them and even question if they did a certain task or had a particular conversation. The most upsetting thing is they lose a sense of who they are and can't seem to perceive themselves as being normal.... The way to move forward out of depersonalisation is not to worry and obsess about it, but to work with it there, to give it as much space as it needs and not be too impressed by it. To see it as your body protecting you and not a sign that something terrible is happening or that you are going mad.'

Dissociation and sect membership
Dissociation has been found to be particularly connected to sect membership as indicated by DSM-IV[645] and it increases the likelihood of developing PTSD. Therefore, current and former sect members may

be more likely to develop PTSD than those exposed to a similar stress-or, but living in environments that do not have group members exhibiting high levels of dissociation. In fact, second-generation former sect members have been found to have high levels of dissociation and PTSD.[646]

For those growing up in groups that practise meditation, chanting, guided imagery, etc., high levels of dissociation in adulthood may be attributable to the lasting effects of these practices.[647] However, some sects do not have practices such as these (e.g., Harry's Sect, Chapter 6) and, in these cases, the reasons for dissociation found in adulthood may be more heavily linked to the trauma that the second generation experienced during sect membership and after leaving the sect.

Some individuals leaving sects have spoken of feeling very wounded and abused after leaving.[648] A number of former members of Harry's Sect and Ted's Sect stated they had trouble sleeping after leaving: others were extremely physically ill and confined to their bed for weeks or experienced panic attacks, faintness or dizziness.[649] Problems like these may stem from subconscious assimilation of threats about the dire personal consequences of leaving. They are also supportive of a wide range of research and theory that has linked stress to ill health, as well as research and theory linking trauma to physical health.[650]

The effects of loss can be traumatic.[651] This links in with the findings of high levels of PTSD and dissociative symptoms in the second generation. There may also be a possible relationship between shame, psychological humiliation and PTSD symptoms, indicating that the traditional causal feature of PTSD of a traumatic stressor may need to be widened.

One Ted's Sect individual explained that after leaving one night he felt as if he was *on the edge of descending into a sort of not being able to trust anyone ever.*[652] A former Harry's Sect member reported having a breakdown and then having to receive medication from their doctor.

PTSD and dissociation were found to correlate with child abuse and maltreatment by parents for both the first- and second-generation former sect members.[653] First-generation former members who had experienced child abuse might be expected to have higher levels of PTSD and dissociation than those who did not. As child abuse and maltreatment might constitute a traumatic stressor, this would be expected. Adults can also have experiences in sects that could constitute traumatic stressors, for example, via physical, sexual and spiritual abuse. Furthermore, where individuals are living in communal groups, it is more likely that they may witness or be confronted with the abuse of others, which might also meet DSM-IV criteria for a traumatic stressor. The finding of high levels of PTSD in former sect members is in line with the view that those experiencing higher levels of trauma are more likely to develop PTSD.[654]

POST-SECT VULNERABILITIES

Introduction to Benjamin Zablocki's post-sect vulnerabilities model
Clinicians who have worked with those raised in sects have put forward some cautious trends regarding the effects of being raised in a sect. Table 8.4 contains a post-sect vulnerability model developed by Benjamin Zablocki[655] from work with children who had been raised in and then left sects. He describes three types of responses that children raised in these groups have: 'hallmark', 'hooligan' or 'hostage'. He goes on to look at the dominant attitude of the child while in the sect, the control mechanism the sect used towards them, how the group viewed them, their post-sect vulnerabilities, the emotional legacy they have and what their birth order with respect to their other siblings is likely to be.

Table 8.3: Benjamin Zablocki's second-generation model

	Hallmark	Hooligan	Hostage
Dominant attitude	I must be better than my parents. I must make up to the sect for the shortcomings of my parents	I must be bad and escape for my own sake and for the sake of my parents	I must stay and be good for the sake of my parents.
Control mechanism	Reward	Direct punishment or isolation	Indirect threat of harm to loved ones
Group orientation towards	Pride	Struggle	Take for granted
Post-sect influence group vulnerability	Scams, rackets, date rape, marital instability and promiscuity	Substance abuse	Fundamentalism and other sect belief systems; abusive or co-dependent marriage
Emotional legacy	Guilt, credulity (depression; grandiosity)	Rebellion (impulsiveness)	Resignation (Paranoia)
Birth order probability	Eldest	Middle	Youngest

However, he views this model with caution, and states that much more research needs to be carried out in order to have valid theories and models for the psychological effects of sects on children. This model seems to indicate that second-generation members who respond by becoming 'hooligans' are more likely to leave and therefore more likely to be included in a study of former second-generation members. Some may prefer the term, 'rebels,' which is less negative. For those second-generation 'rebels' who were predicted to be most likely to leave the sect and hence participate in research such as that discussed in this book, Zablocki identifies their post-sect vulnerability as substance abuse. He suggests their emotional legacy is rebellion or impulsiveness. (Perhaps this impulsiveness links in some way to the impulsive risk-taking and exposure to danger[656] found in those suffering from trauma.)

Alcohol and drug abuse
Vulnerability to alcohol and drug abuse in the second generation may be similar to the vulnerability of those who have been victims of child sexual abuse, as the drugs and alcohol block out painful memories.[657] Those who suffer from PTSD show a greater incidence of substance abuse.[658] The findings of high levels of PTSD symptoms in former members, as well as the experience of child abuse,[659] has also been linked in prior research to drug and alcohol dependence.[660]

After sect membership, an individual might seek to numb severe psychological pain and therefore be vulnerable to addictive behaviours. This vulnerability might be conscious or unconscious. It may be linked to the loss of a dominant social identity, coupled with a lack of alternative social identities outside the sect.[661]

One researcher proposed the following regarding addiction and self-sedation: 'reaching for a cigarette . . . alcohol, drugs, eating, sex, travel, driving, walking, running, television, conversation'[662] and more, e.g. breathing. When used excessively, these can all be a form of self-sedation to distance ourselves from negative feelings such as shame and painful feelings such as loss and grief. When the need and wish to do so is so great it leads to addiction, then a new shame experience is formed, because somewhere in ourselves we know this is happening, although some may be blissfully unaware of a problem until symptoms arise. Therefore, awareness of post-sect vulnerabilities, including addictive and self-sedative behaviours, might be important for second-generation former members.

A study of children raised in the sect Centrepoint found that one-third had had difficulties with alcohol or drugs since leaving,[663] and a few described how they had 'fried their brains' through drug use since leaving the sect. However, in this particular sect, children in the group were actually prescribed mind-altering drugs, whereas in most sects, this is not the case for the second generation.

Some second-generation former members have a long-term involvement with drugs and alcohol after leaving their sect. Brent Jeffs[664] describes some of the difficulties that he and his five brothers faced as they all left the church as teenagers:

> *Two of my brothers became addicted to heroin and similar drugs, one had a period of methamphetamine addiction, and I certainly smoked more than my fair share of marijuana. Many of us have suffered depression and half have some symptoms of or meet the full criteria for post traumatic stress disorder.*

> *And of course I have lost two big brothers: Clayne and David, whom I still miss every day. Although we do not know whether David's overdose was intentional, his addiction was clearly influenced by what happened to him at the church and the way he left it. Without therapy and the support of the people around me, I might well have joined them.'*

Post-sect vulnerability of abusive relationships and prostitution for former members of a few specific groups
Experiences after leaving the sect might contribute to high levels of trauma found in the second generation. Additionally, though systematic research has not yet been conducted on higher rates of prostitution in second-generation former sect members as compared with the levels in the general population, there is some anecdotal and self-report evidence to suggest that this may be the case for a few groups, where sexual abuse of children was encouraged. An online community at a website named Moving On (www.movingon.org) was put together by and for second-generation former members of The Family

(previously called the Children of God, COG and The Family of Love). The website included written materials by former members documenting the abuses they were subjected to as well as the sexual practices of the group.

An in-depth reading of the Moving On website provided evidence, including from the group's own publications, that quite a number of children witnessed their mothers' prostitution.[665] Some grew up thinking that they would become prostitutes.[666] Some did become prostitutes after leaving their group.[667] This also supports previous findings regarding the link between sexual abuse in childhood and prostitution.[668]

Abusive relationships (expanded on in Chapter 6) are another post-sect vulnerability that may also explain the former sect members' potential vulnerability to prostitution because abusive relationships and psychological domination have been found to be characteristic of pimp–prostitute relationships.[669] One of the second-generation former members participating in the Centrepoint research (a sect in which a significant number of the children experienced child sexual abuse) reported having dabbled in prostitution., Another spoke of the monumental effort it had taken to manage to '*get off the game*' and get a '*9 to 5 job*'.[670]

BENEFITS OF SECT INVOLVEMENT

No support for a general connection between religion and psychopathology
This book is not concerned with a link between religion and psychopathology. A review of the literature on those topics[671] concluded that there is no support for a general connection between religion and psychopathology. Research has shown that the association between religion and well-being tends to be positive,[672] although clearly both adults and children can have experiences within mainstream religion

that leave them very hurt and damaged. This book is concerned not with religion as a whole, but with sects, some of which are religious. Specifically, it has looked so far at possible psychological harm following membership of an extremist authoritarian sect.

Reasons for possible benefits of sect membership
Here we now turn to the possible benefits of former membership of sects. The benefits of former sect membership broadly fit into three categories, including benefits occurring:

1. because of sect membership;
2. despite sect membership; or
3. with hindsight, further away from the sect experience.

For example, some groups encourage members to give up drugs, alcohol, cigarettes and gambling,[673] which may have positive health outcomes for individuals. Research has found a strong link between good physical and psychological health, and there is a branch of psychology 'health psychology' which addresses this area.[674] In addition, most drugs have detrimental effects on the psychological well-being of an individual. Research has shown that those religious groups with the strictest rules regarding smoking, drinking, sex and diet have lower mortality rates among members.[675]

There are instances of adults with mental health issues finding the authoritarian structure and lack of need for decision-making beneficial. 'Religious communities can also provide a haven for those who are disturbed or do not cope well with the world, and they can have a therapeutic value because of that. While religious institutions could carry those influences uniquely, religious (and other group) participation is in and of itself linked to psychological well-being and social integration, simply because it offers social involvement rather than isolation.'[676] However, as has been shown in this book, not all sects offer the social integration which might be assumed by those on the outside looking in. In fact some sects, though not all, have a distinct lack of social integration, not only with those outside the group, but with those inside it as well.

Children brought into sects in childhood or youngish teens who join on their own may find their sense of well-being increases because they experience loving and supportive relationships with other members in the group, or because they experience clear directions for their lives.[677] For example, a child bought to live at Centrepoint by his mother reported as an adult and after he had left the group that as a child before he entered the sect with his mother, he had no good male role model, but once in the sect, he carefully identified and sought out men whom he thought could provide that father- figure attachment.[678]

The researchers[679] who looked at adult adjustment after a childhood spent at Centrepoint noted that:

> 'While the accounts of participants acknowledged very diffi-
> cult experiences at Centrepoint, there was also recognition,
> even amongst some of those who had been abused, that there
> were aspects of their environment that they felt had benefited
> them in their adult lives. Positive narrative themes highlighted
> the sense of belonging in the community, continuous social
> interaction, having access to a variety of adult role models, col-
> lective responsibility and social confidence as being helpful in
> their adult adjustment.'

Benefits of sect membership present for first generation but absent for the second generation
For some of the parents of the second generation, joining a sect might have been akin to falling in love. Initially, there are positive effects. Later on, individuals become more aware of the costs of sect

membership and potential misfits between the individual's predisposition and group's teaching and structure, resulting in a decrease in well-being and eventually in the individual leaving the group.[680] Galanter[681] contends that a sect 'acts like a psychological pincer, promoting distress while at the same time providing relief.' As those raised in sects are generally born into the group or bought into it by parents, both aspects of possible benefits are likely to be absent for the second generation. The initial benefits may be absent because the decision to join is not taken by the child but the parent, and therefore the pincer may be experienced, but sadly no relief is likely to be provided from the pincer, as children can usually only leave sects independently once they reach a certain age or level of maturity.

Health benefits

Some sects may bring physical health benefits due to the simple lifestyle. These may have a prolonged positive effect on those who left the sects, particularly those who remained in the sect for a long time. In Ted's Sect, individuals did a lot of exercise and ate a vegetarian diet, but were also likely to smoke hand-rolled cigarettes. In Harry's Sect, individuals did not smoke or drink, and a number walked a lot or rode bicycles. This may have resulted in long-term health benefits for members and may have contributed positively to their mental health. The psychological benefits of particular types of physical exercise may be wide-ranging and could include reduction of stress, depression and anxiety, as well as an increase in self-esteem and self-confidence.[682]

Wiser for the experience

Almost all of the former members of Harry's Sect and Ted's Sect felt that they had learned a great deal because of their experiences in the sect. For example, they mentioned knowing how to respect other people's space, knowing how not to approach people, being more aware generally, and being more wary of other people.[683] A former Ted's

Sect member mentioned that they discovered a deeper understanding and acceptance of themselves.[684] Some looked back on the experience and viewed it as helpful: they were now stronger.[685] A former Ted's Sect member reported being glad of going through the experience because in the end they did not feel harmed, and they had worked through many things in the process.[686]

Spiritual benefits

A number of former Harry's Sect members mentioned that they had had positive spiritual experiences, including conversion, as a result of their sect membership. They explained that they were able to see things more clearly and clarify their thoughts about what they believe.[687] Former Harry's Sect second-generation members reported positively about a good knowledge of the Bible, and one individual spoke of having learnt good behaviour such as punctuality.[688] One individual commented that they were stronger because of their experiences.[689] Another felt that they had learnt to cope without too much money, and this had given them a clearer perspective on what is important in life and what is not.[690]

Self-reported positive effects of very traumatic experiences

It was interesting to note that research interviews showed that a few of those who had had quite traumatic experiences reported positive effects as a result. This is consistent with other research in the area of trauma. For example, in one study, 6% of pilots whose experiences included being shot down, captured and tortured for years in North Vietnam, viewed those experiences as having been beneficial to them.[691] They reported greater levels of confidence following their ordeal, as well as favourable changes in their personalities. They also felt the experiences had taught them about what is valuable in life. This appears to contradict previous research, which has indicated that the worse someone's current symptoms are, the more severe they remember the trauma to be.[692]

Nevertheless, there are highly resilient individuals who do not develop PTSD symptoms following exposure to severe stressors. These individuals focus on the completion of tasks, are very sociable and have an internal locus of control, i.e. they tend to take responsibility for their actions and feel they have the power to do something about a situation.[693]

Oppression as a catalyst to personal growth
A related study found a significant relationship between loss due to oppression and the extent to which respondents' growth experience from the loss had a positive effect on their life. This indicated that the experience of oppression may serve as a catalyst for personal growth to occur.[694] 'The key to transforming losses into something positive lies in our efforts to give our losses meaning, to learn and gain insights from them, and to impart to others something positive based on the loss experience.'[695] This concurs with Victor Frankl's statement:

> 'Suffering ceases to be suffering in some way at the moment it finds a meaning, such as the meaning of sacrifice.'[696]

This in turn links to work which found creativity benefits in mastering stressors, including stressors relating to illness (incorporating trauma) or disability. There were instances of individuals achieving a transformation of an intensely negative experience into something that is positive for the individual and allows a healthy life. I propose that this is an act of creativity.[697]

SUMMARY OF CHAPTER 8
Who we are in relationship to others is a major aspect of our identity. Those raised in sects commonly lose relationships on leaving and therefore major aspects of their social identities. Some losses following a departure from a sect may be hidden losses such as the loss of

a childhood and missed opportunities. Grief for losses may include stages of denial, isolation, anger, bargaining and depression, and with enough time and support, acceptance. Complicated grief and mourning can occur when loss happens under traumatic circumstances, and therefore it can profoundly impact an individual's identity and life structure – for example, when an adolescent leaves a sect and loses contact with family members and others in the sect, and then has to find accommodation and a means to support themselves.

Some second-generation former members may find decision-making difficult after leaving the sect, they may also experience a great deal of fear and anxiety. Further, they may want to make up for missed experiences and a previous lack of opportunity by living a childhood fast-forward and making up for lost time. Being young, they may experience stigmatisation from others, especially if they view the second generation's exploration of life as rebellion and have little understanding of their experiences.

Statistics from a number of studies show that, on average, second-generation former members spend longer in sects (13 – 19 years) as compared to first generation former members (seven years) in these studies.

Statistical studies[698] on levels of distress in second-generation former members found that many suffered from depression, anxiety, dissociative, avoidance and intrusion symptoms indicative of PTSD. While not everyone raised in a sect has psychological problems after leaving, a New Zealand study found that two-thirds of their research participants had psychological problems after leaving. This is most likely due to interpersonal trauma experienced in childhood. Post-sect vulnerabilities for some of the second generation include alcohol and drug abuse, abusive relationships and for some groups, prostitution.

The benefits of former sect involvement may occur because of sect membership, despite sect membership and with hindsight further away from the sect experience. These might include access to a variety of adult role models, continuous social interaction, health benefits, spiritual benefits, knowing what's important in life and a feeling of being wiser for the experience. Losses suffered as a result of oppression can sometimes have a positive effect on a life and serve as a catalyst to personal growth.

WHAT COMES NEXT IN CHAPTER 9?

The chapters that follow look at how individuals might recover from some of the negative experiences they have experienced, particularly in terms of learning resiliency via healthy relationships with people, as Faris Kermani and Winfried Hempel[699] who now works as a lawyer report:

> Correspondent: *He* [Winfried Hempel] *was lucky. The family he was sent to live with were shocked by his story and helped him overcome the years of neglect and ignorance. He had never gone to a proper school. He couldn't speak Spanish, but he was eager to make up for lost time and was able to get into this university to study law.*

> Winfried Hempel: *So that my peers didn't bother me with questions about Colonia Dignidad, I said I was a German citizen who came to Chile to study. And that's how I went unnoticed in the first years of university. But obviously with time my closest friends knew that I grew up in the Colonia and started asking the typical uncomfortable questions.*

CHAPTER 9

HURT IN RELATIONSHIPS, HEALED IN RELATIONSHIPS

It would be an arduous road, but it was one that we needed to travel.[700]

OVERVIEW

This chapter looks at the importance of healthy relationships and their potential positive impact upon leaving a sect. It provides a summary of possible care and social support, which some of the second generation might find to be of benefit, and it includes a brief explanation of different types of counselling available. The chapter looks at resiliency and how people can best adapt after adversity, trauma and stress.

RESILIENCE AND UNIQUENESS

Chapter Two looked at a study of how personality types were converging towards a single type. Having experienced control and a lack of choice while in the sect, and potentially having been treated like 'clones', it is vital that those raised in sects become aware of and realise their own individual uniqueness. We are all different, and as such we will respond differently to events and experiences in our lives. Our ability to recover from negative experiences will vary from person to person.

Research indicates a general trend of psychological distress following sect membership, and second-generation former members appear to be those most psychologically distressed after leaving their sect. Nevertheless, it is important to be aware that one of the methodologies used in my original PhD was to compare groups of mean scores on measures of psychological distress using statistical analysis. Within any of these groups, there was a range of scores, i.e., there are those who scored high, those who scored low, and those who scored at different points between high and low. It is important to remember that the research reflects summaries based on statistics, and that there are major differences between people in the effects of sect membership on former members.

Our brains are incredibly impressive and capable. The Independent referring to our brains states: "Yet the most complex structure in the known universe – at is often described – is more mysterious than the least- explored regions of the deepest ocean."[701] There is so much more that we have still to learn about humans. Added to that we have each had different experiences and we each respond differently to experiences. So many things impact upon whether an individual is seriously psychologically scarred by experiences, for example, quality and quantity of relationships we had as children and at the present time; the age at which an event occurred; our gender; the developmental stage we had reached; our genetic make-up; and the availability of resiliency-enhancing experiences. Not only may all these things impact us differently, but they can interact with each other in a complicated way. Therefore, it is inadvisable to compare ourselves with others.

Everyone is different, everyone's experiences are different, and some emerge with differing primary needs: developmental gaps, trauma, urgent demands of others, and some with two or all three of these difficulties. While some people are very damaged by their sect experience, others are not. Not all sects are necessarily harmful to children, and some show remarkable resilience, adjusting well afterwards.[702]

Resiliency, according to the American Psychological Association (APA), is

'The process of adapting well in the face of adversity, trauma, tragedy, threats or even significant sources of stress such as family and relationship problems.' [703]

The APA has produced a helpful leaflet on resilience. It reports that some people respond resiliently to challenging, stressful or traumatic events in their childhood or adulthood. They adapt well afterwards. Resilience is not a trait that people either have or do not have; it can be developed in anyone. The leaflet describes a key way to build resiliency is to have caring and supportive relationships, including with people both outside and inside the family where possible. The presence of a range of safe people with whom adults, adolescents and children have healthy relationships are crucial as research supports the view that relationships that offer love and trust, provide role models, as well as encouragement and reassurance, help bolster a person's resilience.[704]

One of the concerns about the situation of children raised in some sects is that many of the social and developmental factors known to increase resilience may not be available. For an example of a resilience-enhancing experience that may be unavailable to sect children in some sects is the formation of relationships with surrogate parents.

Nevertheless, upon leaving the sect, resiliency-enhancing factors such as healthy relationships may become available. The extent to which second-generation former members are able to take advantage of these opportunities and overcome the fear that may be attached to them may directly affect their personal growth. The sections that follow expand more on the importance of relationships for those leaving sects.

RELATIONSHIPS AND THE IMPORTANCE OF SOCIAL SUPPORT

We all need healthy relationships in order to thrive. While we may be hurt in relationships with others, we are also healed in relationships with others.[705] The harm experienced in the sect environment is interpersonal, and could be considered in the context of 'abusive relationships'.[706] Therefore, the opposing experience of 'healthy' relationships will be hugely significant in counteracting harmful effects of the former.

Historically, psychologists have thought that first we need to be able to love ourselves and only then can we love others. However, more recent research reinforces the view that in fact we need to receive love first, then we can love ourselves and love others. In fact:

> 'Relationships are the agents of change and the most powerful therapy is human love.'[707]

Those who have experienced abuse and/or neglect, especially emotional neglect, are doubly in need. This book has shown that some people are very hurt in sects. For relationships to work well, appropriate boundaries are essential. Child abuse, like adult abuse, is an invasion of boundaries. Therefore, those exiting sects who have experienced boundary violations may need to discover or rediscover what appropriate boundaries are and internalise them.

Further, despite having had experiences that others may never have had, or at least are unlikely to have until an older age, second-generation former members may be exceptionally innocent, vulnerable and naive in many respects, for example with regard to the opposite sex and how they sometimes think and act. This presents an additional reason for those who support the second generation to maintain their own boundaries in an appropriate fashion so as not to take advantage of innocence, naiveté and vulnerability.

Failure or near-failure to maintain appropriate boundaries may result in further deep wounds being inflicted upon the second generation, particularly if the second-generation adult previously considered the individual to be a safe individual. If second-generation former members experience a violation of appropriate boundaries by those offering support, they must step back to protect themselves. Others who support second-generation former members may do well to gently inform a second-generation former member that those offering support may not always have their best interests at heart, particularly when they get attached to second-generation former members.

Some of those raised in sects reported the tendency to life a double life after leaving their sect. Lorna Goldberg[708] (2006), a therapist who has worked with those raised in sects, reports that:

'I have seen this duality of personality, looking good on the outside and doing 'bad' things in secret, in many of the former cultists with whom I have worked. Because of the need to project a perfect image, adolescents in cults begin to develop an underground or secret life in order to rebel or continue to hold onto a sense of self –that is, liveliness. Those who have been raised in cults also desire to experience all those activities that had been forbidden to them while in the cult. They often feel that they were robbed of a normal childhood, and they often engage in childish or adolescent activities. However, since they presently are adults, they often feel ashamed of these desires. As trust builds in the therapeutic relationship, former members are able to begin to examine this secret, split-off life. If the therapist is simply curious and open to examining this, rather than being judgemental (the transference expectation), the individual is able to begin to heal this split and become a more authentic person.'

Healthy relationships with others assist former members, where relevant, to realise that it is no longer necessary to live a double life, which in turn might enable former members to experience a true sense of what it is to be 'known' and 'know' others.

Those exiting sects[709], where they have been ostracised by virtually every person they have ever known, are completely alone and clearly will lack social support.[710] Even if other siblings or friends have already left the group, they may have no knowledge of their geographical whereabouts. Some sects allow contact between parents in the sect and children who have left. However, there may still be major issues with the quality of the relationship.

Psychologists have identified social support as positively affecting the mental health of individuals. Specifically it helps individuals to cope with adverse life circumstances.[711] The study[712] of Harry's Sect found that 6% of the second generation recorded talking to friends as a supportive experience after leaving, compared to 58% of the first generation. One reason for this could be that the second generation had few friends 'outside' the sect, having no pre-sect friends to go back to. Of the second generation, 69% also recorded receiving no help after leaving, compared to 33% of the first generation.

Former members of both TS and Harry's Sect reported that talking to other former members and reading, particularly articles written by other former members and some books (such as those on co-dependency), were very helpful on leaving.

Quite a number of former TS members received counselling on leaving, and reported on this very positively, specifically regarding help with relationships with the leaders of their former sects.[713] One former member mentioned that a contact with one of the leaders was helpful for another former member. It ensured that the leader knew they were angry and they felt sure that the leader would therefore not come near them. After seeing the sect leader, they were no longer afraid of bumping into him.[714] Similarly, a Harry's Sect former member commented that, after seeing and briefly speaking to Harry after leaving, they knew they were free.[715] Another TS individual stated that writing a letter to the leader had helped them feel better after leaving their sect.

A former sect child of Harry's Sect reported that having a faith and keeping busy helped him to deal with the fact that he had no contact with his parents, who remained in the sect.[716] Those exiting sects may not maintain or acquire a faith or spirituality after leaving the sect and may find a clear philosophy of life based on a humanist worldview or some other way of thinking about life, or this may be an area on which they do not spend time. Having spent so much of their lives with this as the sole or primary focus, an emphasis on different areas of their life might be very important in terms of moving on from the sect experience. However, if they don't sort through their beliefs, sect-instilled ideas and values are likely to continue to impact their thinking and behaviour, even if they endeavour not to think about such matters. As has often been said, it's easier to get the person out of the sect than the sect out of the person.

In summary, items that softened negative effects following sect membership included social support, reading material relevant to recovery, receiving counselling, maintaining a faith, keeping busy and a brief contact with the former leader.

SUPPORT: SUMMARY OF POSSIBLE SUPPORT AND CARE STRATEGIES
Some former members will neither require nor wish for support. They may engage in a form of self-help through reading and writing, or they may progress well through life with little thought of the past. Some of those for whom this is the case may process their sect experience more at later key stages in life, such as when they have their own children, as this may trigger a psychological reaction and a renewed awareness of an individual's own childhood experiences.

For others, recovery will be about acquiring and actively seeking support resources while simultaneously being cautious regarding whom they trust with intimate details of their story, thus allowing them to receive invaluable support. Because these former members may have come from groups that encourage or insist on confession and the sharing of large amounts of personal and intimate information with people who are not safe or who will misuse that information, it is important that former members learn not to share too much information all at once, but rather, have the opportunity to share parts of their story with people with whom they have first built a relationship of trust, where they don't feel pressured to share, and where relationship is built over time. It is also common to have different layers of trust with different people, such that people are not in or out, but different relationships involve differences in terms of personal information shared and items discussed.

This section gives suggestions about possible support that the second generation might find helpful. However, bearing in mind that second-generation former sect members are a relatively new population, it might be some time before organisations and individuals customarily approached for support have adequate knowledge and understanding of the types of issues facing those who have been raised in sects.

Each source of possible support must first earn the trust of the former member. Without trust, support is unlikely to be effective.

> 'The distinguishing characteristic of post traumatic stress disorder is a pervasive feeling of interpersonal distrust even in the face of existing family and friend relationships'.[717]

Given the high levels of PTSD found in former sect-member samples, earning trust will take time, but will also result in more effective support. Because of the interpersonal nature of trauma suffered by the second generation, positive interpersonal experiences may be at the heart of recovery. In light of the levels of accusation and judgement experienced, coupled with the diminished and often negative concept of themselves found in some former members, it is also imperative to support former members with a high level of acceptance of the individual.

Research conducted on those who had grown up and left Centrepoint found that nearly half of those participating in the research had, since leaving the sect, had experienced significant problems with friendships and intimate relationships. As one participant said *'The intimacy problem I have? You know, like I can get in a relationship but I just so can't handle the work in a relationship, I can't bear the intimacy because it's... I don't tend to trust.'*[718]

Vulnerability while bringing intimacy is also a scary experience, especially for those whose trust has been betrayed. Rebecca Mitchell's book 'New Shoes'[719] was written for those stepping out of the shadow of sexual abuse. She describes how when someone has been betrayed, core trust is lost and it becomes very frightening to be close to someone again. There is then a fear of intimacy, as shown in the poem below:

The dance of relationships and intimacy

Move closer,
Fear, I draw back
Retreat to the comfort of myself
Come towards, fear
Retreat to safety
Back and forth

Slowly, slowly, trust is built
Tender gentleness
Moving closer
Trust is built, slowly, slowly
Come towards, retreat
Feel the space,
Enjoy freedom
Come towards, stay

Another crucial factor to bear in mind in light of the fact that sect members very often experience very high levels of control in sects is that 'a therapist who sees her role as authoritarian may try to impose her perceptions, beliefs and need for control on a client who may be struggling to free herself from such control in the past'.[720] With no intention of causing harm and with a sincere desire to be helpful, it is easy for a therapist to impose their beliefs upon a client by insisting on interventions that their clients do not accept or by talking about experiences the client isn't yet ready to talk about.[721] This might be the case for anyone offering support to a former sect member. Audrey Findlay,[722] a foster parent who has supported a number of second-generation former members in her home, expands upon support offered to those raised in sects by stating that:

The one phrase I have repeated more than any other during the reha-bilitation process is, 'What do YOU think?' When every thought and behaviour has been open to scrutiny and judgement and subject to condemnation, it is vitally important to encourage these young people to think for themselves, to have their own ideas and opinions, their own choices and preferences and to feel that these are valid and need no justification or comment.

One observation from the interviews with former TS and Harry's Sect members was that the sect experience characteristically 'lacked compassion'. If former members have not experienced compassion, then the experience of true compassion might be powerful and crucial to their recovery. Compassion is defined[723] as having a deep awareness and understanding for another's suffering. Further, since it involves doing something about the suffering of others, compassion compels action.

SHARING OUR EXPERIENCES
For a variety of reasons, including that second-generation former members have often had experiences that others haven't had or don't share readily, and because we are affected and influenced by those experiences in our day-to-day life, we can easily be in a position where no-one understands what it is like to experience the world as we know it. Even if we are surrounded by people, we can experience acute feelings of loneliness if no-one understands life from our viewpoint. Consequently, it is vital that, bit by bit, we share thoughts, feelings (if we can), ideas, dreams and experiences with other safe people. One of the ways of deciding whether someone is safe is watching to see if they respect other peoples' boundaries, and it is to boundaries we now turn.

BOUNDARIES
Where we start and end, and where someone else starts and ends, can be a confusing topic for those exiting sects. Sects routinely ignore and

trample over boundaries. Therefore, it is no surprise that the second generation might find that boundaries are something they want to learn more about. Setting appropriate boundaries with others is important, whether that's with an individual or in a group setting or a physical boundary, such as who touches you and where, or a psychological boundary, such as whom you tell what to and how much you tell them about yourself. Often, those initially exiting sects may need to learn how to share about themselves a little at a time as opposed to giving away large amounts of information about themselves without knowing if the person they are speaking to is trustworthy or will respond appropriately. It is imperative that others are not intrusive in their questioning of former members as this can be unhelpful to second-generation former members who are still grappling with boundaries.

Dating and romantic relationships

Romantic relationships, by their nature are likely to be both the most rewarding and yet also the most difficult. As well as the possible difficulties with intimacy discussed earlier, it is in romantic relationships that the psychological issues or difficulties an individual has will most likely come to the fore. This is no less and no more the case for second-generation former members than for anyone else. Remembering that all relationships at times can be hard work and if both parties are willing to do the hard work, then conflict can bring about positive change and an enhancement of relationship.

In romantic relationships, we may be known best and loved the most, which also makes us at our most vulnerable, and therefore we risk being more hurt. Maintaining relationships with other people is crucial, even when we are in the most satisfying romantic relationship. This has the advantage of putting less pressure on a relationship and is especially helpful should our romantic relationship break down irreparably.

For those exiting sects with no or limited experience of dating and romantic relationships, they may find that seeing them as an extension of other relationships might be helpful. In all relationships we need to respect the boundaries of others and maintain our own boundaries. And we need to take the time to communicate well, including taking care to communicate in a respectful manner with others. It takes time to get to know someone and have others get to know us. Second-generation former members may feel very unique and indeed may have had some experiences that others do not share. Being a little bit different can make one very attractive. Knowing that the myth of a single soul mate is indeed a myth can be very helpful when it comes to dating. We all have a number of options in terms of people with whom we could have a positive romantic relationship.

Livia Bardin[724] has written an internet book entitled *Starting Out in Mainstream America* for those raised in sects. This is available online at http://startingout.icsa.name. It contains extensive information which may be very helpful to second-generation former members. It covers many topics including: communication, boundaries, dating and romantic relationships. For example, she includes a whole section on how to break off a dating relationship and a section on dating and sex.

Family support

Key sources of family support for second-generation former members might include first-generation parents, grandparents, aunts, uncles, cousins and/or siblings, etc., usually those who have either never been in the group or who have already left the sect. The next chapter has a section entitled 'The smallest kindness', which discusses the amazing impact that those not in sects can have on current members. A child in a sect may have grandparents, aunts, uncles or other blood relatives who are not in the sect, but who may be important relational lifelines. Maintaining those relationships can be difficult, but is extremely important to the child. Some relatives of children in sects are very concerned for their loved ones, yet feel powerless – they may have tried every means to assist, but may now have very limited (if any) contact with their child relatives. This can be particularly difficult, painful and devastating for a parent who is not in the sect.

It is important to hold opposites simultaneously, both hope and resignation: hope that one day it is likely (though there is no guarantee) that the child will leave the group, perhaps when they reach their later teenage years or are in their 20s. Resignation, for it is important for grandparents, parents, uncles and aunts to live their own lives and not be consumed with this. Therefore, opposites are held in tension, hope and despair, and yet one's own life moves on.

Blood relatives have the potential to make a huge difference in the lives of those raised in sects, especially after the children have left the sect and the sect no longer has any power or control to impact the relationship, except for implanted notions about the badness of these relatives that may complicate their perceptions, e.g., 'women who wear trousers are evil' or are seen as prostitutes, which can be difficult to overcome.

Receiving social support from a blood relative maintains a sense of family identity and offers a former member an important bond. Given the second generation's possible experience of ostracism by family members still in the sect, which might be experienced as a loss, grandparents (or aunts, uncles and cousins) who have never been a part of the sect might lessen and in some ways fill in for that loss.

Peer and mentor support might be particularly important for second-generation former members with no or limited family support.

THE IMPORTANCE OF GRANDPARENTS FOR THE SECOND GENERATION
Of those younger than twenty years old in the general population, 96% have a living grandparent.[725] Compared to those grandparents who have gone before, today's grandparents with medical advances, live longer, are better educated, younger and richer. According to the Foundation for Grandparenting, a common mistake that grandparents in general make, is not to realise their importance to their grandchildren, perhaps this is even more the case for grandparents with grandchildren in sects.

Anecdotal evidence from autobiographies of second-generation former members[726] reveals that, where grandparents have contact with their grandchildren, they can play an important role in the lives of both current and former second-generation sect members. Truman Oler, who grew up in Bountiful, British Columbia, in a polygamous Fundamentalist Latter Day Saints group, testified at the Canadian trial on whether to legalise polygamy in 2011. Oler grew up in a family consisting of six mothers and 47 children. At age 19, he wanted to leave the FLDS, but did not trust those outside the group and did not know where to go. He testified that[727]:

> One of the biggest factors in my leaving was my Grandma Lorna [who had left Bountiful years earlier], Oler said through tears. "Grandma Lorna told me no matter what I did I was always going to have a place to come back to. That meant so much to me because I just didn't know where I'd go if I left.

It is not just in the leaving of sects that grandparents may have an important role in the lives of their grandchildren, if they are able to have contact with them. Kornhaber[728] has identified and defined specific roles that grandparents play with their grandchildren which are emphasized at different times dependent on the circumstance and age of the child. For example, Kornhaber[729] identifies that a grandparent is a living ancestor and a family historian whom children will naturally question to learn what life was like in the old days. Grandparents then might be able to provide the child in the sect with a sense of history and family roots and a sense of belonging to something and someone other than the sect.

Grandparents might also give input in terms of being nurturers, mentors who inspire and fire the imagination of their grandchildren in terms of dreams of their futures. Other roles might include that of wizard and hero, role model, student, buddy and teacher. Each of these roles may be important to the grandchild in a sect and while dissected here, may be occurring very naturally in a relationship. Grandparents need to understand that being an emotionally stable individual who is sensitive to the needs of the grandchildren, may be vital to the success of children who succeed against the odds.[730] Your role is important! Those little interactions which result in a close bond with your grandchild may be vital experiences that have real significance for the future, and most especially for the grandchild in a sect.

To the degree to which a grandchild in a sect is isolated from the outside world so on leaving the sect that grandchild will likely benefit, to that same degree, from the input of a grandparent/s. The roles of a grandparent might be paramount at that point, a blood relative to offer encouragement, support, motivation and assistance with all the developmental, skills, and social gaps that may exist in their grandchild. A grandparent can be a vital life-line to a grandchild both in a sect and after they leave.

Some of those born and raised in sects on leaving, leave not only parents behind, but also leave behind their grandparents, or their grandparents are no longer living when they leave the sect. Research on learnt resilience has found that children who grow up in difficult circumstances, but who are good at finding surrogate parents do well, i.e.

they grow up into competent, confident and caring adults.[731] Equally, this may apply to finding surrogate grandparents or just other supportive elderly people. Brent Jeffs in his autobiography records the following about a kind elderly woman named Sandy who he had met when she was a cleaner:

> She did not belong to our church but lived in the neighbourhood. When I met her, she was probably in her sixties and used a wheelchair. She lived on her own in a big rambling house. Her husband had left her and she had several grown children who visited only rarely. Her companions were her two Siamese cats.[732]

Brent Jeff's describes how Sandy listened to him, didn't judge him and how he was able to talk to her. She also helped him out by purchasing a car which made a real difference in his life. He writes:

> For a while I'd spend every Sunday with Sandy, just talking and helping around the house a bit. She had done me a huge favor and I wanted to do right by her, but I enjoyed it too and it felt good to make her feel less lonely. She helped me to understand people outside the church, and to figure out what I wanted and who I was. I could talk to her about most things and I only hope I helped her half as much as she helped me."[733]

GRANDPARENTS AND THE FIRST GENERATION

In order for a child to have a relationship with and receive support from their grandparent, the relationship between the parent and grandparent is also important. Maintaining that relationship during their adult child's sect involvement may be impossible or possible, but difficult at times. The Foundation for grandparenting have identified a number of key mistakes that grandparents can make and I quote these below as they may be particularly relevant for grandparents whose family are involved in a sect. They are:

- *"Not realizing that parents are the linchpins of grandparent's relationship with grandchildren.*
- *Not listening to parents and respecting their right to make their own mistakes and learn from them. Not understanding the insecurities of new parents and being controlling, bossy, critical, judgmental, non-supportive.*
- *Not putting oneself in parents' shoes to understand their experience."[734]*

Amy Siskind[735] who was born and raised in a sect had grandparents who despite having a very limited relationship with their adult daughter in the sect, did provide for her financially while she was in the sect and therefore were able to have a relationship with their granddaughter. Interestingly, Amy Siskind states that her grandparents never spoke negatively about the group her parents were involved with. Amy Siskind discusses how her grandparents support was vital to her, both in the sect and afterwards.

Of course, providing financially to an adult child may not be an option or it might not be an option that an individual can choose in good conscience, however sometimes there are other ways of positively impacting a relationship. For example, via a very small practical gift given to the community of which one's adult child is a member.

A book for a grandchild that might be beneficial and may be allowed by both the sect and parents in a sect and could be given as a gift, is the book Heidi by the Swiss author Johanna Spyri published in 1880 is about the events in the life of a young girl in her grandfather's care, in the Swiss alps.

Maintaining a relationship with an adult child in a sect will not always be possible for grandparents, no matter how diplomatic, gentle and sensitive they are, as it may cut across the teachings and demands of the sect. For a grandparent who has no contact, one possibility is to consider writing a journal style item for their child, grandchild and/or grandchildren. This might include photographs and writing happy birthday on their birthday and marking other events in their lives. It can be brief. If the grandparents do aquire contact or are able to leave this journal to their child/grandchild as an inheritance, it will show that they have thought about them all these years, even though there has been no contact. Upon receiving this, a child or grandchild will receive a powerful message of love and care.

However, for grandparents who are able to maintain a relationship with both their adult children in a sect and their grandchildren, if the time comes when the grandchild wishes to leave the sect, then this is a pivotal moment in time, when their relationship with their adult child in a sect is very important.

For surgeons, where mistakes are made in surgery, it is often at the beginning or at the end of an operation and therefore extra care needs to be taken at beginning and endings when we may lack concentration. There is a truth here, that I think can be applied to our lives generally and that is to take extra care during beginnings and endings. A young person leaving a sect is at both an ending and a beginning. They are at an end of one type of life and at the beginning of another, with all sorts of opportunities and challenges. Grandparents may be a part of being able to facilitate a good ending for their grandchild leaving a sect. This may be via their relationship with either their adult child in a sect and/or their grandchild, or all parties. If a grandparent is able to facilitate and support their grandchild and adult child having the chance to say goodbye to each other, they will have done them a big favour, particularly where the parent is not expected to have contact with the child from that point on.

In terms of a grandchild leaving a sect, this may be a sweet bitter experience for the grandparent/s. Sweet because they may gain relationship with their grandchild, but bitter because they recognise the loss that their adult child, the first generation parent, is suffering. It may also be bitter because it may be a reminder of the loss of relationship that the grandparent/s themselves may have suffered, when their first generation child became involved in a sect. Sect membership can involve a large amount of loss for a number of people. Loss is painful and loss needs to be grieved. However, the second generation leaving and connecting with their grandparents may be a healing balm for each others loss experiences. Further, the second generation former members and their grandparents may share a common bond of concern for the first generation current member.

The second generation upon leaving are carriers of hope. They are carriers of hope for other siblings and young people who may have been told that dire things might happen to them if they leave. Just by being alive they carry hope for those who were also born into the sect whom they have left behind. They are also carriers of hope for the first generation and their grandparents, hope that one day, their parents, like them, may leave and be reunited with living relatives including the parents of the first generation.

WILL MY PARENTS EVER LEAVE THE SECT?

The love that parents have for their children is huge and even where parents ostracise their own children after they have left, the pain of doing that may be immense and invariably happens because of the sect teaching. At times the second generation leaving may have a domino effect resulting in their first generation parents also leaving.

While many first generation parents do leave sects, some parents do not leave sects, and they may even die while still involved in the sect.

This may be a painful complicated loss experience, for those children who may not even be told in a timely fashion of the death of a parent in a sect, let alone receive an invite to or be involved in the funeral. How difficult must this be?

However, for those with living parents, hope that they might one day leave and hope for an actual relationship is not misguided hope as it is a real possibility which has happened for some, including those who others considered that it was highly unlikely or impossible that they would leave. I was encouraged to hear the following account which I share with permission:

It is an account I was told by a woman born and raised in a sect whose parents were also raised in the sect, For this woman both her parents were born in a sect, she left her sect alone leaving her parents in the sect. However, when this woman's parents reached 70 years old they both left the sect together and she was able to have a relationship with them. This elderly couple had a fantastic 10 years together after the sect, they did all sorts of things together that they had never done before. For example, they went to fayres and enjoyed fayre rides together. Ten years after leaving, one of them died, but for this couple the twilight years of their lives were the best years of their lives. On that basis I would say that you are never too old to leave a sect and where there is life there is hope.

Some parents do indeed leave sects and some may become a source of support for their children, however at times the relationship between the parents and their children including adult children can be difficult and I therefore address this in a separate section below.

RESTORATION OF RELATIONSHIP BETWEEN PARENTS AND THEIR ADULT CHILDREN

Some second-generation former members left their sect as children with their parents. Clearly, parents who leave with their children are likely to be a major source of support to the children. This might also be the case when young adults/children exit sects and are able to retain some sort of contact with their parents after leaving. However, there may be issues with the quality and/or quantity of the contact, and therefore, support of the second-generation former member from other family members might be important.

Research on one sect found that it was common for those raised in the sect not to talk to their parents about their experiences in the sect, although a few do report speaking openly[736]. Where there has been a loss of respect between parties, talking about the past maybe a key way to regain respect between parties. Tim Guest, who spent a considerable amount of his childhood in a sect, records spending many, many hours discussing with his mother their experiences in the Bhagwan Rashneesh's communes and Jayanti Tamm records the following about her mother and their relationship:

> *Years later, as she shared with me her own painful struggles of her decades in the Center, we began a new relationship of openness and truth. There would be no more secrets, no fear of repercussions.[737]*

In some instances, first-generation parents might leave their sect after their children have already left the sect. The extent to which both a parent and adult child have worked through their own difficulties will clearly affect the relationship, and would certainly affect the degree to which a parent might be able to offer support to their adolescent or adult children. If the parents are unable to work through their own experience, or are still in the process of doing so, they may not be able to acknowledge the second-generation former member's experience (including their part in that).

Difficult family issues may often be present between the second generation and their family after sect membership. Denial, lack of support and lack of acknowledgement of negative experiences may be very detrimental to the second-generation former member's recovery, particularly if the second-generation adult has suffered greatly in or since the sect experience, especially if they suffered at the hands of their parents or were not protected by their parents. Facing ourselves can at times be difficult and painful, and first-generation former members like others, are better able to do this in an environment of acceptance, rather than judgement and where the influence of the sect and its leader is recognised.

Second-generation former members may look for an apology and a show of genuine remorse from parents, which may not be forthcoming. For some parents, it may appear as if they are part of an honour culture – where to say 'sorry' is to lose face. Some people find it exceptionally difficult to say 'sorry'. They just don't do it even when they feel remorse. In one sense, for a parent to do a U-turn and leave a sect, is for them to acknowledge, at some level they got it wrong. A remorseful apology may be exceptionally helpful, and makes trust easier, but a 'sorry' is not necessarily a prerequisite for a relationship.

At times, second-generation adults who have younger siblings who are also minors and still in their parents' home or still in the sect may have a strong desire and sense of responsibility to endeavour to ensure that their siblings have a different experience growing up than the one they had. It takes a great deal of courage for older siblings to initiate conversations with parents regarding suggested changes to how the parents bring up younger children (the brothers and sisters of the older sibling).

It's important to remember that people, including parents, can change hugely following their departure from a sect. However, it takes time to change after the sect. Former members don't immediately ditch aspects of the sect teaching which are destructive to relationships. It may take longer for someone leaving a sect at an older age to change than a younger person. Younger people may find it easier to realise that they are confused, and may be more flexible and amenable to change themselves. They may also have a greater number of opportunities to meet others who will influence their thinking, their hearts and their behaviours. Significant change in the first-generation former members' relationship with their adult children might be necessary in light of the relationship that may have existed during sect membership.

However, the love between parents and their children is powerful. Acknowledging the interference of the sect in the relationship, which resulted in hurt in the relationship, can be helpful to both parents and their adult children. Winfried Hempel's experience of growing up in a Chilean sect where children lived in quarters separate to his parents states the following:

> *Now I have very frank relationship with my parents. I still have some time to... share with them. And I'm not going to waste time with accusations, because I think that regardless of the possible responsibility they may have following Schaefer, I know how hard it was for parents who tried to get close. They were punished and humiliated in public. My father, for example, was publicly humiliated by Schaefer, having to stand in front of the assembly to be punished because he came to see us more often than the other parents.*

It is easy to underestimate the impact of the sect on the relationship between parents and their children – particularly when an individual receives abusive or neglectful treatment from their parents or other first-generation adults, rather than the sect leader with whom they may have had little interaction. To see an individual change after the sect is helpful in recognising the effects of the sect environment on a person.

Below is a poem I wrote about my relationship with my mother which some individuals might relate to:

THE MAC

Cult, anti-fashion
Women your beauty must come from within, women look as rough and ugly as possible
Wear dull clothes or clothes your granny's granny might have worn.
Mother, kind, skint, made my clothes, a mac, navy-blue, long,
Other children at school, no cult, only short coats, no macs.
Oh, how I hate you, long navy-blue mac.

Mother, fighting, clothes, hatred, has she not heard of fashion?
Whoops, a forbidden word.
Clothes, she made for me, guilt.
I wear homemade clothes from ancient patterns, then stigma, the looks, the stares, the shame.
Oh, long mac, how I hate you
You're horrible and drab and long and have no colour

Mother, argue, disagree, younger sisters grateful in years ahead
Rain; mother makes me wear mac. Oh how I hate you, but I have to take you to school.
Around the corner, into the bag you go, long mac, whom I hate.
I carry you in bag all day long, navy blue long mac, whom I hate
Around the corner from home, out of the bag you come, long mac whom I hate.
I dip you in a puddle, to hide the secret that I never wore you, long mac.

Oh how I hated you.
I was so glad to leave you behind long mac when I left.
Ha, ha, I say, I never wore you.
And they never caught me.
Ha ha I say. I got away without you, long mac

But now, dear mac, I have a use for you.
As I pull you from my memory, I realise your purpose.
In vain your life has not been, as you help me understand
My mother thought of me, she could not miss the rain,
Alas we lived in England,
Where a millimetre of snow causes cars, trains and planes to halt
To work we do not go
My mother to protect me from the rain, each day, the clouds, the wind, the chill.
My daughter will be dry she thought, protected from the cold.
No coughs and sneezes coming to her.
I will protect and shield

My mother worked and pricked her fingers, her precious blood was spilt
Late in the night, while others slept, you came to be, blue mac
You represent my mother's love, misunderstood;
You never had the chance to achieve your purpose.
But now, dear mac, I have written this poem for you.

I know you would have been colourful if my mother made you now
She left that cult, you see
The one I hated so.
Since then she's made me clothes.
She let me choose, pattern, colour, length.

I know, blue mac, that had my mother not been in a cult, but
free
You would have been bright and beautiful
And short.

The envy of children
I'd have worn you with pride
You represent a mother's love
And because of that I'm grateful
I don't hate you now, blue mac, you signal something else
Made with love, as a protection, my mother did her best.

SUPPORT FROM BROTHERS AND SISTERS (SIBLINGS)

Siblings who choose to support an older or younger sibling bring
with them a very important depth of understanding of the shared
sect experience. Nevertheless, psychologists recognise that even
identical twins may have quite different experiences growing up,
coupled with different personality types, as well as different coping
strategies, gender differences, interests and talents. Further, there
may be large differences in experiences, depending on when a child
was born in the sect as the rules and culture in these groups can
and do change over time.[738] Therefore, understanding each other
might be difficult. However, given the difference between the sect
environment and the mainstream environment in which they now
find themselves, siblings may be an important source of mutual social support.

Siblings who have acted as parents to other siblings in the sect may
need to realign that relationship. Siblings may carry their own wounds
from the sect experience, so external support for all siblings might be
important. Older siblings may feel a sense of responsibility and therefore guilt, and a feeling of having abandoned younger siblings in a
group. It is vital that this is recognised as false guilt and that a sibling,

no matter how much older, is a sibling and not a parent. As such, they do not have the option of bringing children out of a group. Only a parent has this right.

Mentors

Research on creativity over the course of peoples' lives has found that having a mentor during one's 20s was one of the most important factors in the development of creativity in the individual (creativity here refers to normal, everyday non-eminent creativity as opposed to creativity at the genius level).[739] Mentors represent a mixture of parent and peer to the mentee, and are usually eight to 15 years older. The ultimate goal of a mentoring relationship is a peer relationship, although this is not fully realised, mentoring can still be helpful even though it does not achieve a full peer relationship. The mentor serves as a guide, teacher and sponsor. Mentoring has both risks as well as rewards. There is the risk of the relationship becoming dysfunctional, and the risk of a bad ending, which is expanded on later and there are also rewards. Mentors can encourage an individual to explore and identify what they are good at. Every individual has things that they are good at, whether it be sport, painting, writing, diving, encouraging people or a host of other possibilities. For those coming from an environment where their gifts were not identified or developed, to do so after exiting their group is part of their discovery of who they are.

Daniel Levinson[740] a developmental psychologist described in his work on lifespan development that individuals need to develop and articulate a 'Dream'. He states that 'In its primordial form, a Dream is a vague sense of self-in-world, an imagined possibility of one's adult life that generates excitement and vitality';[741] a life lived without living out the dream is 'at best a compromise and at worst defeat'.

Children raised in sects may have no dreams of the future, or a foreshortened sense of the future, as well as the shattering of dreams that do exist on leaving the sect, such as a sect belief that when you have grown up you will save the world. This means that it is important for those raised in sects to form new dreams about how their life may pan out. A first-generation former member who left Jonestown at age 26 three weeks before the massacre described her dream after she left Jonestown this way:

My goal, in fact, was that I wanted to live to be 30 so I could have a rich and full life. Now I have a daughter who's 29, and I'm 60. I've had double what I wished for.[742]

A full mentorial relationship involves the mentor supporting the evolution of the dream through nourishment, belief and definition of the mentee's newly emerging adult self, and by creating space in which the one being mentored can move towards a life structure that includes the dream.[743] Piers Worth states that:

'A mentor looks at a person and says, "I see what you are and your potential, perhaps even more completely than you do yourself. I am willing to listen to what is important to you, your dream, your hopes. I am willing to put time and energy into supporting and sponsoring (often in very practical terms) those things to grow and come through you. What I believe is 'right' or 'wrong' is not necessarily the point. I want to know what you believe and want, and will support that coming into life and form."'[744]

Mentoring is not just a set of behaviours; it is a deeply held belief system concerning other people and a willingness to invest energy in others, when there may be no 'return' in conventional terms. Consequently, the end result of the mentoring is for the person mentored to become more fully and completely who they are, and be in a position to be able to express it. The personal identity of the one being mentored grows and strengthens in its uniqueness in this social context. One can view this as a polar opposite of the sect leader/sect member relationship, where the sect leader knows best and seeks to control and constrain members' identities. Consequently, by reversing this denial of individuality and personal identity, good mentoring might have the potential to reverse the 'developmental trauma' I have hypothesised is occurring in sects.[745]

While a positive mentorial relationship might be very beneficial to a former member, a negative relationship is likely to be detrimental. Mentorial relationships can be dysfunctional especially if they become 'unproductive or characterised primarily by conflict'.[746] Before and during the ending of a mentorial relationship, both parties might benefit from being aware and appreciative of the potential pitfalls and outcomes. Dysfunction in a mentoring relationship might stem from healthy maturation of the relationship.[747] Mentoring relationships last on average for two or three years and up to 10 years at most.[748] 'Potentially the biggest gift a mentor can give at the end of the process is to know when to step back and "let go", and to say "please go and live in this space and manifest these talents and ways of being on your own", i.e., "I believe in you enough to say please fly, and that you can do this without me"'.[749]

Ending a mentoring relationship in this way might ensure that it is less painful and that neither party experiences the most 'intense feelings of admiration and contempt, appreciation and resentment, grief, rage, bitterness and relief', as has often been found in mentorship endings.[750] The mentor is often regarded at this point as a tyrannical father or smothering mother, and the mentee is regarded by the mentor as 'inexplicably touchy, unreceptive to even the best counsel, irrationally rebellious and ungrateful'.[751]

In the case of second-generation former members, the ending of the mentorial relationship may be particularly important bearing in mind the difficulties encountered in leaving the sect and the possible experience of ostracisation by parents and peers. If the termination of the mentoring relationship is not handled well, it might represent a negative re-enactment of this prior experience of the second generation. Mentorial relationships do not become characterised by conflict only because of the mentor or mentee, but conflict in the relationship may also stem from environmental factors and/or original poor matching of the mentor and mentee.[752]

Peer support

Former members reported that talking to others who had similar experiences was helpful to their recovery. Interactive websites for second-generation former members of various sects can be helpful. The peer support found on these sites allows former members to know they are not alone in what they are and have experienced. The sites allow former members to reconnect with their childhood peers after leaving the sect, whichever country they are in. Research conducted on one of these sites concluded that 'The virtual community… seems to function as a source of therapy and healing for many participants, besides giving them a chance to reconnect with childhood friends and estranged family members'.[753] As well as interactive websites, there are blogs and discussion groups available. Some of these may lead to face-to-face meetings with others, as do support groups and conferences organised for those raised in sects.

However, many (e.g. Harry's Sect), though not all, sects do not allow their members to have computers at home, and former members may have no or very limited technological skills. Therefore, other forms of peer support are important. These could involve telephone help lines, informal networks of former members, former member groups and workshops. However, these may not be available in an individual's local area.

SPIRITUAL SUPPORT AND CARE

Interviews revealed that individuals often had difficulty in the area of spirituality after sect membership such as concern with matters of the spirit or existential questions like, 'Is there a purpose in life?'. These included confusion, difficulty in knowing whom to trust and the problems of reading religious texts, particularly those that were also used in the sect from which they had exited.

Working through spiritual issues and sect beliefs may facilitate recovery, since former members will most likely still be influenced by the sect beliefs and codes of conduct even when they have left the sect, unless they have sorted through what their beliefs actually are.

Former members need to make their own decisions about their moral views and values. It is important for second-generation former members to learn not to spiritualise everything, for example most everyday events such as the colour of your napkin at the table do not have special spiritual significance.[754]

Furthermore, second-generation former members need to able to choose their own religion, spirituality, or lack thereof at their own pace, in their own time. While acknowledging sensitivity in this area, former members of religion-based sects also need the opportunity and space to discuss these issues if they wish. To experience acceptance, regardless of their religious views, might enable these individuals to know that their value and worth is not based on their adherence to a belief system or a code of conduct.

Second-generation former members who move towards religion or spirituality with the same basic beliefs as their former sect (e.g. Bible-based or Buddhist) might need spiritual support in areas like redefinition of the meanings of words that were used in the sect context to mean something other than their usual meaning in the English language. Interview reports indicated that Harry, the sect leader, used parts of the Bible against people.

For those with traumatic memories associated with words often used in a spiritual context, this aspect of recovery might be particularly difficult. For example, repetitive use of a particular phrase or sentence from the Bible may have been associated with a painful sect experience such as humiliation, beration, or threat to one self or a family member. These words taken from the Bible may then become associated with trauma. Thus, former members may have what is known as advanced priming, meaning that the use of those same words in a different context still results in those words acting as triggers for intrusive re-experiencing of past events.[755]

In terms of Christianity, using a different version of the Bible than that used in the sect can be helpful.[756] A sensitive, gentle, non-condemnatory approach might best enable the former member to move forward in this area. Interview reports indicated that experiencing spirituality, religion, martial arts or a different practice context of the original sect belief as non-controlling and non-manipulative was beneficial for former members. Interviewees reported that it assisted them in working through the confusion they experience about spiritual matters. As St James wrote, 'Everyone should be quick to listen, show to speak and slow to become angry.'[757] Having someone listen to our story affirms our sense of value.

PROFESSIONAL ASSISTANCE AFTER THE SECT: IS IT WORTH IT? SHOULD I BOTHER?

Particularly for young people leaving sects who have not experienced healthy relationships, and therefore don't know what they look like, professional assistance such as counselling can be very helpful. Individuals exiting sects that were supposedly therapeutic environments may be understandably particularly reticent, mistrustful and cautious about therapy. However, research with second-generation former members who have sought professional assistance after leaving their sect has shown that the second generation respond very well to it. One of my studies[758] found that for those former second-generation members who have received counselling, as the time since leaving the sect increases, so their scores on psychological distress decreases unlike those who didn't receive counselling.[759]

Those second generation former members who do acquire counselling for themselves are in good company. Many former members seek out counselling. Details on the numbers and percentages can be found in the end notes of this chapter.[760]

Many colleges, universities and youth support groups as well as doctors' surgeries will refer individuals to a counsellor and, in the UK and some other countries, at least the first six counselling sessions will be free. A therapist or a counsellor can be a compassionate witness to your personal history.[761]

THERAPEUTIC SUPPORT: WHAT KIND?
There are a number of different schools or types of counselling that all provide therapy or counselling, but which use different approaches for this, much like there are numerous ways of making a light – various colours, disposable, refillable, open-flame lighters, matches, open fire, or a combination of the former, etc. Each essentially do the same job – provide us with a light – but people differ in their preferences, what they get on with best, what is available in a given situation.

Having some sort of familiarity with the different schools of therapy might be helpful to those who decide to opt for counselling or therapy. Suggested below in alphabetical order is how each school of therapy might help an area of harm, although it is recognised that each of the therapies is likely to be effective in other areas. I propose that any one of the therapies below (as well as others[762]) might be beneficial in terms of treatment and support of former sect members.

a. Client-centred therapy

A psychologist named Carl Rogers developed client centred therapy in the mid-20th Century, and it is still widely used today. He thought that people are at their core good and this view influenced his style of therapy. The view of people being good might be a useful balancing factor for those who have been raised in groups where they were repeatedly told they were bad. Rogers further thought that people have a desire to fulfil their potential and become the best people they can be.[763]

He believed that rather than a therapist offering interpretations to a client, the therapist should let the client be in control. Sect environments are heavily controlling and usually have a hierarchical structure. The self-directional approach of client-centred therapy might be particularly beneficial to former sect members, encouraging them to maintain and develop their own authority. Further while Rogers did believe that the therapeutic relationship could lead to lasting insights and changes in a client, he felt it to be very important that the therapist endeavour not to offer suggestions or solutions and not pass judgements on the client's feelings. Former sect members have usually experienced a very judgemental and accusatory sect environment as well as double binds. The acceptance that is such an important aspect of client-centred therapy might be a valuable therapeutic element in an individual's recovery, as might having the therapist strive to meet the client as a person in as genuine a manner as possible.[764]

b. Cognitive Behavioural Therapy

Earlier chapters discussed cognitive distortions (distortions in our thinking). Cognitive therapies directly address how people think and specifically uncover cognitive distortions.[765] Cognitive therapies successfully treat conditions such as depression and anxiety. Some studies indicate that this therapy can be at least as effective as prescription drugs even if the depression is severe[766]. Cognitive therapy treatments involve the therapist working alongside the client to enable them to change their thinking about, evaluation of and interpretation of an experience. For example, Aaron Beck,[767] who has created his own theory for treatment, found that those who are depressed have a negative view of themselves, the world as a whole and the future.

Aaron Beck's work and treatment of individuals who are anxious led him to conclude that cognitive distortions centering around an individual's perception of a major physical or social threat and their perceived lack of ability to cope with the threat, are what cause the anxiety. 'The true aim of cognitive therapy is to have the client become his or her own therapist'.[768] Assuming this does not leave the former member lacking in social support, this aspect of cognitive therapy might be particularly empowering.

c. Psychodynamic therapy

Psychodynamic therapy is concerned with how someone's past impacts their present-day life, particularly how our childhood impacts our present relationships with others. Chapter 5 of this book looked at developmental stages[769] and discussed how each stage impacts the stage that follows, and how those raised in sects may have had negative outcomes at some of the stages. I proposed that there may be a possible cumulative 'developmental trauma' occurring as a result of a negative outcome in the first or second of the life development stages, which consequently would affect the stages that follow. However, a negative outcome at one stage might be altered or changed later in life[770].

Michael Jacobs[771] in his book, *The Presenting Past*, shows how this might be achieved using psychodynamic therapy. He demonstrates how clients' past conflicts and unresolved issues relate to their present difficulties, as well as the actual counsellor–client relationship. Resolving these conflicts enables an individual to better negotiate the future. In view of this, psychodynamic therapy might be useful in seeking to alter negative outcomes from the developmental phase. Whether it is possible fully to overcome 'developmental trauma' of this degree within the lifespan, without resultant scars, is discussed further in the next chapter on 'recovery time scale'.

d. Therapists and counsellors specialising in the treatment of trauma
Therapists and counsellors may have specialist areas including a special interest in assisting those with PTSD and other trauma-related conditions and syndromes. Within that specialisation, therapists might utilise different schools of counselling and therapies and different techniques and skills for assisting those with trauma. A register of trauma support specialists in the UK provides on its website[772] an overview of trauma specialities for information purposes, including information on:

- Cognitive Behavioural Therapy
- Emotional Freedom Technique
- Grovian Metaphor Therapy
- Rewind Technique
- Thought Field Therapy
- Trauma Counselling Skills and
- Stress Management.

e. Sect specialist counselling
There is a need for counsellors and psychotherapists to undergo professional training in the area of sects, as would commonly occur in other specialist areas such as sexual abuse.[773] Specialist training is likely to be important, however, in cases where a first-generation former member experiences a therapist engaging too much with their pre-sect history as opposed to fully recognising their sect experience. As

second-generation former members are often born into their sect, this is unlikely to occur in therapy for them.

Many therapists take a psychodynamic approach, which means they are likely to look at their clients' childhood experiences, therefore addressing the sect experience at some level. Nevertheless, specialist psychological assistance from mental health professionals who specialise in the treatment of trauma and have an understanding of sects might be beneficial. Furthermore, if a therapist or counsellor has the humility to recognise that they don't know much about sects, and are willing to be pointed to reading material and have the client educate them about this area, this is a positive sign about the individual therapist and may be therapeutic for the client, who finds that they are an expert in one field, at least.

CHOOSING A THERAPIST

In addition to providing information on the different therapy schools, it is worth noting that research examining which counselling approach is best generally has found that there is not one best style of counselling.[774] All are similar in their positive benefit to people. Therapy is essentially a personal relationship between two people, the client and the therapist, and the particular complexities of that relationship are not very amenable to scientific testing.[775] However, some therapists are more experienced, others less experienced. Some therapists and counsellors are good and others are not good at what they do.

There are also therapists who can be harmful to a client. It is therefore important that if you are considering therapy or counselling to be selective about whom you choose and select a therapist that is right for you. Every client is different and also every therapist or counsellor is different. It therefore follows that a therapist whom your co-worker thinks is wonderful may leave you uncomfortable, or a therapist you find excellent may not appeal to your friend.

The initial session with a counsellor or therapist is as much about your finding if this person is right for you, as it is about them getting to know you a little. Ask pertinent questions. A therapist who is not comfortable with the questions below will probably not be a good therapist for former sect members.

Suggested questions that you might ask a therapist, along with some thoughts on responses include:

1. How much does the therapy cost?
   If you are unable to cover this cost or think it is very high, you might try and find a therapist who charges less or ask whether the therapist has a sliding scale for those on lower incomes or benefits.
2. What school of therapy/counselling do you use?
   If it is a school of therapy you have not heard of, you might want to look it up to see what you think about it and talk to others before making a decision about the therapist.
3. For how long have you been doing counselling/therapy?
   It is possible that a person might be a good therapist after 10 months of experience or a poor therapist after 10 years of experience, however, as a general rule of thumb, the more experienced a therapist, the more time they have had to improve and become a better therapist.
4. What counselling/therapy qualifications do you have?
5. Are you an accredited counsellor or do you belong to an association of counsellors, if so which one? (If you are in the US you could ask if they are licensed.)
6. Do you receive supervision?
   In the US, experienced therapists tend not to have regular supervision, so having supervision might or might not be a useful indicator of a good therapist.
7. Have you counselled former members of sects before?
8. How long might the counselling process be likely to take?

Further questions suggested by Dr Margaret Singer and Janja Lalich[776] in their book *Crazy Therapies: What are they? Do they work?* include:

9. 'Do you usually set treatment goals with a client? How are those determined? How long do you think I will need therapy?
10. Will you see my partner, spouse, or child with me if necessary in the future?
11. Are you reachable in a crisis? How are such consultations billed?'

It is important for those in the UK to be aware that in this country at the moment you can set yourself up as a counsellor/therapist and charge clients a lot of money for counselling, and yet have had no training or even experience of giving therapy. Some of the questions above are suggested with a view to your finding out whether this is the case with the therapist/counsellor you are speaking with. However, these are not must ask questions, rather they are suggestions of the types of questions that you could ask. You may have questions of your own which are very different from those above.

The register of Trauma Specialists report that: 'A therapist is there to work for your best interests within an ethical framework. They are responsible for respecting boundaries and their behaviour towards you can be summed up as forming part of their 'duty of care' towards you. In short, their job is to help you to get better. It is always best to avoid therapists who:

- insist that you need to recover hidden or repressed memories
- tell you all about their own problems
- attempt to make contact with you socially
- ask questions that make you uncomfortable'[777]

Clearly, as the therapist does not know you, initially if a therapist seems like someone who might work well with you, it may be worthwhile giving that person a little time, such as four therapy/counselling sessions, before making a firm judgement on whether you wish to continue therapy/counselling with them.

SUMMARY OF CHAPTER 9

Healthy relationships are vital to recovery from a sect experience, but we are all different and none of us are identically affected by an experience and so recovery from an experience does not happen in an identical fashion either. However, human love, care and support can take many different forms, and can come from all sorts of different people. Having slowly built trust, 'what do you think?' might be a crucial question that those supporting second- generation former members might often find themselves asking.

Support may come from family members such as grandparents or other blood relatives who might be really important relational lifelines, both for second generation who are in a sect and those who have left. Relationships between parents and the second generation may be good, non-existent or strained. Acknowledging the interference of the sect in the relationship between parents and children can be helpful to both parties. Intimacy with others requires trust and vulnerability, but allows us to know we are not alone, and gives us the opportunity of receiving input. Siblings may be an important source of support as may a good mentor who comes with both risks and benefits. Support from peers who were also raised in groups can be helpful. Second-generation former members who acquire or keep a faith or spirituality may feel confused and have particular difficulties with spiritual groups, knowing whom to trust and reading religious texts.

Counselling can be an important source of social support. Different types or schools of counselling exist each could contribute positively to a second-generation former member's recovery, e.g. a specialist trauma therapist or a client-centred or psychodynamic therapist. It is important to choose the right therapist, and asking questions of a therapist prior to commencing counselling can be a good way of gauging whether they are the right counsellor for you.

What comes next in Chapter 10?

Not everyone who has been hurt or harmed by a sect experience wants or needs a therapist. It is relationships that are essential to our recovery, but not necessarily a therapist or counsellor. The next chapter looks further at different factors that might also assist with recovery from a sect experience, including how long it might take to recover from such an experience.

> *Even though I registered for college, I needed to learn subjects and skills about the outside world that would never appear in their course catalogues. Timid and uneasy, I had switched from being the Chosen One, the bold, confident leader, fully comfortable performing on stage before hundreds of people, to a shy, back-row observer. Watching the natural reactions of students and faculty, I was jealous of their seeming unity. They shared a background and culture of American normality. After time, I discovered that Queens College had a large percentage of recent immigrants enrolled, eager to begin their American experience, and it was with this group of students that I felt the most in common.[778]*

CHAPTER 10

HOW LONG?

Sometimes an ordinary life is an extraordinary achievement.'

[Second-generation former member – Moving On]

OVERVIEW

For those former sect members who have been very negatively affected by a sect experience, this chapter examines the time it might take to recover from such an experience. It looks at psycho-educational support, when guilt is irrational and when it is helpful, shame, learning about a culture, decision-making, 'feet of clay', and forgiveness. It moves on to discuss the suffering of the first generation and the human need for comfort, humour and enjoying life. The chapter finishes by firstly discussing how we can impact the lives of current members in sects and briefly examines the potential positive impact the second generation can have on other people.

RECOVERY TIME SCALE

Second-generation former members are each completely unique and have differing experiences both during and after sect membership. Recovery for some second-generation former members might take many years and may still leave scars. Furthermore, an initial lack of psychological distress might be indicative of the sense of freedom and

288

enthusiasm initially felt on exiting the sect, although psychological distress might follow.

Former members in some of the samples discussed in this book had what psychologists call 'clinical levels of harm' (i.e. serious levels of harm), despite it being many years since they left their sect. Even with therapy, harm of this level and intensity in the formative years of an individual's life may leave long-term damage, some parts of which may remain with the individual throughout their life. Especially in these circumstances, the perseverance displayed by second-generation former members is noteworthy, and perhaps it is these former members who specifically, in light of developmental trauma and despite the cliché, consider that it is about 'the journey, as opposed to the destination'. The emotional wounds and scars from sect membership may be used creatively[779] to impart something positive to others[780] and perhaps it is these former members who are most aware that meaning can be found in suffering[781] as discussed in Chapter 8.

Perseverance may well be familiar to second generation former members as it is related to their ability to get through their childhood and to keep going after leaving. Given the sheer quantity of new skills they may need to acquire, knowledge gaps that need filling, as well as the emotional, spiritual and cognitive aspects of their experience that they often have to work through, (although done in a sequential way where possible, one at a time, as opposed to simultaneously, so as not to be overwhelmed) it is perseverance, determination and the support of others that make this possible.

Some second-generation former members reported an initial feeling of psychological health after leaving, reflecting the feeling of freedom and relief on first exiting the sect. Former members, who experience delayed-onset PTSD (i.e., PTSD which comes after a period of time), might initially be dissociated after sect membership and consequently may report a feeling of numbness as opposed to any strong feeling. They may also experience depersonalisation, a sense of being outside looking in. This may be because of the loss of identity and life structure after leaving the sect or it could be related to dissociative experiences in the sect.[782]

However, one study I did found that for those who had received counselling, the further the time away from their sect experience, the less psychological distress symptoms they displayed.[783] Different types of counselling are discussed in Chapter 9.

Psycho-educational support

Those who have been raised in sects may have a sense of not being 'normal'.[784] Perhaps one of the primary needs of those exiting sects is to feel a sense of understanding and belonging with others. Integrating into another culture may be difficult, and they may feel a sense of alienation. While the research area of sects and access to resources, particularly with reference to the second generation, is still growing, it may be beneficial to the second generation to access the resources of others. An area of psycho-educational support might include information on 'third culture kids' (defined in Chapter 7 as 'a person who has spent a significant part of his or her developmental years outside the parents' culture.'[785]). As discussed, some second-generation former members are in fact third-culture kids (TCK's) or may relate to the experience of TCK's. There are resources available for TCK's, including books and conferences, which some second-generation former members might find helpful. Research on first-generation former sect members indicates that counselling and psychotherapy are only marginally helpful before they have learned about the influence techniques that affected them.[786] In addition to the different topics already discussed in this book, there are a number of psycho-educational topics that might also be helpful for second generation former members, such as:

- social influence processes
- the dynamics of traumatic bonding;
- the difference between unjustified or irrational guilt and standard guilt;
- shame; and
- self esteem

How we learn about a culture, and other psycho-educational topics, will now be briefly discussed:

LEARNING ABOUT A CULTURE
Bandura's social learning theory states that:

> 'Those who figure prominently in children's lives serve as indispensable sources of knowledge that contribute to what and how children think about different matters. Indeed, children's intellectual self-development would be stunted if they could not draw on this heritage of knowledge in each realm of functioning and, instead, had to rediscover it, bit by bit, through their own trial and error activity'.[787]

If the second generation is able to understand how individuals raised in normal societies learn, it might help them understand their need for what is sometimes embarrassing (as in the example below) social support, or understand their own frustrations with trial and error in the realms of social functioning.

What follows is a personal anecdote from my own life, which is then discussed in terms of Bandura's model:

> *As probably some of you are aware, pubs are a major source of recreation here in the UK. I was 17 when I first left my group and I was working at a local supermarket. Everyone I worked with always*

went on about the pub really positively, and I thought that pubs must be amazing places judging by the way people talked about them. So I decided that I would visit one. I mentioned this to one of my work colleagues and they helped me with this. One of them invited me to their home and I had a bit of a tasting session with various drinks that they had. I found one that didn't tasted as disgusting as the others and memorised the name of it.

A couple of weeks later on my day off from work I plucked up the courage and decided to go to the pub. At around 3 pm I entered the pub, went to the bar and asked for the drink whose name I had memorised. They gave me the drink and I went and sat down with drink in hand. As I continued to sit there with my drink, I started to wonder why everyone at work went on about the pub being such an amazing place. I had failed to realise that part of the appeal of going to a pub is socialising with others and I had entered the pub on my own. At that point in time, I still hadn't grasped the importance of relationships with others; that other people's company can be a very enjoyable experience. Of course a group of my colleagues took me to the pub for my 18th birthday and this significantly helped me in understanding why my colleagues seemed to so enjoy going to pubs.

In this case, I received some limited instruction. I received encouragement (motivation) to try new behaviours. However, I suspect I did not share my individual pub experience with anyone at the time and so I did not receive any feedback, which is perhaps why it was many years later before I fully understood this experience, because I didn't know, what I didn't know. Doubtless the best learning that I received here was actually going to the pub with my colleagues for my 18th birthday, an experience I still remember to this day. I am grateful to have had such supportive colleagues when I left my group.

When one thinks about the sheer number of new behaviours, rules and limits that must be learned, usually without the social support that kids get, the wonder is how well we all adjust, rather than how many problems we have. Somebody once described second-generation former members as a bunch of kids (actually adults now) trying to get an education without any teachers. Those of us who succeed develop character, for sure. But how many fail, or limp along hampered by a lack of cultural comfort, but still holding down jobs and functioning?

SOCIAL SKILLS TRAINING

It is likely that those second-generation former members who have been in very isolated groups will, over time in mainstream society, begin to pick up social skills in a very natural way. However, bearing in mind the lack of socialisation experiences of those raised in groups like Harry's Sect or more isolated groups where there is no interaction in mainstream society, a few individuals might benefit from social skills training. Social skills are those skills that enable people to understand and interact well with others. In addition to those who struggle with mental health issues, 7% of the general population could benefit from social skills training, particularly the young.[788]

The most effective way of teaching social skills involves modelling, instructions, realistic role-play practice and an instructor to give feedback.[789] These are extremely similar to Albert Bandura's[790] social learning theory on how children learn different social behaviours in childhood. Acquiring the skills to be able to assert oneself, where appropriate, is a subset of interpersonal skills found within social skills training,[791] which some former members might find useful depending on which sect they have left and their role within the sect.

Conversely, again depending on group and experience, some second-generation former members might want to think about becoming a little less assertive, particularly if their assertiveness has a negative effect on those whom they interact with, e.g. if people seem fearful – a sure sign that we are overdoing it! The black-and-white mentality of the sect, either total subservience or total dominance can make it hard to learn alternative perspectives.

GUILT: IRRATIONAL OR HELPFUL

Unjustified or irrational guilt, as well as sometimes being one of the outcomes of traumatic experiences, can also result from emotional abuse and other experiences within the sect. Irrational guilt can be an issue that those exiting sects have to really grapple with after leaving. Guilt is a human feeling that we have not measured up to a standard. Guilt is a conflict we experience when we have done something we believe we should not have done or when we haven't done something we believe we should have done. Distinguishing between irrational guilt and helpful guilt is important. If we experienced no guilt in life we would likely be a psychopath, some guilt is useful. For example, if I think about punching an old woman and then feel guilty, that may stop me punching the old woman and I would not violate my own standards.

Guilt involves a lot of 'shoulds' and 'oughts' to do and not do, and whether we are meeting a particular standard or not. But the question is where is that standard coming from? Is it a standard set by a sect leader whose primary aim was to control you? Or is the guilt representing a useful standard that you want to live by, or the law of the land that we must obey or risk the consequences? This guilt is useful. Irrational guilt, on the other hand, doesn't ask us to do anything. It instead has a crushing effect on us.

Whose standard we are meeting is a legitimate question which can help us distinguish between irrational and justified guilt. Unjustified and irrational guilt can block relationships with other people. Identifying and getting rid of irrational guilt is important. Helpful guilt can result in positive change in our lives, either in terms of reparation in some way, or a resolve to make changes for the future. Ruminative guilt –gnawing repetitive guilt that won't go away – may be linked to misplaced or false responsibility.

A feeling of responsibility for events beyond our control is a classic example of false or irrational guilt, which is unlikely to go away unless we recognise it for that. It may be very difficult or impossible to repair damage that you didn't do or to make constructive changes for the future, because it wasn't your fault anyway. Ruminative guilt could be a result of irrational guilt. It might be present because of an absence of positive change, or it could be that someone has moved to the feeling of shame, which is discussed in the next section.[792]

SHAME

While guilt says that we have done something wrong – e.g., made a mistake – shame says there is something wrong with us. In its extreme, it says we are a mistake. Shame is a very painful feeling that can come attached with guilt. If we have an experience of guilt that starts with the thought 'Phew, what a horrible thing I have done', but then we think further and increase and generalise that thought to 'and aren't I a horrible person?' then we have moved from tension and remorse over a specific behaviour to self-directed feelings of contempt and disgust about ourselves. We have moved from guilt to irrational shame in our thinking, which is essentially unhelpful and damaging to ourselves.[793]

Shame is viewed by most as essentially very destructive. It can lead to a profound sense of hopelessness and despair, and may be of central importance in our understanding of suicidal behaviour. Furthermore, research[794] seems to indicate that there is no apparent benefit from the pain of shame, it is generally thought that it does not stop problematic behaviours such as deterring people from engaging in criminal activities. However, perhaps this is only because people think they won't get caught and therefore I am inclined to think that perhaps more research needs to be done to see whether shame can at times affect our behaviour.

It is still, however essential that we move away from either external or internal voices that exploit shaming for abusive purposes. It is important that those raised in sects ensure that they adjust their thinking, particularly those raised in sects that promote and encourage shame, including through beliefs about self. For example, in Harry's Sect there was what is referred to in theological circles as 'worm-based' theology, which is a very negative view of self. Beliefs such as these about oneself need correcting or our self-esteem will continue to be at rock bottom. I think the following quote, commonly attributed to Winston Churchill,[795] deals quite succinctly with this particular type of theology 'I know that we are all worms, but I do think that I am a glow-worm?' It is to self-esteem that we now turn.

SELF-ESTEEM

How we view ourselves is important. Those raised in sects may have been given negative labels and words while in the sect. We enjoy life more when our self-esteem is of a good level, allowing us to experience more positive relationships with others. Part of a healthy level of self-esteem includes recognising that each and every person on this planet, including ourselves, is valuable and has worth and rights as is expanded on in the Universal Declaration of Human Rights[796] (a declaration adopted by the United Nations General Assembly which outlines the rights that human beings are inherently entitled to). Much has been written about self-esteem but rather than going into details about it, I am going to simply make two suggestions that might be particularly applicable to those exiting sects:

1. Avoid making negative statements about oneself. Most of us in our lifetime will generally hear enough negative statements

about ourselves from others. Despite trying not to, if you still find that you make negative statements about yourself, think about where you got the idea from and why you think like this. Is it possible that the negative statement is not true?

2. Do not let other people put you down. In the same way, it's not a good idea to make negative statements about ourselves, it's also not a good idea to let others make them about us. If you are unsure how to do this, a simple response, like 'I'd appreciate it if you don't make that sort of comment, thank you', can often work.

A healthy level of self-esteem can assist us in feeling a sense of belonging and feeling connected to others in a positive way.

DECISION-MAKING

After involvement in a sect, decision making can be tough, especially when our sense of who we are is diminished or when we are heavily dissociated, at which point all major decision-making might be best delayed where possible. For those former members who are not used to taking decisions, the sheer quantity of decisions that need to be made can be overwhelming. Even shopping can be tough, with its vast array of different types, prices, shapes and sizes of everything. Decisions that we never had to take are suddenly ours to be taken. While some of these decisions may be a welcome freedom, others may feel like a bind and a burden, but still the decisions need to be taken. So how do we decide?

> Depending on the particular sect an individual has exited, it may be that former members may be accustomed to seeing all decisions from a moral compass. However, the reality is that the majority of decisions have no moral consequences, there are no rights and wrongs to them. We could go either way, or perhaps there is a third or fourth option that we haven't yet thought of that we might want to choose.

According to the American Psychological Association (APA),[797] part of resilience is sticking with a decision – following it through. While the application of sticking with a decision is not an entirely rigid thing, nevertheless it might be a good general rule of thumb once a decision has been made. So how do we take decisions, generally smaller decisions, like what colour shirt to wear. They are made according to the activities expected during the day – for example, work uniforms, hiking clothes, etc. – or they are made according to our likes and dislikes, according to our whims on a particular day. For larger decisions which have greater consequences, weighing up the pros and cons and even talking to a non-directive friend can be helpful. Whole books have been written about decision-making. However, as we take more and more decisions, they get easier and on the whole we gradually learn that many, if not most, decisions that we take are not concerned with right and wrong, and don't have eternal consequences or even much consequence at all. Furthermore, making a poor decision can act as a learning experience for us and as such can be useful.

FEET OF CLAY

As others have expanded on, all human beings have feet of clay. Nancy Kohen writes on the area of leadership, in an article entitled 'On the Fallacy of Perfection'.[798] She says:

> 'Flawlessness, like worthlessness, in any human being is an illusion. The more we uncover about any person's life, no matter how perfect it seems at first glance, the more complicated we see that it really is. Alongside each positive personal trait, such as my father's intelligence, live vulnerabilities, like his diffidence. In a similar vein, an individual's weaknesses coexist with his or her strengths. If we had the luxury of reading an honest biography of any successful person, there would be not only paragraphs but whole chapters on their frailties and

failures: stories of the lost election, the broken marriage, or all the deals that fell apart.'

Current members, former members, sect leaders, friends, enemies, therapists and every other human being we meet do in fact have feet of clay, and as we get to know a person, either their weaknesses become apparent or they are hiding their weaknesses, or they just don't stand out obviously. In sects, leaders are put on pedestals. The second generation are sure to have witnessed and may have had to take part in adoration and/or flattery of the leader/s in order to avoid suffering, to avoid being emotionally or even physically hurt in the sect.

In his autobiography, Mike Finch expands on the cycle of reinforcement between a guru and his followers, and discusses how adoration can affect us. Flattery too can have a very detrimental effect on people. Following the rule of thumb of being careful to only give honour to people where honour is due breaks the cycle of reinforcement and also ensures that we do not disparage others in our attempts to break the negative cycle of reinforcement,.

Realising that others are imperfect can assist us in realising that we too cannot expect perfection from ourselves, as Nancy Kohen[799] writes:

'As we set our sights on perfection – on an all-encompassing, no-holds-barred embrace of specific ways of being – an even bigger problem emerges: we apply that same expectation to ourselves. Unrelenting success – being at the top of that hill, all the time – becomes our barometer, the impossible but seductive standard against which we have to measure up. When we fall short – and, invariably, we all do – and make mistakes or encounter failure, the result is a deep sense of shame, which can lead to a sense of overwhelming inadequacy. We often swing from one extreme to another in our opinion of ourselves. Those feelings, produced by the inability to live up to our own mythologized view of success, can be corrosive. They are frequently draining and all-consuming, and prevent us from learning from our mistakes, seeing others and ourselves more realistically, and productively moving forward in our lives and careers.'

FORGIVENESS

I am tentative about discussing forgiveness because of the way that too many groups misuse it. Forgiveness is defined by the Oxford Minidictionary[800] as to 'cease to feel angry or bitter towards or about.' For former members it can be a very difficult concept. However, following on from feeling angry over injustices we and others such as family members have suffered, looking at forgiveness may be helpful to former members. Forgiveness cannot be rushed and it cannot be coerced. After acknowledging harm experienced and after feeling angry, former members may find it helpful to think about what they consider forgiveness is and what they consider it is not.

If working out what forgiveness is and what it is not proves difficult, then reading what others have written on the topic could prove useful[801]. However, if you don't feel the need to forgive or you aren't at a place where you are ready to consider it, or if you have already heard far too much about forgiveness to want to hear anything else about it, or if you would prefer not to read about what others have said about forgiveness, you might want to skip this section.

Marina Cantacuzino set up the Forgiveness Project and the F word exhibition which is a collection of personal narratives as well as images that explore forgiveness in the face of atrocity. She[802] writes that:

'forgiveness cuts public opinion down the middle like a guillotine. There are those who see forgiveness as an immensely noble and humbling response to atrocity – and then there are those who simply laugh it out of court. For the first group, forgiveness is a value strong enough to put an end to the tit-for-tat settling of scores that has wreaked havoc over generations. But for the second group, forgiveness is just a cop-out, a weak gesture, which lets the violator off the hook and encourages only further violence. This is why we called the exhibition, The F Word. For some people, forgiveness is a very dirty word indeed.'

In describing the vengeful comments of some about the killers of two-year-old James Bulger (who was abducted from a shopping centre by two 10-year-old boys, walked over two miles to a railway line where he was tortured and his body left on the track to be cut in two. The 10-year-old boys were later found guilty of murder and the full awful details of the events of that day resulted in widespread grief and anger across the UK[803]), Marina Cantacuzino[804] states that

'I do not believe revenge makes anyone feel any better, but also it seems to me that the desire to mete out equal injury to those who have harmed others means we become a little like them ourselves.'

There is a growing body of research indicating that forgiveness is good for our mental well-being. In short, forgiveness does us good, is transformative and is essential to recovery.[805] Not forgiving results in us holding onto pain and negative emotions, that, if allowed to continue could harm us psychologically and physically.[806] I see forgiveness as a bit like cutting ourselves off from a festering ball and chain, however, I also recognise that reaching a point of forgiving an individual does not mean that a person necessarily stops being negatively affected by an experience, although it may bring significant release, nor does it mean forgetting. I would say that forgiveness is a process, which doesn't happen overnight and yet can happen too quickly. It is necessary to acknowledge harm and hurt and it is essential not to have forgiveness short-circuit this process.

Some view forgiveness as a choice, an intensely personal one.[807] However, I would argue that while forgiveness may start as a choice in our heads, it is in fact something that needs to happen in our hearts. Realising the negative impact that unforgiveness can have on us, such as keeping us locked up in an experience and unable to be free of it, as well as impacting us in other ways such as our health, can assist us with the head choice.

Forgiveness is a dignified response. Marina Cantacuzino[808] states that:

> 'For many people forgiveness is no soft option, but rather the ultimate revenge. For many, it is a liberating route out of victimhood; a choice, a process, the final victory over those who have done you harm. As Mariane Pearl, the wife of murdered journalist Daniel Pearl, said of her husband's killers, "The only way to oppose them is by demonstrating the strength that they think they have taken from you."'

Nevertheless, as she explains, the cost of forgiveness is high and can be intensely painful. However, it is transformative. Sometimes the hardest person to forgive is ourselves, but forgiving ourselves is a necessity. Forgiveness is pricey, but the cost of unforgiveness can be higher, as it doesn't only affect us emotionally but can impact our physical health and relationships. Sometimes we may think that by withholding forgiveness we harm someone, and in that way exact revenge for what has been robbed, however, I think that the reality is that by not forgiving, as well as having been originally robbed of something by someone else (the original offence), we do further damage to and rob and harm ourselves.

Personally (in this instance I am not talking about anything sect-related and it was a relatively minor item), I have at times experienced physical symptoms from allowing resentment to grow within me. Forgiveness is not easy. It is independent of whether or not the person who has wronged us acknowledges their guilt and it is independent of whether they show any remorse. As Kristina Jones[809] records about her stepfather in her autobiography when he appeared to want to repair their relationship, yet did not show remorse for his actions, which included sexual molestation when she was a child: *'There was a place in my heart that pitied him, but though I had forgiven him, it was too late. The past could not be undone.'*

Expressing forgiveness for someone who has wronged us in a serious way before they have demonstrated any remorse by word and action may be inadvisable. Those who have wronged us can either hinder or make forgiveness a little easier. The absence of remorse; glossing over of wrongs; denial of actions; the minimising or justification of actions, particularly when they have caused serious harm to another; and doing, saying, or omitting to do things can make forgiveness harder. But a timely, sincere, heartfelt apology that includes an acknowledgement of harm and responsibility for actions without justification of actions can make forgiving a person easier, as at times can their positive actions or words as well.

Responding appropriately to someone who offers us forgiveness is also important. A simple 'thank you for saying that, I can hear you really mean it' can go a long way in being helpful to the person expressing forgiveness.

Forgiveness then is not being blind, thoughtless, wimpy or weak. It may well not include reconciliation, a bigger process of which forgiveness is just a part. Reconciliation for some second-generation former members may not be possible, for example with the sect leader, or family members in a sect who refuse all contact, and it's not letting the person 'off the hook' legally, it's not glossing over wrongs, it's not pardoning, condoning or excusing. Forgiveness does not remove consequences.

THE SUFFERING OF THE FIRST GENERATION AND THE HUMAN NEED FOR COMFORT

The suffering of parents and the suffering of others who joined sects in adulthood can be enormous. Those who have not received comfort previously may be uncomfortable and mistrustful of those who seek to provide it.

Acknowledging the harm experienced and effects of the second generation's upbringing on into adulthood does not diminish in any way the suffering of adults who join sects. Suffering is not about comparisons. There will always be people who have suffered less and people who have suffered more. The suffering of the first generation has already in part been documented elsewhere. In contrast, less has been known about the suffering of the second generation and resultant effects in adulthood and therefore this area has received comparatively little attention in the writing in this field. It is my hope and desire that through this book at least some of those raised in sects will know that they are not alone in their experiences. There are others, too, who have experienced what they have experienced, who have felt what they have felt, or who have had similar thoughts, similar challenges, difficulties, joys and sorrows.

Suffering involves experiencing pain, and where there is pain there is a need for comfort which is defined in the Oxford minidictionary as:

'relief of suffering or grief'.[810]

Some second-generation former members may have lived much or all of their life with little or no comfort, which lends itself to a life of despair. Further, without the experience of being comforted, we are, as discussed in Chapter 8, likely to seek comfort in other things such as drugs or alcohol as we seek to dull the pain. Comfort is something that we receive.

Being able to express ourselves, perhaps through words or tears, allows others to see and realise our need for comfort, and therefore invites the compassion of others and the delivery of comfort. Therefore, the ability to be vulnerable with safe others, increases our chances of having others seek to provide comfort. The ability to receive comfort may be something that we have to work towards.

Finances and opportunities after the sect

Some children in sects grow up in relative poverty. This may be because their parents give a significant part of their income to the sect, or because they are one of many children, or because their parents earn very little or no money (they may work for the sect or be part of a communal group) or some combination of the former. I have spoken to second-generation former members who when growing up didn't have coats and warm clothing despite bitterly cold weather. I have spoken to those who did not have enough to eat as children. They experienced such poverty that their basic needs were not met. In other sects while children's basic needs were met, the children had no luxuries and may, for example, have only worn clothes also worn by other children in the sect or family, have never visited a restaurant and had very limited possessions.

After leaving such an environment and having now to fend for themselves, habits learned in the sect can be difficult to shed. For those who leave with their parents, the first generation themselves may be having to start out from scratch at older ages.

> I remember a second-generation former member (who has given me permission to share this here), telling me about how when he first left his sect, the landlord of the place he was renting came to speak to him because the electricity bill was so low. It turned out that my second generation former member friend owned one lightbulb. When he went into another room in the accommodation, he unscrewed the one light bulb and then screwed it back into the ceiling in the next room. He did not realise that most people have a light bulb in each room.

While second-generation former members might rightly see knowing what's important in life and learning to live with little money as positive things that they learnt from the sect environment, living and spending time with people who don't come from poverty can assist former members with understanding how others operate in the area of finances and the choices open to us in terms of how we spend our money. It is possible for individuals to expect to be poor and feel hopeless about changing that, and indeed some second-generation former members may have been taught that poverty was a good thing.

Reassessing our beliefs about finances may be important as is valuing ourselves, having dignity and realising that there is no reason that we can't, for example, if we are self- employed, charge the going rate for work we do.[811] To some extent, in today's culture money is a measure of self-worth, if we have been influenced by this thinking then an increase in self-worth may be directly related to our willingness to look for and accept a higher wage.

Becoming aware of our choices in life, such as our options in terms of gaining education, training in a particular field, and changing employment is important in terms of us understanding that change in life circumstances can be possible. Seeing different events and changes as opportunities that we are determined to make the most of can be helpful particularly in terms of overcoming negative or depressive thoughts and moving forward with our lives.

Transferrable skills

Those raised in sects may have learnt skills that others who have been raised in mainstream culture did not acquire in their childhood. After the sect these skills can be very useful and may even form the basis of a lucrative career. For example, those raised in sects where they had to earn money for the group via selling flowers or talking to people outside the group to evangelise them, may find that they have transferrable skills which enable them to become excellent sales people. Skill sets will vary dependent on the group and experiences in the group. Identifying these skills and then utilising them may be a very important part of the transition to finding ones way after the sect. Transferrable skills are an asset to an employer and are likely to be valued. Discussing these skills in job applications in a way that shows their usefulness in terms of the job applied for is important, as it may make the difference between getting a job and not getting a job.

Former membership of a sect may at times result in some individuals discovering talents and gifts and again these can be important indicators of potential areas of enjoyable employment for the individual or an area the individual might want to explore further within education.

Identifying skills and gifts is also important for our self-concept and self-esteem, so regardless of the group and experiences in the group, it might just be the case that careful consideration of this area might throw up some unexpected but useful items that can be helpful to us as people both for ourselves and our lives.

HUMOUR

Some second-generation former members may have had to produce a plastic smile on cue, although the sect environment itself may have been mostly painful, and/or scary and/or boring. In some sects, humour was not an option. Tears and laughter can be very similar and while tears may elicit compassion and comfort from others, if we are not in a place where we can receive that, then laughter may at least be a way of our expressing some of our emotions. Black humour can certainly be therapeutic and some second-generation have a lively black-humour wit, which should not be underestimated in terms of its therapeutic benefit.

Perhaps one of the readers of this book will be encouraged to begin, with permission from their storytellers, to document the bizarre and hilarious stories that so many former members have. They could perhaps form a rather mind-boggling, interesting and humorous read, perhaps in the form of a book, blog or website.

ENJOYING LIFE

For those raised in Harry's Sect and some other sects, the time taken in sect-related activities, coupled with the restrictions and rules by which most sect members have to abide, means that most current members have had very little time to enjoy life and engage in the type of play that those not raised in sects may experience. In some groups, engaging in play activities purely for the purpose of enjoyment is discouraged or forbidden. A startling example of the withdrawal of children's toys by the imprisoned leader of the FLDS, Warren Jeffs, is found below:

'A year-long investigation by ABC News' '20/20' revealed that Jeffs' presence extends far beyond his prison walls and into the daily lives of his faithful followers. It started when he ordered followers to destroy all of their children's toys.

At home you couldn't have any toys. You couldn't ride bikes either. 'Cause he gave away all our bikes. I didn't even get a chance to ride mine before I gave it away,' said 6-year-old Nellie Steed, who left the sect after her mother was banished by Jeffs.'[812]

On exiting Harry's Sect and other sects, former members might very much benefit from seeking to enjoy their life and newfound freedom, where possible. This relates to the finding that some of those raised in Harry's Sect, reported really struggling after leaving, but also living their childhood fast-forward.[813] They made up for lost time and did all sorts of activities that they had previously not had the freedom to do.

The smallest kindness

Before concluding this book, which has discussed former members in some depth, some readers may want to know how they can positively impact the lives of current members in groups. What can be done? Aside from ensuring that charities have available, adequate resources to assist and support people when they choose to leave these groups, there is another key thing that can be done: I call this the smallest kindness.

We have all heard that sometimes it's the smallest things in life that matter the most. In reading a number of autobiographies of those who have spent time in sects, it is evident that the smallest kindnesses sometimes have the most impact. For example, Masoud Banisadr, a first-generation former member who is also a father to two children born in a sect, records the following in his book:[814]

On the plane I fell asleep immediately, as I hadn't slept for almost two days. When I woke up, an elderly African-American woman in the next seat offered me some food and drink. 'I kept everything that was brought for you because I knew you would be very hungry when you

woke up,' she said, adding, 'I felt that it was not only sleep you needed.'
I was so moved I wanted to hug her and weep my heart out. It had been
so long since I had received an ordinary kindness from anyone.

He goes on to reflect on the experience and how the sect rules meant
he had to report negatively on the experience:

For us everything was black and white: we in the organisation were white;
those outside, black. Yet here was a 'black' person with a heart of purest
white. Inevitably, I had to write a report about this in which I censured
myself for showing so much weakness in response to a kind gesture: a clear
sign that I was turning from a Mojahed [member of the sect he belonged
to] into an ordinary human being with ordinary needs and desires.

Another example of kindness involves the grandparents of Kristina
Jones, who visited her and her siblings when they were children in the
sect and living in India. She records that[815]:

For the last night of their visit, Nan and Papa said they would take
us to eat at Bombay's grandest hotel, the Taj Mahal. We had a lovely
meal accompanied by a string quartet. We chatted together and ignored
Joshua *[their step father] altogether as he sat sulking through the*
meal. As we expected, he waved away the dessert menu.

'Well, I'm having dessert! Papa insisted and ordered the king of ba-
nana splits.

As soon as Joshua left to go the toilet, Papa pushed the amazing
mountain of ice-cream, cherries and nuts over and told us to tuck
in. It was a rare moment of defiance, so we quickly stuffed our faces
while Nan kept watch. By the time Joshua returned the banana split
was gone. When we took them to the airport, we were all in tears as
we hugged goodbye. I was heart broken to see them go. On the train

back to Bangalore, I was silent. It was difficult to come down from the high of their visit.

Some of those with loved ones in a sect do not have the opportunity to give a kindness to their loved ones because contact is forbidden. Therefore, when we give a kindness to someone in a sect, we may never know when we are giving a kindness where loved ones want to, where they long to do just that, but their kindness would not be received and therefore they cannot. We may be impacting the life of a second generation in a sect who shrinks in fear away from siblings who have left as the siblings who have left have been 'demonised'.

It is important that we never underestimate the impact we can have on the lives of others. The more difficult their circumstances, the darker the times, and the greater the need, the larger our potential impact can be.

In answer then to the question – what can be done for current members? We can gift to current members small kindnesses that have the potential to radically impact lives, although we will likely never find out in what ways.

Strengths and the potential impact of the second generation

In a summary of their findings, researchers writing about adults who had been raised in Centrepoint recorded that it may be important to recognise that:

'although dysfunctional communities have the potential to create difficulties for adult life, they may also provide former child members with some strengths and capacities that they can draw on in this process. While this cannot justify the abuse of children that can and does occur in communities like Centrepoint, it is an important consideration in supporting and empowering the former child members of such communities to tackle the challenges they face in their lives. It may also help former child members to resist stigmatised representations. Allowing for the possibility of both good and bad experiences as well as advantages in adulthood may give children who have grown up in such communities the space to find meaning for themselves out of the complex social environment in which they spent their childhood.'[816]

As I write, some second-generation former members are putting themselves through university and gaining experience in different fields of work, including the legal field, social work, therapy, sociology, research, cross-cultural studies, creative arts, media studies, anthropology, religious studies and teaching. Some have a great deal of empathy and compassion for children in sects as well as for those who have left. Of all people, they have a very deep understanding of that experience.

In the years to come, the area of sects will have an increasing number of educated, experienced professionals who care deeply about the issue of children in sects and have a depth of experience and a burning compassion. I expect that the sect field as a whole will change as a result of these individuals. From this pool of people, our knowledge about children raised in sects will increase dramatically the number of available books, articles as well as internet and media information and understanding available to assist and empower the second generation will expand. The second generation will not only assist each other but will reach to the third and fourth generations and beyond that come after them. The poem below highlights some of the creativity that can come forth from the second generation:

A poem for my peers: No more disbelief

I've spoken to my peers
Listened to their stories
Each one unique and yet a common theme
Speaking of their lives:
'It wasn't so bad, not like so and so
No Kool aid did we drink'

Yet when they open their mouths and speak
Tell their stories with stilted tone
Or pour them out, like a gushing overflow
A burst pipe, through which, water must proceed

I watch the realisation hit
It really was that bad, can't believe that happened
But happen it really did
The stories they tell beggar belief
And yet their truth is not up for sale

A brave few write their autobiography
Then submit it to the fire
Memories purged
Burned up forever
Or out there for all to see
To risk the scalding eye
Of those who want to question,
Who disbelieve and judge from distance far

My peers and I we must express
Overcome the fear of disbelief
Fear that you'll question
That you will dismiss

Tell us were crazy
That really didn't happen

We need to talk, tell our stories
We'll write our poems and songs,
Our novels, plays and dramas
We get poetic licence
Of that we're really glad
You can't call into question

Creativity will burst forth
Our locked insides, have come undone
Plugged no longer
Out of us will emerge

Ruthless, random, surging, colourful, creativity
Bursting out from depths unseen
We will blind you with the vibrance of the colours
You will have to shield your eyes
There will be no more disbelief

> Second-generation former members can and have at times managed to change the landscape of sects for the benefit of their younger brothers and sisters and all those second-third-and-fourth generation former members and beyond who have come after them. There actions may even effect a sect in terms of it disbanding and it being no more.

As a sociological researcher, Amanda van Eck Duymaer van Twist speaking of former members from some of the larger groups who have sought to effect change in the groups that they come from records in her PhD[817]:

'Over time, they frequently can expect change. The 'outside' presence of young former members can initiate changes within groups over time, as the parents and the group realise that some of their children are unhappy and aim to accommodate them more and minimise criticism. But with rigid sectarian groups this is not always possible. The presence of KIT... [a group of former members] did change dynamics within the Brüderhof, but these were not the changes KIT requested – the group intensified its rigidity and became more litigious towards former members and critics. However, they do have more flexibility towards younger cohorts of former members.'

Over and above the field of sects, second-generation former members have a lot to offer this world. The depth of their experiences can powerfully impact others. Their creative skills can be huge. Here is a quote from a second-generation former member from Centrepoint:

So I'm learning about resilience and patience and my, and my [work in the arts] is.... I'm just bloody lucky to have found something that stabilises me, and really is giving me an opportunity to experience the wonderfulness of me.[818]

The second generation's ability to form deep bonds with others should not be underestimated. Their unique way of viewing the world can shed light on different circumstances. Their desire to change the world for good can be immense. Their knowledge and insight into human behaviour can potentially benefit different organisations and countries in so many ways. Their compassion and empathy for others, especially those who suffer, can be immense. Their strength in adverse circumstances may develop special attributes of perseverance. Time will tell how these different traits, attributes and skills will impact in many different spheres of life.

Given what has been discussed above it is my hope that second generation former members, especially those reading or listening to this are able to think positively about themselves. That you would realise your wonderfulness, if not today then at some near future point in your life. That one day, you will, like the second generation former member from Centrepoint *'experience the wonderfulness of'* you. [819]

SUMMARY OF CHAPTER 10

The experiences of people raised in sects may differ greatly dependent on numerous factors. We are all unique, and therefore uniquely affected by experiences, therefore there is huge variety in terms of the time it takes to recover from a sect experience. However, for some it may be many years, and so perseverance is an important characteristic of recovery.

Second-generation former members may have a large number of new skills as well as knowledge they need to acquire. Learning about a new culture and social functioning takes time, and includes both trial and error, however with time and opportunity, we invariably do learn. Resources former members might relate to include those currently developed for third-culture kids – those who have spent a significant part of their developmental years outside of the parent's culture.

Guilt can be helpful at times, as it lets us know that we haven't measured up to a standard, but it is important to know whose standard have we not measured up to: The sect leaders? Our own standard? Our parents' standard? Sometimes guilt can be irrational, and like shame, it can have a crushing and debilitating effect on us and therefore it is another area of recovery that former members may need to address.

Similarly, a healthy level of self-esteem is important as it allows us to experience more positive relationships with others and ourselves.

With practice decision-making gets easier. All decisions do not have moral consequences and many decisions have no right or wrong to them. There may also be third or fourth options that we might want to consider.

Flattering others can be a survival skill learnt in the group, but nevertheless it can have a very detrimental effect on others. Forgiveness is also discussed at length in this chapter, both the fact that it is misused by the groups and people's reticence towards it, as well as the fact that it is costly but brings benefits.

While suffering is not about comparisons as there will always be people who have suffered more and people who have suffered less, many first-generation former members, including parents and their children, have suffered enormously in sects. Where suffering has occurred, there is pain and consequently, there is a human need for comfort, something which is often lacking in sect environments. Receiving comfort allows us to avoid seeking comfort in other things such as drugs and alcohol to dull the pain.

Second-generation adults who have grown up in relative poverty, which was justified and encouraged via the group's doctrine may need to reassess their beliefs about finances, allowing themselves for example to charge the going rate for work undertaken. The black humour present in some second-generation former members can in itself be wonderfully therapeutic and fun to be around. Enjoyment of life is important especially because too many groups frown upon, discourage or forbid play activities that are merely for the purpose of enjoyment. Former members report very positively on having the freedom to finally enjoy forbidden items.

Those reading this book who are not themselves former members but instead are moved by the stories contained herein and wonder what they can do might be encouraged to be aware that the more difficult someone's circumstances, the more positive impact the smallest kindness can have, even when it comes from a stranger.

The second generation have fantastic potential to positively impact the lives of others in many different fields. They have strengths and creative potential; they may have a burning passion to ensure that future generations of children receive support and have childhoods that are different to their own. History has shown that some second generation former members that grow up in sects have at times and doubtless will continue to make a difference in the lives of the generations to come.

Conclusion

It is my hope that this book will be helpful to at least some second-generation former members. However, there is still a need for further research and writing in this area. There may be a high price to pay for going public with one's personal story, but those who choose to let their voice and experiences be heard in this way will doubtless positively impact the lives of others who have grown up in sects.

I hope that some of the readers of this book will take up the challenge to conduct research, write, develop plays and documentaries, and use other media, so that all second-generation former members might find other people whose experiences they can relate to and whose communication style and type is easily accessible and that each and every person raised in a sect will come to know that they are definitely not alone in what they have experienced.

Endnotes

Acknowledgements
1. Kanigel, 1986; Worth, 2000

Introduction
2. Barnett, Miller-Perrin and Perrin, 1997: 17

3. Out at Last, 2005

4. Wooden, 1981

5. Gibson, Morgan, Woolley, and Powis, 2010

6. Kendall, 2006

7. Ted's Sect practised hand-reading. A major part of what went on in Ted's Sect was self-analysis, which, as one former member put it, in the end amounted to the leaders telling you what you were like, and who you were and therefore what you needed to do to change. Another former member said of it:

   > 'So Darren was an expert in hand-reading so of course he knew what everybody was like much more than we knew what we were like.' Ted's Sect:2

   Szurko (Kendall, 2006: Appendix 32) talks of the use of hand-reading in the following way:

   > 'In practice, it sounds as though their hand-readings were done in such a way as, once more, to focus on either your existing negative cognitive structures or to create negative cognitive structures, which then could be used to control, manipulate and if necessary to discipline you. That would appear to be one of the major functions of it in the

group, as opposed to what people wanted to study for. As I say there were people who really got into studying it, who were interested because they were looking at it as a way of understanding their own character, a way of understanding their own tendencies. Well, I would say that the way the leadership used it was as a way of exposing ... '

8. Theroux, 2011

9. Burks, 2002

10. Anthony and Robbins, 1992

11. Burks, 2002

12. Barker, 1986

13. Cowan, 2002

14. Langone, 1992a

15. Giambalvo, 1992

16. Barker, 1986

17. MacHovick, 1991

18. Burks, 2002

19. Robbins, 2001: 73

20. Singer, 1995

21. Rubin, 1998

22. Burks, 2002

23. Kent and Krebs, 1998

24. Beit-Hallahmi, 2001; Robbins, 2001

25. Harry's Sect:195

CHAPTER 1

26. Ted's Sect:103

27. Giambalvo, 1999

28. Barker, 1989

29. Pfeifer, 1992

30. Saliba 1995: 1

31. Langone, 2003a

32. Barker, 1989

33. Langone, 1993

34. Mytton, 1993

35. Langone 1993

36. Singer, 1995

37. Martin, 1993

38. Barker, 1989: 4

39. Beckford and Levasseur, 1986: 29

40. Singer, 1995

41. Saliba, 1995

42. Saliba, 1995: 1

43. Szurko, 2002

44. Zablocki, 1997

45. Enroth, 1992

46. E.g. Langone, 1993

47. He suggests that some sects are benign, but this contradicts his own definition, which states that they necessarily cause psychological harm to members.

48. Langone, 1993: 5

49. Singer, 1995

50. Lifton, 1961

51. Lifton, 1961

52. Funari, 2004

53. Funari, 2005; 1

54. Barker, 1984; Anthony, 2001

55. Martin, Pile, Burks and Martin, 1998; Zablocki, 2001

56. Chambers, Langone, Dole and Grice 1994

57. Langone, 1992b

58. Gibson, Morgan, Woolley and Powis, 2010; Funari, 2005

59. Szurko, 2002: 1

60. Chorpita and Barlow, 1998

61. Finch, 2009

62. Herman, 1992

63. Harry's Sect:140

64. Szurko, 2002: 1

65. Milgram, 1974; Meesus and Raaijmakers, 1995

66. Smith and Bond, 1993

67. Haslam and Reicher, 2012: 1

68. Harry's Sect:71

69. Harry's Sect:123

70. McNally, 2003

71. E.g. Gross, 1992

72. Haslam and Reicher, 2012: 3

73. Haslam and Reicher, 2012: 2

74. Packer (2008) cited in Haslam and Reicher, 2012: 2

75. Burger, Girgis, and Manning (2011) cited in Haslam and Reicher, 2012: 2

76. Reicher and Haslam (2011) cited in Haslam and Reicher, 2012: 2

77. Szurko, 2002: 1

78. Langone, 1993

79. Harry's Sect:148

80. Ted's Sect:44

81. Dutton and Painter, 1981, 1994

82. Aronoff, Lynn and Malinoski, 2000

83. Dutton and Painter, 1981, 1994

84. Dutton and Painter, 1994

85. Ward, 2000

86. Harry's Sect:203

87. Ted's Sect:105

88. Haney, Curtis and Zimbardo, 1995

89. Szurko, 2002: 1

90. Szurko, 2002: 1

91. Szurko, 2002: 1

92. Jones, 2011a

93. Jones, 2014b

Chapter 2

94. Melton, 2008

95. Bardin, 2005

96. Bird and Reimer, 1982

97. Langone, 1993

98. Jansa, 2005

99. Informed consent to share this quote was obtained from this individual

100. Informed consent to share this quote was obtained from this individual

101. Barker, 1989

102. Bergman n.d.; Bergman, 1996

103. Bergman n.d.; Bergman, 1996: 1

104. Galanter, Rabkin, Rabkin, & Deutsch, 1979

105. Barker,1983

106. Langone, 1993

107. Taylor,1982

108. Langone, 1993

109. Langone, 1993:33

110. Sirkin, 1990: 119

111. E.g. West, 1993; Burks, 2002

112. Galanter, 1982

113. Stone, 1992

114. Galanter, 1982; Martin, 1989; Langone, 1995; Singer, 1995

115. Martin, 1989

116.   Maron and Braverman, 1988

117.   Ozer, Best, Lipsey and Weiss, 2003

118.   Clark, Langone, Schecter and Daly, 1981; Singer, 1986; Goldberg and Goldberg, 1982; Maron and Braverman, 1988; Langone, 1995

119.   Cushman, 1984

120.   Ted's Sect: 8, 9 and 10.

121.   Ted's Sect:9

122.   Ted's Sect:10

123.   Ted's Sect: 39

124.   Ted's Sect: 11

125.   Yeakley, 1988

126.   Yeakley, 1988

127.   Yeakley, 1988

128.   Eysenck and Eysenck, 1980

129.   Yeakley, 1988

130.   Beit-Hallahmi and Argyle, 1997; Richardson, Stewart and Simmonds, 1979

131. Kosmin and Lachman, 1993

132. Bergman, 1996

133. Refer to note six in the introduction for more information on what hand reading refers to in this context.

134. Bandura, 1982

135. Ted's Sect: 15.

136. Harry's Sect: 97, 98, 99, 100, 101.

137. Gibson, Morgan, Woolley, and Powis, 2010

138. Hochestetler, 2007: 9

139. Ted's Sect:29

140. Ted's Sect:30

141. Whitsett and Kent 2003: 495

142. Ayella, 1998

143. Asser and Swan, 2000

144. Helfer, 1983

145. Erikson 1959: 97

146. This links into Erikson's psychosocial state of generativity versus stagnation and self-absorption discussed in more depth in Chapter Four.

147.   Levinson, 1996: 365

148.   Levinson 1996

149.   Stein, 1997

150.   Bardin, 2005

151.   Wall, 2008: 22

152.   Tamm, 2009:22. Jayanti and Ketan's plan worked and they managed to acquire a bunny, selected on a trip out with their mother. The bunny later received a spiritual name from the guru. Jayanti, once even tried to teach the bunny to meditate but gave up when the bunny bit her.

CHAPTER 3

153.   Perry and Szalavitz, 2006: 69

154.   Siskind, 2001.

155.   A theory has been developed which integrates current research and theory in attachment behaviour, developmental psychopathology, trauma, dissociation and experiential psychotherapy (Thomas, 2003). This theory investigates the long-term effects of child abuse, and argues that children abused in childhood do not receive adequate caregiver protection, do not form internal representations of an effective protector, and consequently have on-going difficulties in defending themselves against interpersonal aggression and internal self-criticism (Thomas, 2003). Given the high levels of child abuse found in the samples and discussed further in the next chapter, testing the theory might be appropriate with this population, particularly since

the theory accounts for many of the clinical symptoms found in adult survivors of child abuse. Specific strategies for treatment are suggested in light of this theory (Thomas, 2005).

156.   Rajneesh, 1984: cited in Puttick, 1999

157.   Rajneesh, 1984:508 quoted in Puttick, 1999; 90

158.   Winfried Hempel quoted in Aljazeera, 2013

159.   Kendall, 2006, Appendix 5: 39-40

160.   Harry's Sect:54

161.   Harry's Sect: 63

162.   Harry's Sect: 58

163.   Osherow, 1984

164.   Harry's Sect:58

165.   Harry's Sect:73

166.   King, Akande and Dong, 1996

167.   Kendall, 2006

168.   Perry and Szalavitz, 2006:64

169.   Kochanska, Gross, Lin and Nichols, 2002

170.   Kochanska, Gross, Lin and Nichols, 2002

171.   Gullone and King, 1997

172.   Ollendick, and Yang, 1996

173.   Perry and Szalavitz, 2006:64

174.   Harry's Sect: 132.

175.   Harry's Sect:132

176.   Ted's Sect: 35, Harry's Sect: 12, 142.

177.   Harry's Sect: 140, Ted's Sect: 97.

178.   Kendall, 2006: Appendix 5: 31-32, 143

179.   Stein, 1997

180.   Wooden, 1981

181.   Moos and Moos, 1986

182.   Moos and Moos, 1986:2

183.   Moos and Moos, 1986:2

184.   Moos and Moos, 1986:2

185.   Beit-Hallahmi and Argyle, 1997: 111–12

186.   Moos and Moos, 1986

187.   Moos and Moos, 1986: 5

188.   Orme-Collins, 2002

189.   Aaslid, 2003

190.   Orme-Collins, 2002

191.   Orme-Collins, 2002: 45-46.

192.   Orme-Collins, 2002: 44.

193.   One study examined 172 current members, most of whom were born, raised and educated in The Family (formerly known as the Children of God) and were aged 15 to 25, with an average age of 19 (Sell, 2000). These were individuals living in a few homes in either the USA or Canada. Cattel's Sixteen Personality Factor Questionnaire (fifth edition) and the Structural Analysis of Social Behaviour (SASB) were completed for both 'self-at-best' and 'self-at-worst' scenarios. Sell (2000) reports that the mean scores on the Sixteen Personality Factor Questionnaire were within the average personality domain, with no pathological trends. He states that reports for the SASB did not suggest psychopathology and were in the 'relatively healthy' range. However, looking at the tables in the study, there are numerous significant differences between the sample and norms scores for both 'best self' and 'worst self'. For 'best self', the family members scored significantly lower on 'free', 'affirm' and 'love' self and significantly higher on 'control', 'blame', 'attack' and 'neglect' self, as compared to norm scores. Sell records that 'the average group participant tended to devalue free thinking and place greater value on loyalty to group needs than most peers their age' (Sell, 2000: 6).

194.   Aljazeera, 2013

195.   Cunningham, 1993; Steinberg, 1993

196.   Marwan, 2004

197.   Bee, 1992

198.   Chang, 2007

199.   Marwan, 2004

200.   Baumrind, 1991: Harwood, 2003

201.   Kendall, 2006, Appendix 5: 36-37, 143

202.   Olapegba and Emelogu, 2004

203.   Marwan, 2004

204.   Cooper, 1985 cited in Daniel, Gilligan and Vassell, 2010: 52.

205.   Brenner and Fox, 1999

206.   Prevatt, 2003: 470

207.   Easterbrooks and Graham, 1999: Frick, Christian and Wooton, 1999

208.   Prevatt, 2003

209.   Harry's Sect:70

210. Kendall, 2006: Appendix 5: 39-40

211. Easterbrooks and Graham, 1999; Frick, Christian and Wooton, 1999

212. Baumrind, 1991; Harwood, 2003

213. Maccoby and Martin, 1983

214. Osho, 1991, 52,62 *The NewChild* quoted in Puttick, 1999: 90

215. Guest, 2004: 96-97

216. Gibson, Morgan, Woolley, and Powis, 2010

217. This appearing to look good to those outside the group relates to (Goffman, 1959) impression management by group members who ensure the group appears in a good light to those outside the group.

218. Maccoby and Martin, 1983

219. Harry's Sect:60

220. Stein, 1997:28-37

221. Stein, 1997:33

222. Stein, 1997:33

223. Franzoi, 2000: 271

224. Osherow, 1984

225. Osherow, 1984: 70

226. Asch, 1956

227. Ted's Sect:58

228. Milgram, 1974

229. Asch, 1956, 1987

230. Langone, 1993; Singer, 1995

231. Singer, 1995

232. Wooden, 1981: 184

233. Wooden, 1981: 190

234. Harry's Sect:69

CHAPTER 4

235. Szurko in Kendall, 2006: Appendix 5:46

236. Zablocki, 2005

237. Higgins 2004

238. Smith & Fong, 2004

239. Fish, 2001

240. Langone and Eisenberg, 1993

241. Gaines, Wilson, Redican and Baffi, 1984

242. Gary Dorrien in Vitello, 2010; Kramer, 2000

243. Fraser, 1995

244. Asser and Swan, 2000

245. Asser and Swan, 2000: 1

246. "Convention on the Rights of the Child", Office of the High Commisioner for Human Rights, UN General Assembly resolution 44/25 of 20 November 1989, Article 24.

247. Jeff's, 2009: 51

248. Barnett, Miller-Perrin, & Perrin, 1997

249. Smith & Fong, 2004

250. Gibson, Morgan, Woolley, and Powis, 2010:55

251. Langone and Eisenberg, 1993, citing Gaines, Wilson, Redican and Baffi, 1984: 13

252. Gaines, Wilson, Redican and Baffi, 1984

253. Gaines, Wilson, Redican and Baffi, 1984: 13, cited in Langone and Eisenberg, 1993

254. Egholm, 2005

255. Helfer, 1983

256. Helfer, 1983: 261

257. Kent, 2010

258. Wooden, 1981; Kent, 2010

259. Harry's Sect:66

260. Harry's Sect:67

261. Barnett, Miller-Perrin and Perrin, 1997

262. Aljazeera, 2013

263. Ted's Sect:64

264. Frankl, 1963: 36

265. American Psychiatric Association, 1994

266. Ted's Sect:68

267. Taft, Murphy, King, Dedeyn and Musser, 2005

268. Ward, 2000

269. Dutton and Painter, 1994, Cassidy, 2001

270. Barnett, Miller-Perrin and Perrin, 1997

271. Langone, 1992b: 209

272. Harry's Sect: 27

273.   Barnett, Miller-Perrin and Perrin, 1997

274.   Barnett, Miller-Perrin and Perrin, 1997:123

275.   Harry's Sect: 118, 120.

276.   Harry's Sect: 111, 119.

277.   Harry's Sect: 117

278.   Harry's Sect:122

279.   Harry's Sect: 117

280.   Barnett, Miller-Perrin and Perrin, 1997

281.   Van Eck Duymaer van Twist, 2007

282.   Barnett, Miller-Perrin and Perrin, 1997

283.   Rochford, 1998

284.   Perry and Szalavitz, 2006

285.   Gibson, Morgan, Woolley, and Powis, 2010:72

286.   Lilliston, 1997

287.   Egholm, 2005

288.   Avert, 2008

289.   Sedlak & Broadhurst, 1996; Irenyi, Bromfield, Beyer, and Higgins, 2006

290.   Jeffs, 2009

291.   Ted's Sect:98

292.   Ted's Sect:95

293.   Langone, 1992b

294.   Fortune 1995: 33

295.   Ted's Sect:97

296.   Fortune, 1995: 33

297.   Ted's Sect:98

298.   2Frankl, 1963

299.   Home Office Communications Directoratet, 2003, Section 74: 48

300.   Home Office Communications Directorate, 2004: 3

301.   Frankl: 1963

302.   Ted's Sect:98

303.   Ted's Sect:99

304.   Rutters, 1989; Ditsch and Avery, 2001

305.   Luepker, 1995

306.   Johnson and Van Vonderen, 1991: 20

307. Harry's Sect:208

308. Harry's Sect:121

309. DSM-IV; American Psychiatric Association, 1994

310. Michael, Ehlers and Halligan, 2005

311. Ehlers and Clark, 2000, cited in: Michael, Ehlers and Halligan, 2005: 103

312. Loewenthal, 2000

313. Kent, 1993: 239

314. Ted's Sect:144

315. Harry's Sect:120

316. Aljazeera, 2013

317. Rochford, 1998

318. DSM-IV; American Psychiatric Association, 1994

319. Ted's Sect:65

320. Harry's Sect: 110.

321. Harry's Sect:109

322. Osherow, 1984

323. Cartwright and Kent, 1992

324. Bandura, 1992

325. Bandura, 1992

326. Bandura, 1992: 41

327. Bandura, Barbaranelli, Caprara and Pastorelli, 1996: 368

328. As was found by Osherow, 1984

329. Harry's Sect: 192, Harry's Sect: 35

330. Tobias and Lalich, 1994

331. Marowitz and Halperin, 1984

332. Kendall, 2010

333. Marowitz and Halperin, 1984

334. Rochford, 1998: 50

335. Marowitz and Halperin, 1984; Landa, 1990/1991, Tobias and Lalich, 1994

336. Singer, 1995

337. Rochford, 1998

338. Furnari, 2004

339. DSM-IV-TR, American Psychiatric Association, 2000

340. Furnari, 2004

341. Siskind, 2003: 59

342. Furnari, 2005

343. Langone and Eisenberg, 1993

344. Irenyi, Bromfield, Beyer and Higgins, 2006

345. Siskind, 2001

346. Aronoff, Lynn and Malinoski, 2000

347. Balch, 1996; Goffman, 1959

348. Entitled 'Alternative religions and their academic supporters'

349. Kent and Krebs, 1998

350. Marowitz and Halperin, 1984: 3

351. Langone and Eisenberg, 1993: 339

352. Beit-Hallahmi, 2001, 61; citing from 'Richardson and Dewitt 1992: 561

353. Pollock and Van Reken, 1999

354. Aljazeera, 2013

CHAPTER 5

355. Bowlby, 1980

356. Malim and Birch, 1998: 446-447

357. Perry and Szalavitz, 2006

358. Smith & Fong, 2004

359. Siskind, 2003

360. Association of Therapeutic Communities, 2009

361. Siskind, 1999; Siskind, 2003

362. Gibson, Morgan, Woolley, and Powis, 2010: 129

363. Van Eck Duymaer van Twist, 2007:84

364. Hounam and Hogg, 1984: 15

365. Aljazeera, 2013

366. Van Eck Durmaer van Twist, 2007

367. Kent, 2005

368. Worth, 2000; Erikson, 1980

369. Erikson's theory originated from his therapeutic work with healthy adolescents and with the Sioux and Yurok American Indian tribes, and therefore his work is intended to be

cross-cultural. However, others have criticised the theory as slanted towards Western culture due to the focus on individualism (Perlmutter and Hall, 1992; Stevens, 1983). Nevertheless, Erikson's theory has been commended because he identified how a child's environment influences their development, including the fit between the child's needs and the society's needs at each point in development, and how the society tries to deal with the biologically based changes in the child's needs (Miller, 1993).

370. Miller, 1993

371. Harry's Sect:189

372. A 2002 documentary about Amish children experiencing 'Rumspringa' was entitled 'Devils Playground'. The title refers to the 'English' or the outside world.

373. Katchen, 1997; Kendall 2006

374. Macias, Young and Barreira, 2000: 16–17

375. Erikson, 1980

376. Tamm, 2009:10

377. Harry's Sect:88

378. Hounam and Hogg, 1984: 272

379. Hounam and Hogg, 1984: 216

380. Harry's Sect:120

381.   Erikson, 1980

382.   Bee, 1992

383.   Hounam and Hogg, 1984: 16

384.   Jeffs, 2009:50

385.   Hollenhorst, 2011

386.   Gibson, Morgan, Woolley and Powis, 2010

387.   Smith & Fong, 2004

388.   Erikson, 1959: 82

389.   Miller, 1993

390.   Gibson, Morgan, Woolley, and Powis, 2010: 198

391.   Miller, 1993

392.   Tajfel and Turner, 1979

393.   Erikson and Erikson, 1981

394.   Gibson, Morgan, Woolley and Powis, 2010

395.   Perry and Szalavitz, 2006: 234

396.   Harry's Sect:126

397.   Harry's Sect:127

398.   Erikson 1959: 97

399.   Jeffs 2009: 207

CHAPTER 6

400.   Harry's Sect: 76

401.   Refers to Bandura's Social Cognitive Theory referred to here as Social Learning Theory for ease of understanding

402.   Bandura, 1992

403.   Bandura, 1986

404.   Harry's Sect: 107

405.   Bandura, 1992

406.   Harry's Sect: 63

407.   Grusec, 1992

408.   Harry's Sect: 82

409.   Harry's Sect: 85

410.   Harry's Sect: 212

411.   Harry's Sect: 83

412.   Goffman, 1971 cited in Entwistle, 2000

413.   Entwistle, 2000:123-124

414.   Zadro, Williams and Richardson, 2004

415.   Ted's Sect:117

416.   Luck, 1992

417.   Harry's Sect: 74

418.   Haney, Curtis and Zimbardo, 1995

419.   Ribeiro, 1992

420.   Livia Bardin, 2011, personal communication regarding a research interview she had completed

421.   Gibson, Morgan, Woolley, and Powis, 2010

422.   Ribeiro, 1992

423.   Wilson 1992: 4

424.   Rochford, 1999

425.   Rochford 1999:37-38

426.   Jeffs, 2009

427.   Rochford, 1999:37

428.   Miller and Major, 2000

429.   Luck, 1992

430.   Luck, 1992

431.   Harry's Sect: 80

432.   Miller and Major; 2000: 262–3

433.   Harry's Sect: 111, 119

434.   Harry's Sect: 75

435.   Harry's Sect: 77

436.   Harry's Sect: 78

437.   Guest, 2004:97

438.   Jeffs, 2009: 57

439.   Miller and Major, 2000

440.   Kendall, 2006

441.   Harry's Sect: 79

442.   Mostow, Izard, Fine and Trentacosta, 2002

443.   Jeffs, 2009, 136

444.   Hounam and Hogg, 1984:212

445.   Muster, 2012; Van Eck Duymaer van Twist, 2007

446.   Van Eck Duymaer van Twist, 2007

447.   Van Eck Duymaer van Twist, 2007:230

448.   Office of the High Commissioner for Human Rights, 1989

449.   Eg. Jeffs 2009

450.   Aljazeera, 2013

451.   Harry's Sect: 93

452.   Harry's Sect:45

453.   Gibson, Morgan, Woolley, and Powis, 2010:50-51

454.   Siskind, 2003

455.   Harry's Sect: 50

456.   Harry's Sect:49

457.   Osherow, 1984

458.   Harry's Sect: 64

459.   Gibson, Morgan, Woolley, and Powis, 2010: 74

460.   Cochran and Brassard, 1979; Crinic, Greenberg, Ragozin, Robinson and Basham, 1983

461.   Findler and Taubman-Ben-Ari, 2003

462.   Miller, 1993

463.   Erdley, Nangle, Newman and Carpenter, 2001

464.   Szurko, 2002; Appendix 5: 41-42

Chapter 7

465.   Harry's Sect:174

466.   Beck, 1976

467.   Whetherick 2002: 1

468.   Tobias and Lalich, 1994

469.   Beck, 1976

470.   Burks, 2002

471.   Cherry Lane Collection, 2008

472.   Ted's Sect:89

473.   Copi 1972; Haight 1999; Bowell and Kemp, 2002

474.   Copi 1972; Haight 1999; Bowell and Kemp, 2002

475.   Copi 1972; Haight 1999; Bowell and Kemp, 2002

476.   Enroth, 1992; Martin, 1993

477.   Cialdini, 1984

478.   Singer, 1995

479.   Cialdini,1984: 116

480.   Harry's Sect: 118

481.   Martin, 1989

482.   Cialdini, 2005

483.   Harry's Sect:173

484.   Harry's Sect: 29

485.   Harry's Sect: 163

486.   Harry's Sect: 87

487.   Mytton, 1993

488.   Kendall, 2006

489.   Kendall, 2006

490.   Mytton, 1993

491.   Tobias and Lalich, 1994

492.   Dickens, 1846 – 1848: 322

493.   Ted's Sect: 119

494.   Harry's Sect:175

495.   Van Eck Duymaer van Twist (2007:231) reports in her PhD thesis that in a group known as The Family, 'During the 1990's between half and two-thirds of their children were leaving'.

496.   Kendall, 2006

497.   Ozorak, 1989

498.   Hollingworth, 1933

499.   Borger, 2005:1

500.   Langone and Ryan, 2005

501.   Robbins and Anthony, 1980:31-32

502.   Bird and Reimer, 1982; Barker, 1984

503.   Bromley, Shupe, and Ventimiglia 1979; Bromley & Shupe, 1981

504.   Lewis and Bromley, 1987

505.   Zablocki, 2001

506.   Lewis and Bromley, 1987

507.   Burks, 2002

508. Kirsch and Glass, 1977

509. Harry's Sect: 191

510. Aljazeera, 2013

511. Chirkov, Rya, Kim, and Kaplan, 2003: 97

512. Self-determination theory Deci and Ryan, 1985; Ryan and Deci, 2000

513. Chirko, Ryan, Kim, and Kaplan, 2003

514. Triandis, and Gelfand, 1998

515. Chirkov, Ryan, Kim and Kaplan, 2003

516. Harry's Sect: 88

517. Singer, 1995

518. Perry and Szalavitz, 2006, 69

519. Berry, Poortinga, Segall and Dasen, 1992

520. Berry, Poortinga, Segall and Dasen, 1992

521. Furnham and Bochner, 1986

522. Harry's Sect:190

523. Cockburn, 2002

524. Pollock and Van Reken, 1999: 19

525. Kebshull and Pozo, 2006

526. Ted's Sect: 132, Harry's Sect: 177, 185.

527. Harry's Sect: 176, 187, 190, Ted's Sect: 130.

528. Ted's Sect: 131.

529. Ted's Sect: 132.

530. Ted's Sect: 133.

531. Harry's Sect: 181.

532. Harry's Sect: 179, 180, 183.

533. Harry's Sect: 173.

534. Harry's Sect: 188.

535. Harry's Sect: 184.

536. Harry's Sect: 186, 187

537. Harry's Sect: 176

538. Harry's Sect: 176

539. Harry's Sect: 224

CHAPTER 8

540. Ray Connolly, 2011. This quote has had abbreviations put in full length to tie in with their use in the rest of this book

541. Tajfel and Turner, 1979

542. Mlicki and Ellemers, 1996

543. Kübler-Ross, 1970

544. Rando, 1993

545. Kendall, 2006; Mytton, 1993

546. Jeffs, 2009:191

547. Kübler-Ross, 1970

548. Rando, 1993

549. In one UK study I did, the sample included 49% of the first- and 48% of the second-generation former members reporting having no children, compared to just 21% of the comparison group, despite the first generation having a mean age of 40 years (SD = 9.48), the second generation having a mean age of 38 years (SD=12.21) and the comparison group having a mean age of 47 (SD = 12.70).

550. Pollock and Van Reken, 1999: 172

551. Kübler-Ross, 1970

552. Kübler-Ross, 1970: 123

553.   Pollock and Van Reken, 1999

554.   Rando, 1993

555.   Reported by some former members of both Ted's Sect and Harry's Sect

556.   Harry's Sect: 188

557.   Harry's Sect: 189

558.   Harry's Sect:188

559.   Martin, 1993

560.   Harry's Sect: 193

561.   Berger, 1998

562.   It is probably the case though that most of those participating in the research studies recorded in the table are those who have spent longer time in sects than former sect members in general and particularly for the first generation, the average length of time in a sect may be shorter than that recorded in the table. It could also be longer, especially for those who don't ever leave the sect.

563.   Conway and Siegelman, 1982

564.   Walsh, Russell and Wells, 1995; Kendall, 2006

565.   Langone, 2003b

566.   Langone, 1999: 1

567.   Barker, 1989

568.   Kaplan, 2001

569.   Beit-Hallahmi, 2001

570.   BBC News Online, 2000

571.   Langone, 1999

572.   Ted's Sect: 133

573.   Ted's Sect: 140

574.   Ted's Sect: 141

575.   Harry's Sect: 134, 182

576.   Ted's Sect: 132, 133, 134

577.   West, 1993

578.   Keiser & Keiser, 1987

579.   Kendall, 2006

580.   Aronoff, Lynn and Malinoski, 2000; Singer and Ofshe 1990;
        Keiser and Keiser, 1987

581.   Questions exist about the research such as questions regarding
        the number of research participants, the low incidence of the
        involvement of comparison groups and whether some of those
        involved could be self-selecting research participants (do they
        really have free choice about being a part of the research?).

582. Aronoff, Lynn and Malinoski, 2000; Singer and Ofshe, 1990; Keiser & Keiser 1987; Gasde and Block, 1998; Martin, Langone, Dole and Wiltrout, 1992; Malinoski, Langone and Lynn, 1999

583. Malinoski, Langone and Lynn, 1999

584. Winocur, Whitney, Sorenson, Vaughn and Foy, 1997; Martin, Langone, Dole and Wiltrout, 1992; Schwartz, 1985

585. Tylden, 1995

586. Tylden, 1995: 78

587. Singer, 1995

588. Singer 1995: 263–5

589. Craig and Weathers, 1990

590. Ted's Sect:47

591. Tobias and Lalich, 1994

592. Tobias and Lalich, 1994

593. Tobias and Lalich, 1994

594. Tobias and Lalich, 1994

595. McFarland, 2010

596. Clinically significant levels of distress

597. Beck Depression Inventory II (BDI-II)

598. State-Trait Anxiety Inventory (STAI-Y)

599. State-Trait Anger Scale (STAS)

600. Dissociative Experiences Scale

601. Putnam, 1999

602. Clinically significant scores on the Impact of Events (IES) scale were found.

603. Kessler, Sonnega, Bromet, Hughes and Nelson, 1995

604. Kendall, 2006

605. Clinically significant scores on the IES

606. Kendall, 2006

607. On the SCL-90-R, State Anxiety, Trait Anger and Dissociative Experiences scales the second-generation sample was significantly more likely to have clinically significant levels of distress than the first generation, as measured by Fisher's exact test.

608. Kendall, 2006

609. Langone, 1998

610. Gibson, Morgan, Woolley, and Powis, 2010: 147, 157

611.   See Chapter Four for more details: Barnett, Miller-Perrin and Perrin, 1997

612.   Analysis of covariance found that after removing the variable physical abuse significant differences between the first and second generation were still present.

613.   Removing the effect in terms of the statistical test

614.   Lourie, 1996

615.   NHS Choices, 2010

616.   Hewstone, Fincham, and Foster, 2005

617.   Weissman, Bland, Can Ino, Greenwald, Hwu, Joyce, Karam, Lee, Lellouch, Lep Ine, Newman, Rub, Ipec, Wells, Ickramaratne, Wittchien, and Yeh, 1999

618.   Szalavitz, and Perry, 2010

619.   Perry and Szalavitz, 2006

620.   Perry and Szalavitz, 2006

621.   Gray, Bolton, and Litz, 2004

622.   American Psychiatric Association, 1994

623.   Mind, 2012

624.   Lourie, 1996

625. Dutton and Painter's (1994)

626. Kendall, 2006

627. Andrews, Brewin, Rose and Kirk, 2000

628. American Psychiatric Association, 1994: 425

629. van der Kolk 1996b cited in Scott and Stradling, 2001:15

630. Herman, 1992

631. Mind, 2012

632. McNally, 2003; Support for the dose response model has been found by 16 of 19 studies, which found that the stressor magnitude is directly proportional to the subsequent risk of developing PTSD March, 1993

633. Lloyd and Turner, 2003; McKeever and Huff, 2003

634. Lloyd and Turner, 2003: 381

635. Lloyd and Turner, 2003

636. Nielsen, 2003

637. Koenen, Stellman, Stellman and Sommer, 2003

638. Blank, 1993: 9

639. BBC health, 2012

640. Davison and Neale, 1998

641. Ted's Sect:134

642. Putnam, 1999

643. West and Martin, 1994

644. David, 2010-2012

645. American Psychiatric Association, 1994

646. Kendall, 2006; Katchen 1997

647. Garvey, 1993; Goldberg, 1993; Szurko, 1995; Tylden, 1995

648. Ted's Sect: 133

649. Ted's Sect: 135, 136, 140

650. Schnurr and Green, 2004

651. Carlson, Johnston, Liiceanu, Vintila and Harvey, 2000

652. Ted's Sect: 133

653. Kendall, 2006

654. Kendall, 2006

655. Zablocki, 1998

656. Herman, 1992

657.   Krahe, 2000

658.   Macias, Young and Barreira, 2000

659.   Kendall, 2006

660.   Krahe, 2000

661.   Turner and Oakes, 1997

662.   Kaufman, 1989: 127

663.   Gibson, Morgan, Woolley, and Powis, 2010: 147 and 153

664.   Jeffs, 2009: 235

665.   Jules, 2005

666.   EyeWideShut, 2002

667.   Jules, 2002

668.   Cahill, Llewelyn and Pearson, 1991

669.   MacInnes, 1998

670.   Gibson, Morgan, Woolley and Powis, 2010: 151 and 160

671.   Gorsuch, 1988

672.   Loewenthal, 2000

673.   Beit-Hallahmi and Argyle 1997; Barker, 1989

674.   Cardwell, Clark, and Meldrum, 2008

675.   Jarvis and Northcott 1987; Levin, 1994

676.   Brown 1988, cited in Beit-Hallahmi and Argyle, 1997: 121

677.   Murken, 2005

678.   Gibson, Morgan, Woolley, and Powis, 2010

679.   Gibson, Morgan, Woolley, and Powis, 2011: 49

680.   Namini, 2005

681.   Galanter, 1989: 93

682.   Scully, Kremer, Meade, Graham, and Dudgeon, 1998

683.   Harry's Sect: 217, 220, 221, Ted's Sect: 150, 162, 163

684.   Ted's Sect: 162

685.   Ted's Sect: 158

686.   Ted's Sect: 156

687.   Harry's Sect: 218, 219, 225

688.   Harry's Sect: 221, 223

689.   Harry's Sect: 222

690.   Harry's Sect: 224

691. Schnurr, Rosenberg and Friedman, 1993

692. McNally, 2003

693. Herman, 1992

694. Carlson, Johnston, Liiceanu, Vintila and Harvey, 2000

695. Harvey, 1996 cited in Carlson, Johnston, Liiceanu, Vintila and Harvey, 2000: 98

696. Frankl, 1963: 179

697. Worth, 2000

698. Gibson, Morgan, Woolley, and Powis, 2010; Kendall 2006; Katchen 1997,

699. Aljazeera, 2013

CHAPTER 9

700. Wall, 2008:329

701. The Independent, 2014

702. Langone, 1998

703. American Psychological Association 2011

704. American Psychological Association, 2011

705. Perry and Salavitz, 2006

706.   Dutton and Painter, 1994

707.   Perry and Szalavitz, 2006:230

708.   Goldberg, 2006:16

709.   Eg. Harry's Sect.

710.   Although, some second-generation former members may have secret friends in the outside world who are unknown to the group or family.

711.   Holtzman, Newth and Delongis, 2004

712.   Demographic study of Harry's Sect: Kendall, 2006

713.   TS: 147

714.   TS: 148

715.   Harry's Sect: 216

716.   Harry's Sect: 213

717.   Macias, Young and Barreira 2000: 16–17

718.   Gibson, Morgan, Woolley, and Powis, 2010, p 138

719.   Mitchell, 2011

720.   Pearlman and Saakvitne, 1995: 270–1

721.   Thomas, 2005

722.   Findlay, 2004

723.   Hyper Dictionary, 2003

724.   Bardin, 2011-2013

725.   Hayslip, 2001

726.   Siskind, 2003

727.   Bramham, 2011

728.   Kornhaber, 1996, 2006

729.   Kornhaber, 1996, 2006

730.   Werner, 2005

731.   Werner, 2005

732.   Jeffs, 2009, p148

733.   Jeffs, 2009, p149

734.   Foundation for Grandparenting, 1982, p1

735.   Siskind, 2010

736.   Gibson, Morgan, Woolley, and Powis, 2010

737.   Tamm, 2009:286

738.   van Eck Duymaer van Twist, 2007

739.   Worth, 2000: Schuldberg, 2000-2001

740.   Levinson, 1978, 1996

741.   Levinson, 1996: 238

742.   Gritz, 2011

743.   Levinson, Darrow, Klein, Levinson, and McKee, 1978

744.   Worth, 2005: 1

745.   Worth, 2005

746.   Johnson and Huwe, 2002:45

747.   Johnson and Huwe, 2002

748.   Levinson, Darrow, Klein, Levinson, and McKee, 1978

749.   Worth, 2005

750.   Levinson, Darrow, Klein, Levinson, and McKee, 1978: 334

751.   Levinson, Darrow, Klein, Levinson, and McKee, 1978: 101

752.   Johnson and Huwe, 2002

753.   Egholm, 2005: 2

754. Findlay, 2004

755. Michael, Ehlers and Halligan, 2005

756. Johnson and VanVonderen, 1991

757. James 1:19: Holy Bible, New International Version

758. Kendall, 2006, UK study looking at former members from multiple groups

759. This was a correlational finding and therefore we cannot assume causation.

760. Table 9.1 records the percentage of those first- and second-generation former sect members and former members of non-sect-like groups receiving professional help after leaving their sect. It shows that the second-generation samples were consistently more likely to have a higher percentage seeking counselling after leaving their sect. The results of the two UK studies demonstrated that between 25% and 50% of the second-generation samples have had counselling after leaving their sect. This is similar to Jill Mytton's study of former members of the Exclusive Brethren, which found that 30% of her sample of 201 former second-generation sect members had received counselling or consulted a professional after leaving their sect. It is also consistent with a poll, which included 133 second-generation former members of The Family who were part of an online community at Moving On, 32% of whom have met with a psychiatrist or psychologist to discuss their upbringing and a further 28% who would like to.

Table 9.1: Receiving professional help after group membership across research studies

	Percentage receiving counselling or consulting a professional		
Study	First generation	Second generation	Comparison group
Mytton (1993) UK		30% (N = 201)	
Kendall (2006) UK – Harry's Sect	8% (N = 12)	25%(N = 16)	
Kendall (2006) US, before attending Wellspring	58% (N = 113)	91% (N = 22)	
Kendall, (2006): UK	38% (N = 47)	50%(N = 26)	12.1% (N = 32)61
Bella (2003) International, Moving On poll		32% (N=133) A further 28% would like to consult a professional	

761.   Shaw, 2007

762.   Identified by Roth and Fonagy, 1996

763.   Cherry, 2013

764.   Rogers, 1951

765.   Beck, 1976

766.   Antonuccio, Danton, and DeNelsky, 1995

767.   Beck, 1976

768.   Sanders and Wills, 2003: 38

769.   Erikson, 1980

770.   Erikson, 1988

771.   Jacobs, 1985, p5.

772.   Register of Trauma Specialists 2007-2012

773.   Jenkinson, 2005

774.   Bergin and Garfield, 1994: 822; Woolfe and Dryden, 1996

775.   Marzillier, 2004: 1

776.   Singer and Lalich, 1996

777.   Register of Trauma Specialists, 2007-2012

778.   Tamm, 2009:282

CHAPTER 10

779.   Worth, 2000

780.   Harvey, 1996

781.   Frankl, 1963

782.   American Psychological Association, 1994

783.   Please note this study found a correlation between these variables as opposed to a causal relationship, as such this needs further research to asertain whether this a causal relationship or not.

784.   Kendall, 2006

785.   Pollock and Van Reken, 1999: 19

786.   Jenkinson, 2005

787.   Bandura, 1992: 9

788.   Argyle, 1994

789.   Argyle, 1994

790.   Bandura, 1992

791.   Bull and Frederikson, 1995

792.   Tangney and Dearing, 2002

793.   Tangney and Dearing, 2002

794.   Tangney and Dearing, 2002

795.   National Churchill Museum

796.   A full text copy of the Universal Declaration of Human Rights
        can be found on the United Nations website.

797.   American Psychological Association, 2011

798.   Koehn, 2006

799.   Kohen, 2006:1

800.   Hawkins, 1991

801.   E.g. the work of Hughes, 2011

802.   Cantacuzino, 2011

803.   Siddique, 2010

804.   Cantacuzino, 9 March 2010

805.   Fincham, 2002; Thoresen, 2002; DiBlasio, 2004

806.   Fincham, 2002; Thoresen, 2002; DiBlasio, 2004

807.   Richmond 1997-2010

808.   Cantacuzino, 2011: 1

809.   Jones, 2007:291

810.   Hawkins,1991

811.   Goldberg, 2006

812.   Pearson and Diaz, 2012

813.   Harry's Sect: 193

814.   Banisadr, 2004, 424

815.   Jones, 2007: 196-197 in Jones, Jones, and Buhring, 2007

816.   Gibson, Morgan, Woolley and Powis, 2011: 49

817.   van Eck Duymaer van Twist, 2007, 247

818.   Gibson, Morgan, Woolley and Powis, 2010: 162

819.   Gibson, Morgan, Woolley and Powis, 2010: 162

REFERENCES

Aaslid, F.S. (2003) 'On the Outside Looking In: Growing Up in the Moonies,' *Cultic Studies Review*, 2 (1): 1–7.

Aljazeera, (2013) 'The Colony: Chile's dark past uncovered' Documentary. Available online from http://www.aljazeera.com/programmes/aljazeeracorrespondent/2013/11/colony-chile-dark-past-uncovered-2013114105429774517.html (accessed 9 December 2013).

American Psychiatric Association (1994) *Diagnostic and Statistical Manual of Mental Disorders* (4th edition) (Washington; DC: Author).

American Psychiatric Association (2000) *Diagnostic and Statistical Manual of Mental Disorders* (4th edition) Text Revision. (Washington; DC: Author).

American Psychological Association (2011) *The Road to Resilience*. Available online from http://www.apa.org/helpcenter/road-resilience.aspx# (accessed 16 July 2011).

Anthony, D. (2001) 'Tactical Ambiguity and Brainwashing Formulations: Science or Pseudo Science,' in Zablocki, B. and Robbins, T. (eds) *Misunderstanding Cults: Searching for Objectivity in a Controversial Field* (London: University of Toronto Press), pp. 215–317.

Anthony, D. and Robbins, T. (1992) 'Law, Social Science and the 'Brainwashing' Exception to the First Amendment,' *Behavioural Sciences and the Law* 10: 3–29.

Antonuccio, D.O., Danton, W.G. and DeNelsky, G.Y. (1995) 'Psychotherapy versus medication for depression: Challenging the conventional wisdom with data,' *Professional Psychology: Research and Practice*, 26: 574–85. Available online from http://www.apa.org/journals/anton.html (Accessed 7 December 2004).

Argyle, M. (1994) *The Psychology of Interpersonal Behaviour*, 5th edition (London: Penguin Books).

Aronoff, J.B., Lynn, S.J. and Malinoski, P.T. (2000) 'Are Cultic Environments Psychologically Harmful?' *US Clinical Psychology Review*, 20: 91–111.

Asch, S.E. (1956) 'Studies of Independence and Submission to Group Pressure: 1 A Minority of One Against a Unanimous Majority,' in *Psychological Monographs*, 70 (9) (Whole no. 416).

Asch, S.E. (1987) *Social Psychology* (Oxford, UK: Oxford University Press; originally published in 1952), cited in J.R. Harris (1998) *The Nurture Assumption* (New York: The Free Press).

Asser, S. and Swan, R. (2000) 'Child Fatalities From Religion-Motivated Medical Neglect,' *Cultic Studies Journal*, 17: 1–14.

Association of Therapeutic Communities (2009) *What is a TS?* Available online from http://www.therapeuticcommunities.org/index.php?option=com_content&view=article&id=76&Itemid=94 (accessed 28 May 2011).

Ayella, M. (1998) *Insane Therapy: Portrait of a Psychotherapy Cult.* (Philadelphia: Temple University Press), cited in Whitsett, D. and Kent, S.A. (2003) 'Cults and Families,' *Families in Society: The Journal of Contemporary Human Services*, 84 (4): 491–502.

Balch, R. (1996) 'Review of Sex, Slander, and Salvation Investigating the Family/Children of God,' *Journal for the Scientific Study of Religion*, 35 (1), cited in Kent, S. and Krebs, T. 'When Scholars Know Sin: Alternative Religions and their Academic Supporters,' in *Skeptic* 6 (3): 14–26.

Bandura, A (1982) 'The Psychology of Chance Encounters and Life Paths', *American Psychologist*, 37: 747–755, cited in Bandura, A. (1992) 'Social Cognitive Theory', in Vasta, R. (ed.) *Six Theories of Child Development* (London: Jessica Kingsley).

Bandura, A. (1986) *Social Foundations of Thought and Action: A Social Cognition Theory* (Englewood Cliffs, NJ: Prentice-Hall), cited in Bandura, A. (1992) 'Social Cognitive Theory', in Vasta, R. (ed.) *Six Theories of Child Development* (London: Jessica Kingsley).

Bandura, A. (1992) 'Social Cognitive Theory', in Vasta, R. (ed.) *Six Theories of Child Development* (London: Jessica Kingsley).

Bandura, A., Barbaranelli, C., Caprara, G.V. and Pastorelli, C. (1996) 'Mechanisms of Moral Disengagement in the Exercised of Moral Agency', *Journal of Personality and Social Psychology*, 71 (2): 364–74.

Banisadr, M. (2004) *Masoud: Memoirs of an Iranian Rebel*, (London: Saqi Books).

Bardin, L. (2011-2013) *Starting Out in Mainstream America* (US: ICSA) Available online from http://startingout.icsa.name (accessed 4 July 2014).

Bardin, L. (2005) 'Child Protection in an Authoritarian Community; Culture Clash and Systematic Weakness'. *Cultic Studies Review* 4(5).

Barker, E. (1983) 'The Ones Who Got Away: People Who Attend Unification Church Workshops and Do Not Become Moonies', in E. Barker (ed.), *Of Gods and Men: New Religious Movements in the West* (Macon, GA: Mercer University Press), pp. 309–36.

Barker, E. (1984) *The Making of a Moonie. Brainwashing or Choice?* (Oxford: Basil Blackwell).

Barker, E. (1986) 'Religious Movements: Cult and Anticult since Jonestown,' *Annual Review Sociology* 12: 329–46.

Barker, E. (1989) *New Religious Movements: A Practical Introduction* (London: HMSO).

Barnett, O.W., Miller-Perrin, C.L. and Perrin, R.D. (1997) *Family Violence Across the Lifespan: An Introduction* (London: Sage).

Baumrind, D. (1991) 'Parenting Styles and Adolescent Development', in J. Brooks-Gunn, R. Lerner and A.C. Peterson (eds), *The Encyclopaedia of Adolescence* (New York: Garland), pp. 746–58, cited in Prevatt, F.F. (2003) 'The Contribution of Parenting Practices in a Risk and Resiliency Model of Children's Adjustment', *British Journal of Developmental Psychology*, 21: 469–80.

BBC News Online (29 March 2000) *'Quiet Cult's Doomsday Deaths'.* Available online from http: //www.hartford-hwp.com/archives/35/142.html (accessed 12 November 2003).

BBC Health (2012) *'Post-traumatic stress disorder'* The Royal College of Psychiatrists Available online from http://www.bbc.co.uk/health/

emotional_health/mental_health/disorders_ptsd.shtml (accessed 6 February 2012).

Beck, A.T. (1976) *Cognitive Therapy and the Emotional Disorders* (London: Penguin).

Beckford, J.A. and Levasseur, M. (1986) 'New Religious Movements in Western Europe,' in J.A. Beckford (ed.) *New Religious Movements and Rapid Social Change* (London: Sage), pp. 29–54.

Bee, H., (1992) 6th Ed *The Developing Child* (USA, New York: Harper Collins Publishers).

Beit-Hallahmi, B. (2001) 'O Truant Muse: Collaborationism and Research Integrity,' in Zablocki, B. and Robbins, T. (eds) (2001) *Misunderstanding Cults: Searching for Objectivity in a Controversial Field*. (London: University of Toronto Press), pp. 35–70.

Beit-Hallahmi, B. and Argyle, M. (1997) *The Psychology of Religious Behaviour, Belief and Experience* (London: Routledge).

Bella (11 June 2003) *'Moving On Poll: Have you ever met with a psychologist and/or psychiatrist to discuss your upbringing?'* Available online from http: //movingon.org/results.asp?pID=139 (accessed 16 July 2004).

Berger, K.S. (1998) *The Developing Person Through the Life Span* (New York: Worth), cited in Zerbrowitz, L.A. and Montepare, J.M. (2000) '"Too Young, Too Old": Stigmatizing Adolescents and Elders' in Heatherton, T.F., Kleck, R. E., Hebl, M.R. and Hull, J.G. (eds) *The Social Psychology of Stigma* (New York: The Guildford Press).

Bergin, A.E. and Garfield, S.L. (1994) 'Overview, Trends and Future Issues,' in Bergin, A.E. and Garfield, S.L. (eds), *Handbook of*

Psychotherapy and Behaviour Change (4th Edition) (New York: Wiley), pp. 821–30, cited in Woolfe, R. and Dryden W. (1996) (eds) *Handbook of Counselling Psychology* (London, Sage).

Bergman, J. (n.d.) 'Why Jehovah's Witnesses have Mental Problems'. Available online from http://www.premier1.net/~raines/mental. html (accessed 14 August 2005).

Bergman, J. (1996) 'Paradise Postponed…and Postponed: Why Jehovah's Witnesses Have a High Mental Illness Level,' *Christian Research journal*, 19 (1): 36-41.

Berry, J.W., Poortinga, Y.H., Segall, M.H. and Dasen, P.R. (1992) *Cross-cultural Psychology: Research and Applications* (Cambridge: Cambridge University Press).

Bird, F. and Reimer, B. (1982) 'Participation Rates in New Religious and Para-Religious Movements,' *Journal for the Scientific Study of Religion*, 21 (1): 1–14.

Blank, A.S. (1993) 'The Longitudinal Course of Posttraumatic Stress Disorder', in Davidson, J.R.T. and Edna, B.F. (eds) *Post Traumatic Stress Disorder: DSM-IV and Beyond.* (Washington: American Psychiatric Press).

Borger, J. (2005) 'The lost boys, thrown out of US sect so that older men can marry more wives' *The Guardian* 4 June 2005. Available online from http://www.guardian.co.uk/world/2005/jun/14/usa.julianborger (accessed 2 March 2010).

Bowell, T. and Kemp, G. (2002) *Critical Thinking: A Concise Guide* (London: Routledge).

Bowlby, J. (1980) *Attachment and Loss: Vol. 3. Loss, sadness and depression* (New York: Basic Books).

Bramham, D. (2011, Jan 18th) 'Former Bountiful resident gives tearful testimony on polygamy.' *The Vancouver Sun.* Available online from http://www.vancouversun.com/life/Opinion+Former+Boun tiful+resident+gives+tearful+testimony+polygamy/4129050/story. html#ixzz1BZaDC2ry (accessed 29 August 2011).

Brenner, V. and Fox, R. (1999) 'An Empirically Derived Classification of Parenting Practises,' *The Journal of Genetic Psychology,* 160(3): 343–56.

Bromley, D. G., Shupe, A. D., & Ventimiglia, J. C. (1979). Atrocity tales, the Unification Church and the social construction of evil. *Journal of Communication,* 29: 42-53.

Bromley, D. G. and Shupe, A.D. (1981) 'Apostates and atrocity stories: some parameters in the dynamics of deprogramming,' in Wilson, B. (eds) (1981) *The Social Impact of New Religious Movements.* (New York, Rose of Sharon Press).

Beit-Hallahmi, B. (2001) 'O Truant Muse: Collaborationism and Research Integrity,' in Zablocki, B. and Robbins, T. (eds) (2001) *Misunderstanding Cults: Searching for Objectivity in a Controversial Field.* (London: University of Toronto Press), pp. 35–70.

Brown, L.B. (1988) *The Psychology of Religion: An Introduction* (London: SPCK), cited in Beit-Hallahmi, B. and Argyle (1997) *The Psychology of Religious Behaviour, Belief and Experience* (London: Routledge).

Bull, P. and Frederikson, L. (1995) 'Non-Verbal Communication', in Argyle, M. and Colman, A.M. (eds) *Social Psychology* (London: Longman).

Burger, J.M., Girgis, Z.M. and Manning, C.M., (2011) 'In their own words: explaining obedience to authority through an examination of participants comments', in *Social Psychological and Personality Science* 2: 460–466. Cited in Haslam, S.A. and Reicher, S. D. (2012) 'Contesting the "Nature" of Conformity: What Milgram and Zimbardo's Studies Really Show', in *PLOS Biology* 10 (11): 1-4.

Burks, R. (2002) *'Cognitive Impairment in Thought Reform Environments,'* Ph.D. Thesis, Ohio University. Available online from http://oak. cats.ohiou.edu/~rb267689/ (accessed 7 May 2002).

Cahill C., Llewelyn, S.P. and Pearson, C. (1991) 'Long-Term Effects of Sexual Abuse which Occurred in Childhood: A review', *British Journal of Clinical Psychology*, 30: 117–30, cited in Krahe, B. (2000) 'Childhood Sexual Abuse and Revictimization in Adolescence and Adulthood', in Harvey, J.H. and Pauwels, B.G. (eds) (2000) *Post-Traumatic Stress Theory: Research and Application* (E. Sussex: Brunner/Mazel Taylor & Francis Group).

Cantacuzino, M. (2011) *'Forgiveness: a way out of the darkness'* Available online from http://theforgivenessproject.com/about-us/founder/ (accessed 24 February 2011).

Cantacuzino, M. (9 Mar 2010) What Redemption for a Child Killer? *Huffington Post* Available online from http://www.huffingtonpost. com/marina-cantacuzino/what-redemption-for-a-chi_b_489215. html (accessed 24 February 2011).

Cardwell, M., Clark, L., and Meldrum, C., (2008) *Psychology AS for AQA A*, 4th edition (London: Harper Collins Publishers Limited).

Carlson, E.B. and Putman, F.W. (1993) 'An Update on the Dissociative Experiences Scale,' *Dissociation*, 6: 16–27.

Carlson, H.R., Johnston, A., Liiceanu, A., Vintila C. and Harvey, J.H. (2000) 'Lessons in the Psychology of Loss: Accounts of Middle-aged Romanian Women', in Harvey, J.H. and Pauwels B.G. (eds) (2000) *Post-Traumatic Stress Theory: Research and Application* (E. Sussex: Brunner/Mazel Taylor & Francis Group).

Cartwright, R.H. and Kent, S.A. (1992) 'Social Control in Alternative Religions: A Familial Perspective,' *Sociological Analysis,* 53 (4): 345–61.

Chang, M,, (2007) *'Cultural differences in parenting styles and their effects on teens' self-esteem, perceived parental relationship satisfaction, and self-satisfaction',* Dietrich College Honors Theses. Paper 85. Available online from http://repository.cmu.edu/cgi/viewcontent.cgi?article=1084&context=hsshonors (accessed 22 April 2014).

Chambers, W.V., Langone, M.D., Dole, A.A. and Grice, J.W. (1994) 'The Group Psychological Abuse Scale: A measure of the Varieties of Cultic Abuse,' *Cultic Studies Journal,* 11 (1): 88–117.

Cherry, K. (2013) *'Client Centred Therapy',* Available online from http://psychology.about.com/od/typesofpsychotherapy/a/client-centered-therapy.htm (accessed 6 March 2013).

Cherry Lane Collection (2008) 15th Century English Proverbs Available online from http://www.famous-proverbs.com/15th_Century_Proverbs.htm (accessed 17 May 2011).

Chirkov, V. Ryan, R.M., Kim, Y. and Kaplan, U. (2003) 'Differentiating Autonomy From Individualism and Independence: A Self-Determination Theory Perspective on Internalization of Cultural Orientations and Well-Being', *Journal of Personality and Social Psychology,* 84 (1): 97–110.

Chorpita, B. and Barlow, D.H. (1998) 'The Development of Anxiety: The Role of Control in the Early Environment,' *Psychological Bulletin*, 124 (1): 3–21.

Cialdini, R.B. (1984) *Influence: the Psychology of Persuasion* (New York: William Morrow).

Cialdini, R.B. (2005) *'You Don't Have to Be a Fool to Be Fooled'* Paper presented at plenary session at International Cultic Studies Association Conference 'Psychological Manipulation, Cultic Groups and Other Alternative Movements', 14–16 June, University of Madrid, Spain.

Clark, J.G., Langone, M.D., Schecter, R.E. and Daly, R.C. (1981) *Destructive Cult Conversion: Theory, Research, and Treatment* (Weston, MA: American Family Foundation).

Cochran, M. and Brassard, J.A. (1979) 'Child Development and Personal Social Networks,' *Child Development*, 50: 601–16, cited in Bee, H. (1992) *The Developing Child*, 6th edition (New York: Harper Collins).

Cockburn, L. (2002) 'Children and Young People Living in Changing Worlds: The Process of Assessing and Understanding the Third Culture Kid', *School Psychology International*, 23 (4): 475–85.

Connolly, R., (2011) *Something Somebody Stole* (Charleston, South Carolina: CreateSpace).

Conway, F. and Siegelman, J. (1982) 'Information Disease: Have Cults Created a New Mental Illness?' *Science Digest*, 90 (1): 86–92.

Cooper, C., (1985) *Good-enough parenting– a framework for assessment.* British Agencies for Adoption and Fostering, London, 55-80, in

Daniel, B., Gilligan, R. and Vassell, S., (2010), *Child Development in Child Care and Protection Workers*, 2nd revised edition (London, UK: Jessica Kingsley Publishers).

Copi, I.M. (1972) *Introduction to Logic*, 4th edition (New York: Macmillan).

Cowan, D.E. (2002) *'Cult Apology: A Modest (Typological) Proposal'*, Paper presented to the 2002 Society for the Scientific Study of Religion Conference, Salt Lake City, Utah, 1–3 November. Available online from http://www.cornerstonemag.com/cart/txt/cowanSSR02.htm (accessed 17 December 2002).

Craig, N.W. and Weathers, R. (1990) 'The False Transformational Promise of Bible-Based Cultic Groups: Archetypal dynamics,' *Cultic Studies Journal*, 2: 17–30.

Crinic, K.A., Greenberg, M.T., Ragozin, A.S., Robinson, N.M. and Basham, R.B. (1983) 'Effects of Stress and Social Support on Mothers and Premature and Full-Term Infants,' *Child Development*, 54: 209–17, cited in Bee, H. (1992) *The Developing Child*, 6th edition (New York: Harper Collins).

Cunningham, B. (1993) *Child Development* (New York: Harper Collins Publishers).

Cushman, P. (1984) 'The Politics of Vulnerability: Youth in Religious Cults,' *Psychohistory Review*, 12 (4): 5–17.

David, P. (2010-2012) *'Recovery from Depersonalisation and Derealisation: Understanding Feelings of Unreality'* Available online from http://www.anxietynomore.co.uk/depersonalisation_and_derealisation.html (accessed 23 August 2013).

Davison, G.C. and Neale, J.M. (1998) *Abnormal Psychology*, 7th edition (New York: John Wiley & Sons).

Deci, E.L. and Ryan, R.M. (1985) *Intrinsic Motivation Theory and Self-Determination Theory in Human Behaviour* New York: Plenum, cited in Chirkov, V. Ryan, R.M. Kim, Y. and Kaplan, U. (2003) 'Differentiating Autonomy From Individualism and Independence: A Self-Determination Theory Perspective on Internalization of Cultural Orientations and Well-Being', *Journal of Personality and Social Psychology*, 84 (1) 97–110.

Derogatis, L.R. (1994) *Symptom Checklist-90-R. Administration, Scoring, and Procedures Manual*, 3rd edition (Minneapolis: National Computer Systems).

DiBlasio F (2004) *'Forgiveness in Marital & Intergenerational Family Relationships'* University of Maryland, Available online from http://www.forgiving.org/Result_Summaries_2006/Frederick_DiBlasio.pdf (accessed 24 February 2011).

Dickens, C. (1846 – 1848) *Dombey and Son* (Hertfordshire, UK: Wordsworth Editions Limited)

Dutton, D. and Painter, S. (1981) 'Traumatic Bonding: The Development of Emotional Attachments in Battered Women and Other Relationships of Intermittent Abuse', *Victimology: An International Journal*, 6: 139–55.

Dutton, D. and Painter, S. (1994) 'Emotional Attachments in Abusive Relationships: A Test of Traumatic Bonding Theory,' *Violence & Victims*, 8 (2): 105–20.

Easterbrooks, M.A. and Graham, C.A. (1999) 'Security of Attachment and Parenting: Homeless and Low-Income Housed Mothers and infants', American Journal of Orthopsychiatry, 69: 337–45, cited in Prevatt, F.F. (2003) 'The contribution of parenting practices in a risk and resiliency model of children's adjustment', British Journal of Developmental Psychology, 21: 469–80.

Egholm, C.P. (2005) 'Grandchildren of God: An Empirical Investigation of Apostasy Among Former Second Generation Members of the Family (Children of God).' MA Thesis, Department of the Study of Religion, University of Aarhus, Denmark. Summary in English entitled 'Grandchildren of God – the raw statistics', available online from http: //www.movingon.org/documents/summary_ of_statistics.doc (accessed 14 January 2005). And general summary entitled 'summary' available in English online from http: //www.movingon.org/documents/summary.doc (accessed 14 January 2005).

Ehlers, A. and Clark, D. M. (2000) 'A Cognitive Model of Posttraumatic Stress Disorder', Behaviour Research and Therapy, 38, 319–45, cited in Michael, T., Ehlers, A. and Halligan, S.L., (2005) 'Enhanced Priming for Trauma-Related Material in Posttraumatic Stress Disorder', Emotion, 5 (1): 103–12.

Enroth, R. (1992) Churches that Abuse (Michigan, US: Zondervan Publishing House). Available online from http://www.reveal. org/development/Churches_that_Abuse.pdf (accessed 5 July 2014).

Entwistle, J. (2000) The Fashioned Body: Fashion Dress and Modern Social Theory (Cambridge: Polity Press).

Erdley, C.A., Nangle, D.W., Newman, J.E. and Carpenter, E.M. (2001) 'Children's Friendship Experiences and Psychological Adjustment: Theory and Research', in Nangle, D.W. and Erdley, C.A. (eds) *The Role of Friendship in Psychological Adjustment. New Directions for Children and Adolescent Development* (San Francisco: Jossey-Bass).

Erikson, E.H. (1958 and 1980) *Identity and the Life Cycle* (New York: Norton), cited in Worth, P.J. (2000) 'Localised Creativity: A Life Span Perspective.' Unpublished PhD Thesis, The Open University, Milton Keynes.

Erickson, E.H. (1959) *Identity and the Life Cycle. Psychological Issues, Monograph 1.* (New York: International Universities Press), cited in Miller, P.H. (1993) *Theories of Developmental Psychology*, 3rd edition (New York: W.H. Freeman and Company).

Erikson, E.H. (1980) 'On The Generational Cycle: An Address', *International Journal Of Psychoanalysis*, 61: 213–23, cited in Worth, P.J. (2000) 'Localised Creativity: A Life Span Perspective.' (Unpublished PhD Thesis, Milton Keynes: The Open University).

Erikson, E.H. and Erikson, J. (1981) 'On Generativity and Identity: From a Conversation with Erik and Joan Erikson,' *Harvard Educational Review*, 51 (2): 249–69, cited in Worth, P.J. (2000) 'Localised Creativity: A Life Span Perspective.' Unpublished PhD Thesis, The Open University, Milton Keynes.

Erikson, J.M. (1988) *Wisdom and the Senses: The Way of Creativity* (New York: Norton), cited in Worth, P.J. (2000) 'Localised Creativity: A Life Span Perspective.' Unpublished PhD Thesis, The Open University, Milton Keynes

EyeWideShut (2002; 20 October) *'To Mika'.* Available online from http://movingon.org/article.asp?sID=4&Cat=24&ID=877&search Terms=prostitute&qlid= (accessed 16 July 2004).

Eysenck, M.W. and Eysenck, M.C. (1980) 'Effects of Processing Depth, Distinctiveness, and Word Frequency Retention,' *British Journal of Psychology,* 71: 263–74.

Finch, M. (2009) *Without the Guru: How I took my life back after thirty years* (US: Babbling Brook Press).

Fincham, F. (2002) *'Forgiveness in Family Relationships'* Florida State University, Available online from http://www.forgiving.org/Result_ Summaries_2006/Frank_Fincham.pdf (accessed 24 February 2011)

Findlay, A. (2004) *'My Ordinary Self'* Inform Seminar XXXIII: London School of Economics and Political Science, 4 December 2004.

Findler, L. and Taubman-Ben-Ari, O. (2003) 'Social Workers' Perceptions & Practice Regarding Grandparents in Families of Children with a Developmental Disorder,' *Families in Society,* 84 (1): 86–94.

Fish, E. (2001) 'The Prevalence of Child Maltreatment in the UK.' *National Child Protection Clearing House Newsletter,* 9 (1) 6-9.

Fortune, M.M. (1995) 'Is Nothing Sacred? When Sex Invades the Pastoral Relationship', in Gonsiorek, J.C. (ed.) *Breach of Trust: Sexual Exploitation by Health Care Professionals and Clergy* (London: Sage), pp. 29–40.

Foundation for Grandparenting (1982) 'Mistakes Grandparents Make' Available on-line from: http://www.grandparenting.org/ mistakes1.htm (Accessed 05 Oct 2009).

Francis, V.M., Rajan, P. and Turner, N. (1990) 'British Community Norms for Brief Symptom Inventory,' *British Journal of Clinical Psychology*, 29: 115–16, cited in Mytton J.A. (1993) 'An Exploratory Study of the Mental Health of Former Members of the Taylorite Branch of the Exclusive Brethren,' MSc Counselling Thesis, Goldsmiths College, London.

Frankl, V.E. (1963) *Man's Search for Meaning: An Introduction to Logotherapy* (New York: Washington Square Press).

Franzoi, S.L. (2000) *Social Psychology*, 2nd edition (New York: McGraw-Hill Higher Education).

Fraser, C. (1995) 'Suffering Children and the Christian Science Church,' *The Atlantic Monthly* 264 (4): 105-120. Available online from http://www.theatlantic.com/past/docs/unbound/flashbks/xsci/suffer.htm (Accessed 1 April 2013).

Frick, P.J., Christian, R.E. and Wooton, J.M. (1999) 'Age Trends in the Association Between Parenting Practices and Conduct Problems,' *Behaviour Modification*, 23: 106–28, cited in Prevatt, F.F. (2003) 'The Contribution of Parenting Practices in a Risk and Resiliency Model of Children's Adjustment', *British Journal of Developmental Psychology*, 21: 469–80.

Furnari, L. (2004) *'Growing Up in Cults: Developmental Aspects,'* Paper Presented to Annual Conference of the AFF, June 11–12, University of Alberta, Edmonton, Canada.

Furnari, L. (2005) 'Born or Raised in High-Demand Groups: Developmental Considerations', ICSA newsletter, 4 (2).

Furnham, A. and Bochner, S. (1986) *Culture Shock: Psychological Reactions to Unfamiliar Environments* (London: Methuen), cited in Berry, J.W., Poortinga, Y.H., Segall, M.H. and Dasen, P.R. (1992) *Cross-Cultural Psychology: Research and Applications* (Cambridge: Cambridge University Press).

Gaines, M.J., Wilson, M.A., Redican, K.J. and Baffi, C.R. (1984) 'The Effects of Cult Membership on the Health Status of Adults and Children,' *Health Values: Achieving High Level Wellness,* 8 (2): 13–17, cited in Langone, M.D. and Eisenberg, G. (1993) 'Children and Cults' in Langone, M.D. (1993) (ed.) *Recovery From Cults. Help for Victims of Psychological and Spiritual Abuse* (New York: Norton & Co).

Galanter, M., Rabkin, R., Rabkin, J., & Deutsch, A. (1979) '"The Moonies": A psychological study of conversion and membership in a contemporary religious sect,' *American Journal of Psychiatry* 136(2): February, 165-70.

Galanter, M. (1982) 'Charismatic Religious Sects and Psychiatry: An Overview,' *American Journal of Psychiatry,* 139 (12): 1539–48.

Galanter, M. (1989) *Cults: Faith Healing, and Coercion* (New York: Oxford University Press), cited in Zablocki, B. (2001) 'Towards a Demystified and Disinterested Theory of Brainwashing', in Zablocki, B. and Robbins, T. (eds) (2001) *Misunderstanding Cults: Searching for Objectivity in a Controversial Field* (London: University of Toronto Press).

Garvey, K. (1993) 'The Importance of Information in Preparing for Exit Counselling: A Case Study' in Langone, M.D. (ed.) (1993) *Recovery from Cults. Help for Victims of Psychological and Spiritual Abuse* (New York: Norton & Co.), pp. 327–42.

Gasde, I. and Block, R.A. (1998) 'Cult Experience: Psychological Abuse, Distress, Personality Characteristics, and Changes in Personal Relationships Reported by Former Members of Church Universal and Triumphant,' *Cultic Studies Journal* 15 (2). Available online from http://www.csj.org/pub_csj/csj_v0115_n02_98/cutexperiencetext.htm (accessed 24 March 2003).

Giambalvo, C. (1992) *Exit Counselling. A Family Intervention. How to Respond to Cult-Affected Loved Ones* (Bonita Springs, FL: American Family Foundation).

Giambalvo, C. (1999) *'Thought Reform Consultation'*, Paper presented at AFF Conference, 'Cults Psychological Manipulation and Society' May 14–16, University of Minnesota, Minneapolis.

Gibson, K., Morgan, M., Woolley, C., and Powis, T. (2010) A Different Kind of Family: Retrospective Accounts of Growing up at Centrepoint and Implications for Adulthood. Massey University, School of Psychology, Palmerston North: New Zealand. Available online from http://muir.massey.ac.nz/bitstream/10179/1850/3/Centrepoint_Report_2010.pdf (accessed 16 November 2010).

Gibson, K., Morgan, M., Woolley, C., and Powis, T. (2011) 'Life after Centrepoint: Accounts of adult adjustment after childhood spent at an experimental community'
New Zealand Journal of Psychology, 40, (3):41-51. Available online from http://www.psychology.org.nz/cms_show_download.php?id=1422 (accessed 9 April 2013).

Goffman, E. (1959) *The Presentation of Self in Everyday Life* (New York: Doubleday and Anchor), cited in Kent, S. and Krebs, T. 'When Scholars Know Sin: Alternative Religions and their Academic Supporters,' *Skeptic* 6 (3): 14–26.

Goffman, E. (1971) *The Presentation of Self in Everyday Life* (London: The Penguin Press), cited in Entwistle, J. (2000) *The Fashioned Body: Fashion Dress and Modern Social Theory* (Cambridge: Polity Press).

Goldberg, L., (2006) 'Raised in Cultic Groups: The Impact on Development of Certain Aspects of Character', *Cultic Studies Review* 5, (1): 4-19, available online from https://docs.google.com/file/d/0B4dmoPK1tYNjTHhFMHRVcDZ4WDA/edit?pli=1 (accessed 22 April 2014).

Goldberg, L., (1993) 'Guidelines for Therapists' in Langone, M.D. (ed.) (1993) *Recovery from Cults. Help for Victims of Psychological and Spiritual Abuse* (New York: Norton & Co).

Goldberg, L. and Goldberg, W. (1982). 'Group Work with Former Cultists,' *Social Work*, 27: 165–70.

Gorsuch, R.L. (1988) 'Psychology of Religion,' *Annual Review of Psychology*, 39: 201–22, cited in Sunberg, N.D., Latkin, C.A., Littman, R.A. and Hagan, R.A. (1990) 'Personality in a Religious Commune: CPI's in Rajneeshpuram,' *Journal of Personality Assessment*, 55 (1&2): 7–17.

Gray, M.J., Bolton, E.E. and Litz, B.T. (2004) 'A Longitudinal Analysis of PTSD Symptom Course: Delayed-Onset PTSD in Somalia Peacekeepers', *Journal of Consulting and Clinical Psychology*, 72 (5): 909–913.

Great Ormond Street Hospital review this article in June 2007 '*Eye Movement Desensitisation and Re-processing (EMDR)*'Available online from http://www.gosh.nhs.uk/medical-conditions/procedures-and-treatments/eye-movement-desensitisation-and-re-processing-emdr/ (accessed 26 March 2013).

Gritz, J.A. (2011) *Drinking the Kool-Aid: A Survivor Remembers Jim Jones*, The Atlantic, Nov 18 (Survivors name: Teri Buford O'Shea) Available online from http://www.theatlantic.com/national/archive/2011/11/drinking-the-kool-aid-a-survivor-remembers-jim-jones/248723/# (accessed 21 Nov 2011).

Gross, R.D. *Psychology: The Science of Mind and Behaviour,* 2nd edition (London: Hodder and Stoughton).

Guest, T. (2004) *My Life in Orange* (London: Granta Books).

Gullone, E. and King, N.J. (1997) 'Three-year Follow Up of Normal Fear in Children and Adolescents Aged 7 To 18 Years,' *British Journal of Developmental Psychology,* 15: 97–111.

Haight, M. (1999) *The Snake and the Fox: an Introduction to Logic* (London: Routledge).

Haney, C., Curtis, B. and Zimbardo, P. (1995) 'A Study of Prisoners and Guards in a Simulated Prison', in Aronson, E. *Readings about The Social Animal,* 4th edition (New York: W.H. Freeman and Company).

Harvey, J.H. (1996) *Embracing their Memory: Loss and the Social Psychology of Storytelling* (Needham Heights, MA: Allyn & Bacon), cited in Carlson, H.R. Johnston, A., Liiceanu, A., Vintila C. and Harvey, J.H. (2000) 'Lessons in the Psychology of Loss: Accounts of Middle-aged Romanian Women', in Harvey, J.H. and Pauwels B.G. (eds) (2000) *Post-Traumatic Stress Theory: Research and Application* (E. Sussex: Brunner/Mazel Taylor & Francis Group).

Harwood, E.A. (2003) 'Authoritarian Parenting and its Relationship to Aggression in Males Diagnosed with a Learning Disability or

Attention-Deficit/Hyperactivity Disorder.' Dissertation Abstracts International: Section B: the Sciences & Engineering. Vol 61 (1-B), 441 USA: University Microfilms International: Pennsylvania State University.

Haslam, S.A. and Reicher, S. D. (2012) 'Contesting the "Nature" of Conformity: What Milgram and Zimbardo's Studies Really Show', in *PLOS Biology* 10 (11): 1-4.

Hawkins, J.M. (1991) *The Oxford Minidictionary* Third Edition (Oxford: Clarendon Press).

Hayslip, B. (2001) 'Grandparents Raising Grandchildren: New Challenges for Geropsychologists.' *Adult Development and Aging News* Spring 2001, 5.

Helfer, R. (1983, 5 August) *'The Children of the House of Judah,'* unpublished report, East Lansing: Michigan State University, Department of Paediatrics/Human Development.

Herman, J.L. (1992) *Trauma and Recovery: from Domestic Abuse to Political Terror* (New York: Basic Books).

Hewstone, M. Fincham, F.D. and Foster, J. (eds) (2005) *Psychology,* (Oxford: BPS Blackwell), cited in Cardwell, M., Clark, L. and Meldrum, C., (2008) *Psychology AS for AQA A,* 4th edition (London: Harper Collins Publishers Limited).

Higgins, D., (2004) Differentiating between Child Maltreatment Experiences *Family Matters* 69, (spring/summer): 50-55.

Hochstetler, P. (2007) *Delusion: Growing Up in an Amish-Jewish Cult* (Indiana, US: Baker Trittin Press)

Hollenhorst, J. (2011, 30 Dec) 'Marriages dissolved, sexual relationships banned among FLDS faithful'. Available online from http://www.ksl.com/index.php?nid=148&sid=18684356&title=marriages-dissolved-sexual-relationships-banned-among-flds-faithful (accessed 24 June 2013).

Hollingworth, L.S. (1933) 'The Adolescent Child,' in Murchison, C.A. (ed.) A Handbook of Child Psychology (Worcester, MA: Clark University Press), cited in Beit-Hallahmi, B. and Argyle, M. (1997) The Psychology of Religious Behaviour, Belief and Experience (London: Routledge).

Holtzman, S. Newth, S. and Delongis, A. (2004) 'The Role of Social Support in Coping with Daily Pain among Patients with Rheumatoid Arthritis', Journal of Health Psychology, 9 (5): 677–95.

Home Office Communications Directorate (May 2004) 'Adults: Safer from Sexual Crime: The Sexual Offences Act 2003' pp. 1–9. Available online from http: //www.fawcettsociety.org.uk/documents/SOA03_000.pdf (accessed 7 March 2005).

Hounam, P. and Hogg, A, (1984) Secret Cult (England: Lion Publishing).

Hughes, P. M., 'Forgiveness', The Stanford Encyclopaedia of Philosophy (Winter 2011 Edition), Edward N. Zalta (ed.), Available online from http://plato.stanford.edu/archives/win2011/entries/forgiveness/ (accessed 11 December 2012).

Jules (2005, 1 February) 'A Mother and Her Toddler'. Available online from http://www.movingon.org/article.asp?sID=1&Cat=10&ID=2594 (accessed 3 February 2005).

Hyper Dictionary (2003) 'Meaning of Compassion'. Available online from http://www.hyperdictionary.com/dictionary/compassion (accessed 14 February 2005).

Irenyi, M., Bromfield, L., Beyer, L., and Higgins, D. (2006). Child Maltreatment in Organisations: Risk Factors and Strategies for Prevention. *Child Abuse Prevention Issues*, 25, 1-23.

Jacobs, M. (1985) *The Presenting Past: An Introduction to Practical Psychodynamic Counselling* (Milton Keynes, UK: Open University Press).

Jansà, J.M. (2005) 'Updating Cultic Knowledge: A Prevalence Study ✓ and Qualitative Research', Paper presented at International Cultic Studies Association Conference 'Psychological Manipulation, Cultic Groups and Other Alternative Movements', 14–16 June, University of Madrid, Spain.

Jarvis, G.K. and Northcott, H.C. (1987) 'Religion and Differences in Morbidity and Mortality,' *Social Science and Medicine*, 25: 813–24, cited in Beit-Hallahmi, B. and Argyle, M. (1997) *The Psychology of Religious Behaviour, Belief and Experience* London: Routledge.

Jeffs, B (2009) *Lost Boy* (New York, US: Broadway Books).

Jenkinson, G. (2005) 'A Gestalt Therapist's Phenomenological Exploration into What Helps Ex-Members Recover from an Abusive Cult Experience.' Submitted Masters Thesis, The Sherwood Institute and The University of Birmingham, England.

Johnson, W.B. and Huwe, J.M. (2002) 'Toward a Typology of Mentorship Dysfunction in Graduate School,' *Psychotherapy: Theory/Research/ Practise/Training*, 39 (1) 44–55.

Johnson, D and VanVonderen, J. (1991) *The Subtle Power of Spiritual Abuse: Recognizing and Escaping Spiritual Manipulation and False Spiritual Authority Within the Church* (Minneapolis, Minnesota: Bethany House Publishers).

Jones, K. Jones, C. and Buhring, J (2007) *Not Without my Sister* (London: Harper Element).

Jones, S. (2011a) *Call Me Evil, Let me Go: A Mother Struggle to Save Her Children from a Brutal Religious Cult*, Australia, Harper Collins Publishers.

Jones, S. (2011b) '*About the book: Call Me Evil, Let me Go*' *Available online from* http://www.harpercollins.com/books/Call-Me-Evil-Let-Go-Sarah-Jones/?isbn=9780007433568 (accessed 28 February 2014).

Jules (2002, 15 April) 'Comments from a Fallen Woman'. Available online from http: //www.movingon.org/article.asp?sID=8&Cat=19&ID=329 (accessed 4 March 2005).

Jules (2005, 1 February) 'A Mother and Her Toddler'. Available online from http: //www.movingon.org/article.asp?sID=1&Cat=10&ID=2594 (accessed 3 February 2005).

Kanigel, R. (1986) *Apprentice to Genius: The Making of a Scientific Dynasty* (Baltimore: The John Hopkins University Press).

Kaplan, J. (2001) 'The Roots of Religious Violence in America', in Zablocki, B. and Robbins, T. (eds) (2001) *Misunderstanding Cults: Searching for Objectivity in a Controversial Field* (London: University of Toronto Press).

Katchen, M.H. (1997) 'The Rate of Dissociation and Dissociative Disorders in Former Members of High Demand Religious Movements.' PhD thesis, Sociology Department, Sydney University, Sydney, Australia, cited in Zablocki, B. and Robbins, T. (eds) (2001) *Misunderstanding Cults: Searching for Objectivity in a Controversial Field* (London: University of Toronto Press).

Kaufman, G. (1989) *The Psychology of Shame* (London: Routledge).

Kebshull, B., and Pozo, M. (2006). Third Culture Kids/Global Nomads and the Culturally Skilled Therapist, LCSW Available online from http://clinicalsocialworksociety.org/docs/continuing_education/ThirdCultureKids.pdf (accessed 10 Feb 2012).

Keiser, T.W. and Keiser, J.L. (1987) *The Anatomy of Illusion. Religious Cults and Destructive Persuasion* (Springfield, Illinois: Charles C Thomas).

Kendall, L. (2006) 'A Psychological Exploration into the Effects of Former Membership of 'Extremist Authoritarian Sects'' (PhD Thesis, Brunel University, England, UK).

Kendall, L. (2010) 'Physical Child Abuse in Sects', *Paradigm*, 15 (3) 6-8. On-line Available from http://www.addictionrecov.org/Paradigm/DisplayParadigmIssue.aspx?ID=50 (accessed 8 September 2011).

Kent, S. (1993) 'Deviant Scripturalism and Ritual Satanic Abuse Part One: Possible Judeo-Christian Influences,' *Religion* 23: 229–41.

Kent, S. A. (2005) 'Education and Re-Education in Ideological Organizations and Their Implications for Children' *Cultic Studies Review* 4, (2). Available online from http://griess.st1.at/gsk/fecris/english%20Kent.htm (accessed 28th May 2011).

Kent, S. (2010) 'House of Judah, the Northeast Kingdom Community, and 'the Jonestown Problem': Downplaying Child Physical Abuses and Ignoring Serious Evidence,' *International Journal of Cultic Studies*, 1, (1): 29-53.

Kent, S. and Krebs, T. (1998) 'When Scholars Know Sin: Alternative religions and their Academic Supporters,' *Skeptic* 6 (3): 14–26.

Kessler, R.C., Sonnega, A., Bromet, E., Hughes, M. and Nelson, C.B. (1995) 'Posttraumatic Stress Disorder in the National Comorbidity Survey', *Archives of General Psychiatry*, 52: 1048–60, cited in Kubany, E.S., Hill, E.E., Owens, J.A. Iannce-Spencer, C., McCraig, M.A., Tremayne, K.J., Williams, P.L., (2004) 'Cognitive Trauma Therapy for Battered Women with PTSD (CCT-BW)', *Journal of Consulting and Clinical Psychology*, 72 (1): 3–18.

King, J.N., Akande, A. and Dong, Q. (1996) 'Fears in American, Australian, Chinese and Nigerian Children and Adolescents: A Cross-Cultural Study,' *Child Psychology, Psychiatry*, 37 (2): 213–20.

Kirsch, M.A. and Glass, L.L. (1977) 'Psychiatric Disturbances Associated with Erhard Seminars Training: II. Additional Cases and Theoretical Considerations,' *American Journal of Psychiatry*, 134: 1254–8, cited in Sirkin, M.I. (1990) 'Cult Involvement: A Systems Approach to Assessment and Treatment,' *Psychotherapy*, 27: 116–23.

Kochanska, G., Gross, J.N., Lin, M. and Nichols, K.E. (2002) 'Guilt in Young Children: Development, Determinants, and Relations with a Broader System of Standards,' *Child Development* 73 (2): 461–82.

Koehn, N.F., (2006) 'On the Fallacy of Perfection' Personal Excellence, *The Magazine of Life Leadership*. Available online from http://www.eep2.com/images/PE0606.pdf (accessed 19 March 2013).

Koenen, K.C., Stellman, J.M., Stellman, S.D. and Sommer, J.F., (2003) 'Risk Factors for Course of Posttraumatic Stress Disorder Among Vietnam Veterans: A 14-Year Follow-Up of American Legionnaires', *Journal of Consulting and Clinical Psychology*, 71 (6): 980–6.

Kornhaber, A., (1996) *Contemporary Grandparenting* (California, Sage Publications, Inc).

Kornhaber, A., (2006) *The Grandparent Guide*, (New York: McGraw Hill).

Kosmin, B.A. and Lachman, S.P. (1993) *One Nation under God* (New York: Harmony Books), cited in Beit-Hallahmi, B. and Argyle, M. (1997) *The Psychology of Religious Behaviour, Belief and Experience* (London: Routledge).

Krahe, B. (2000) 'Childhood Sexual Abuse and Revictimization in Adolescence and Adulthood', in Harvey, J.H. and Pauwels B.G. (eds) (2000) *Post-Traumatic Stress Theory: Research and Application* (E. Sussex: Brunner/Mazel Taylor & Francis Group).

Kramer, L.S. (2000) *The Religion that Kills, Christian Science: Abuse, Neglect and Mind Control*, (Louisiana: Huntington House Publishers).

Kübler-Ross, E. (1970) *On Death and Dying*, (London: Routledge).

Landa, S. (1990/1991) 'Children and Cults: A Practical Guide,' *University of Louisville Journal of Family Law*, 29(3): 591–634, cited in Langone, M.D. and Eisenberg, G. (1993) 'Children and Cults,' in Langone, M.D. (ed.) (1993) *Recovery from Cults. Help for Victims of Psychological and Spiritual Abuse* (New York: Norton & Co.).

Langone, M.D. (1992a) 'Preface' to Giambalvo, C. (1992) *Exit Counselling. A Family Intervention. How to Respond to Cult-Affected Loved Ones* (Bonita Springs, FL: American Family Foundation).

Langone, M.D. (1992b) 'Psychological Abuse,' *Cultic Studies Journal*, 9 (2): 206–17.

Langone, M.D. (ed.) (1993) *Recovery from Cults. Help for Victims of Psychological and Spiritual Abuse* (New York: Norton & Co.).

Langone, M.D. (1995) 'An Investigation of a Reputedly Psychologically Abusive Group that Targets College Students' (Tech. Rep.). Boston: Boston University, Danielson Institute.

Langone, M.D. (1998) 'Cultic Groups & Children: What does the Literature tell us?' Paper Presented to Annual Conference of the American Family Foundation, May 29–31, Philadelphia, PA.

Langone, M.D. (1999) 'What Should Be Done About Cults?' Available online from http: //www.addictionrecov.org/paradigm/P_PR_SP00/cont_langone.htm (accessed 11 December 2002)

Langone, M.D. (2003a) 'The Definitional Ambiguity of 'Cult' and AFF's Mission.' Available online from http: //www.cultinfobooks.com/infoserv_aff/aff_termdefambiguity.htm (accessed 23 April 2003).

Langone, M.D. (2003b) Personal phone conversation, 20 June 2003.

Langone, M.D. and Eisenberg, G. (1993) 'Children and Cults' in Langone, M.D. (ed.) (1993) *Recovery from Cults. Help for Victims of Psychological and Spiritual Abuse* (New York: Norton & Co.), pp. 327–42.

Langone, M.D. and Ryan, P. (2005) 'Religious Conflict Resolution: A Model for Families,' Paper presented at International Cultic Studies Association Conference 'Psychological Manipulation, Cultic Groups and Other Alternative Movements', 14–16 June, University of Madrid, Spain.

Lee, C.-S., Chang, J.-C. and Cheng, A.T.A. (2002) 'Acculturation and Suicide: A Case-Control Psychological Autopsy Study,' *Psychological Medicine* 32 (1): 133–41.

Levin, J.S. (1994) 'Religion and Health: Is there an association, is it valid, and is it causal?' *Social Science and Medicine*, 38: 1475–82, cited in Beit-Hallahmi, B. and Argyle (1997) *The Psychology of Religious Behaviour, Belief and Experience* London: Routledge.

Levinson, D.J. (1996) *Seasons of a Woman's Life* (New York: Alfred Knopf).

Lewis, J.R. and Bromley, D.G. (1987). 'The Cult Withdrawal Syndrome: A case of misattribution of cause?' *Journal for the Scientific Study of Religion*, 26 (4): 508–22.

Lifton, R.J. (1961) *Thought Reform and the Psychology of Totalism* (New York: W.W. Norton).

Lloyd, D.A. and Turner, R.J., (2003) 'Cumulative Adversity and Posttraumatic Stress Disorder: Evidence From a Diverse Community Sample of Young Adults', *American Journal of Orthopsychiatry*, 73 (4): 381–91.

Loewenthal, K.M. (2000) *The Psychology of Religion: A Short Introduction* (Oxford: Oneworld).

Lord Justice Ward (1995) *The Judgement of Lord Justice Ward* (October 19th 1995 W 42 1992 IN THE HIGH COURT OF JUSTICE). Available online from http: //www.exfamily.org/art/misc/just-ward_ver1.html (accessed 26 March 2003).

Lourie, J.B. (1996) 'Cumulative Trauma: The Nonproblem Problem', *Transactional Analysis Journal*, 26: 276–83, cited in Burks, R. (2002) 'Cognitive Impairment in Thought Reform Environments,' Ph.D. Thesis, Ohio University. Available online from: http: //oak.cats.ohio.edu/~rb267689 (accessed 7 May 2002).

Luck, K. (1992) 'Trouble in Eden, Trouble with Eve: Women, Trousers and Utopian Socialism in Nineteenth Century America,' in J.

Ash and E. Wilson (eds), *Chic Thrills: A Fashion Reader* (London: Pandora).

Maccoby, E.E. and Martin, J.A. (1983) 'Socialization in the Context of the Family: Parent-Child Interaction', in Hetherington, E.M. (ed.), *Handbook of Child Psychology: Socialization, Personality, and Social Development*, Vol. 4 (New York: Wiley), pp. 1–102.

MacHovick, F.J. (1991) 'Cults, Personality, and Pathology,' *Psychotherapy in Private Practice*, 8(4): 77–85.

Macias, C., Young, R. and Barreira, P. (2000) 'Loss of Trust: Correlates of the Comorbidity of PTSD Severe Mental Illness', in Harvey, J.H. and Pauwels B.G. (eds) (2000) *Post-Traumatic Stress Theory: Research and Application* (E. Sussex: Brunner/Mazel Taylor & Francis Group).

MacInnes, R.A. (1998) *Children in the Game* (Alberta, Street Teams).

Malim, T. and Birch, A., (1998) *Introductory Psychology* 1998, (London: Macmillan Press Ltd.)

Malinoski, P.T., Langone, M.D. and Lynn, S.J. (1999) 'Psychological Distress in Former Members of the International Churches of Christ and Noncultic Groups,' *Cultic Studies Journal*, 16 (1): 33–47.

Maron, N. and Braverman, J. (1988) 'Family Environment as a Factor in Vulnerability to Cult Involvement,' *Cultic Studies Journal*, 5(1): 23–43.

Markowitz, A. and Halperin, D.A. (1984) 'Cults and Children. The Abuse of the Young,' *Cultic Studies Journal*, 1: 143–55. Electronic Journal Reprint Version of original version. Received 11 December 2002.

Martin P.R. (1989) 'Dispelling the Myths: The Psychological Consequences of Cultic Involvement,' *Christian Research Journal,* 11: 9–14.

Martin P.R. (1993) *Cult Proofing your Kids* (Grand Rapids, MI: Zondervan).

Martin, P.R., Langone, M.D., Dole, A.A. and Wiltrout, J. (1992) 'Post-Cult Symptoms as Measured by the MCMI Before and After Residential Treatment,' *Cultic Studies Journal,* 9 (2): 219–50.

Martin, P.R., Pile, L.A., Burks, R. and Martin, S. (1998) 'Overcoming the Bondage of Revictimization, A Rational/Empirical Defence of Thought Reform,' *Cultic Studies Journal* 15 (2). Available online from http: //www.csj.org/pub_csj/csj_v0l15_n02_98/defendthoughtreform13.htm (accessed 20 May 2003).

Marwan, D (2004) 'Parenting Styles and Mental Health of Palestinian-Arab Adolescents in Israel,' *Transcultural Psychiatry,* 41 (2): 233–52.

Marzillier, J. (2004) 'The Myth of Evidence-Based Psychotherapy,' *The Psychologist,* 17 (7): 392–5.

McFarland, H. (2010) *Quivering Daughters: Hope and Healing for the Daughters of Patriarchy* (Dallas, Texas: Darklight Press).

McKeever, V.M. and Huff. M.E. (2003) 'A Diathesis-Stress Model of Post Traumatic Stress Disorder: Ecological, Biological And Residual Stress Pathways', *Review of General Psychology,* 7 (3): 237–50.

McNally, R.J. (2003) *Remembering Trauma* (London: The Belknap Press of Harvard University Press).

Meesus, W.H.J. and Raaijmakers, Q.A.W. (1995) 'Obedience in Modern Society: The Utrecht Studies', *Journal of Social Issues*, 51: 155–75, cited in Franzoi, S.L. (2000) *Social Psychology*, 2nd edition (New York: McGraw-Hill Higher Education).

Melton, J.G. (2008) 'Forty Years of the Institute for the Study of American Religion,' paper presented to INFORM, CESNUR, ISORECEA Conference, at the London School of Economics, London, 16-19 April 2008.

Michael, T., Ehlers, A. and Halligan, S.L., (2005) 'Enhanced Priming for Trauma-Related Material in Posttraumatic Stress Disorder', *Emotion*, 5 (1): 103–12.

Milgram, S. (1974) *Obedience to Authority* (New York: HarperCollins).

Miller, C.T. and Major, B. (2000) 'Coping with Stigma and Prejudice', in Heatherton, T.F., Kleck, R.E., Hebl, M.R. and Hull, J.G. (eds) *The Social Psychology of Stigma* (New York: The Guildford Press).

Miller, P.H. (1993) *Theories of Developmental Psychology*, 3rd edition (New York: W.H. Freeman and Company).

Mind, (2012) Understanding Post Traumatic Stress Disorder Available online from: http://www.mind.org.uk/help/diagnoses_and_conditions/post-traumatic_stress_disorder (accessed 6 Feb 2012).

Mitchell, R. (2011) *New Shoes: Stepping out of the shadow of sexual abuse and living your dreams*, Oxford, Lion Hudson plc.

Mlicki, P.P. and Ellemers, N. (1996) 'Being Different or Being Better? National Stereotypes and Identifications of Polish and Dutch Students,' *European Journal of Social Psychology*, 26: 97–114.

Moos, H.R. and Moos B.S. (1986) *Family Environment Scale* (Second Edition) (Palo Alto, CA: Consulting Psychologists Press).

Mostow, A.J., Izard, C.E., Fine, S. and Trentacosta, C.J. (2002) 'Modeling Emotional, Cognitive, and Behavioural Predictors of Peer Acceptance,' *Child Development* 73 (6): 1775–87.

Murken, S. (2005) 'Psycho-Social Motives for Becoming a Member of a New Religious Movement (NRM),' Paper presented at International Cultic Studies Association Conference 'Psychological Manipulation, Cultic Groups and Other Alternative Movements', 14–16 June, University of Madrid, Spain.

Muster, N. (2012, 02 Jan) *Child of the Cult* (Kindle eBook).

Mytton J.A. (1993) 'An Exploratory Study of the Mental Health of Former Members of the Taylorite Branch of the Exclusive Brethren,' MSc Counselling Thesis, Goldsmiths College, London.

Namini, S. (2005) 'Psycho-Social Consequences of Becoming a Member of a New Religious Movement (NRM),' Paper presented at International Cultic Studies Association Conference 'Psychological Manipulation, Cultic Groups and Other Alternative Movements', 14–16 June, University of Madrid, Spain.

National Churchill Museum, *Winston Churchill, The Glow Worm,* Available online from http://www.nationalchurchillmuseum.org/winston-churchill-leadership-the-glow-worm.html (accessed 19 March 2013).

NHS Choices (2010) *Symptoms of Depression.* Available online from http://www.anxietynomore.co.uk/depersonalisation_and_derealisation.html (accessed, 23 August 2012).

Nielsen, M.S. (2003) 'Prevalence of Posttraumatic Stress Disorder in Persons With Spinal Cord Injuries: The Mediating Effect of Social Support,' *Rehabilitation Psychology* 48 (4): 289–95.

Office of the High Commissioner for Human Rights (1989) *Convention on the Rights of the Child*. Available online from http://www.ohchr. org/EN/ProfessionalInterest/Pages/CRC.aspx (Accessed 24 June 2013).

Olapegba, P.O. and Emelogu, V.E. (2004) 'Live and Lets Live: Psychosocial Issues in Parent-Adolescent Conflict,' *Psychologia: An International Journal* 12 (1): 33–9.

Ollendick, T.H. and Yang, B. (1996) 'Fears in American, Australian, Chinese, and Nigerian Children and Adolescents: A Cross-Cultural study,' *Journal of Child Psychology and Psychiatry,* 37 (2): 213–20.

Orme-Collins, D. (2002) 'Death of a Moonie: Reflections of a "Blessed Child"', *Cultic Studies Review,* 1 (3): 44-46. Available online from https:// docs.google.com/file/d/0B4dmoPK1tYNjUWdJYmloNUhKRFE/ edit?pli=1 (accessed 21 April 2014).

Osherow, N. (1984) 'Making Sense of the Nonsensical: An Analysis of Jonestown', in Aronson, E. *Readings about The Social Animal*, 4th edition (New York: W.H. Freeman and Company).

Out at Last (2005, February) 'I'm free'. Available online from http:// www.movingon.org/article.asp?sID=1&Cat=16&ID=2714# (accessed 22 February 2005).

Ozer, E.J., Best, S.R., Lipsey, T.L. and Weiss, D.S. (2003) 'Predictors of Posttraumatic Stress Disorder and Symptoms in Adults: A Meta-Analysis,' *Psychological Bulletin* 129 (1): 52–73.

Ozorak, E.W. (1989) 'Social and Cognitive Influences on the Development of Religious Beliefs and Commitment in Adolescence,' *Journal for the Scientific Study of Religion,* 28: 448–63, cited in Beit-Hallahmi, B. and Argyle, M. (1997) *The Psychology of Religious Behaviour, Belief and Experience.* (London: Routledge).

Packer, D. (2008) 'Identifying systematic disobedience in Milgram's obedience experiments: a meta-analytic review', in *Perspect Psychol Sci* 3: 301–304. Cited in Haslam, S.A. and Reicher, S. D. (2012) 'Contesting the "Nature" of Conformity: What Milgram and Zimbardo's Studies Really Show', in *PLOS Biology* 10 (11): 1-4.

Pearlman, L. A. and Saakvitne, K.W. (1995) *Trauma and the Therapist: Countertransference and Vicarious Traumatization in Psychotherapy with Incest Survivors* (New York: Norton), cited in Thomas, P.M. (2005) 'Dissociation and Internal Models of Protection: Psychotherapy with Child Abuse Survivors', *Psychotherapy: Theory, Research, Practise, Training,* 42 (1): 20–36.

Pearson, M., Diaz, J., (2012) Jailed Polygamist Leader Warren Jeffs Issues Hundreds of Orders from Prison' ABC News Nov 21 2012, Available online from http://abcnews.go.com/US/jailed-polygamist-leader-warren-jeffs-issues-hundreds-orders/story?id=17770090#.UKzk-uTBEt1 (accessed 19 March 2013).

Perlmutter, M. and Hall, E. (1992.) *Adult Development and Aging* (Second Edition) (Chichester: John Wiley and Sons), cited in Worth, P.J. (2000) 'Localised Creativity: A Life Span Perspective.' (Unpublished PhD Thesis, The Open University, Milton Keynes).

Perry, B. D. and Szalavitz, M. (2006) *The Boy Who Was Raised as a Dog* (New York: Basic Books).

Pfeifer, J.E. (1992) 'The Psychological Framing of Cults: Schematic Representations and Cult Evaluations,' *Journal of Applied Social Psychology*, 22 (7): 531–44.

Pollock D. C. and Van Reken R. E. (1999) *The Third Culture Kid Experience: Growing up among worlds* (Maine USA: Intercultural Press).

Prevatt, F.F. (2003) 'The Contribution of Parenting Practices in a Risk and Resiliency Model of Children's Adjustment', *British Journal of Developmental Psychology*, 21: 469–80.

Putnam, F. W. (1999) 'Pierre Janet and Modern Views of Dissociation', in Horowitz, M.J. (ed.) *Essential Papers on Post Traumatic Stress Disorder* (London: New York University Press).

Puttick (1999) '*Osho Ko Hsuan School*' in Palmer, S.J. and Hardman, C.H. (eds) *New Religions and Children* (London: Rutgers University Press).

Rajneesh, S. (1984) *The Book: An Introduction to the Teachings of Bhagwan Shree Rajneesh* (Antelope, Ore.: Rajneesh Foundation International). Cited in Puttick (1999) '*Osho Ko Hsuan School*' in Palmer, S.J. and Hardman, C.H. (eds) *New Religions and Children* (London: Rutgers University Press).

Rando, T.A. (1993) *Treatment of Complicated Mourning* (Illinois: Research Press).

Reicher, S.D. and Haslam, S.A., (2011) 'After shock? Towards a social identity explanation of the Milgram 'obedience' studies', *Brit J Soc Psychol* 50: 163–169. Cited in Haslam, S.A. and Reicher, S. D. (2012) 'Contesting the "Nature" of Conformity: What Milgram and Zimbardo's Studies Really Show', in *PLOS Biology* 10 (11): 1-4.

Register of Trauma Specialists (2007-2012) *'Trauma support skills'* Available online from http://www.traumaregister.co.uk/Skills/index.htm (accessed 26 March 2013).

Ribeiro, A. (1992) 'Utopian Dress,' in J. Ash and E. Wilson (eds), *Chic Thrills: A Fashion Reader* (London: Pandora).

Richardson, J.T. and Dewitt, J (1992) 'Christian Science, Spiritual Healing, the Law, and Public Opinion' *Journal of Church and State* 34: 549–61. Cited in Beit-Hallahmi, B. (2001) 'O Truant Muse: Collaborationism and Research Integrity,' in Zablocki, B. and Robbins, T. (eds) (2001) *Misunderstanding Cults: Searching for Objectivity in a Controversial Field.* (London: University of Toronto Press), pp. 35–70.

Richardson, J.T., Stewart, M. and Simmonds, R.B. (1979) *Organised Miracles: A study of a contemporary youth, communal fundamentalist organisation* (New Brunswick, NJ: Transaction), cited in Beit-Hallahmi, B. and Argyle, M. (1997) *The Psychology of Religious Behaviour, Belief and Experience* (London: Routledge).

Richmond, R. L, (1997-2010) *A Guide to Psychology and its Practise: Forgiveness* Available online from http://www.guidetopsychology.com/forgive.htm (accessed 24 February 2011)

Robbins, T. (2001) 'Balance and Fairness in the Study of Alternative Religions,' in Zablocki, B. and Robbins, T. (eds) (2001) *Misunderstanding Cults: Searching for Objectivity in a Controversial Field* (London: University of Toronto Press).

Robbins, T. and Anthony, D. (1980) 'The limits of "coercive persuasion" as an explanation for conversion to authoritarian sects.' in *Political Psychology*, Summer, 22-36.

411

Rochford, E.B. (1998) 'Child Abuse in the Hare Krishna Movement: 1971–1986,' in *ISKCON Communications Journal* 6 (1). Available online from http: //www.iskcon.com/icj/6_1/6_1rochford.html (accessed 11 December 2002).

Rochford, E.B. (1999) 'Education and Collective Identity: Public Schooling of Hare Krishna youth' in Palmer, S.J. and Hardman, C.H. (eds) *New Religions and Children* (London: Rutgers University Press).

Rogers, C.R. (1951) *Client Centred Therapy* (London: St Edmundsbury Press Ltd).

Ross, J. and Langone, M. (1988) *Cults, What Parents Should Know* (New York: Carol Publishing).

Roth A. and Fonagy, P. (1996) *What Works for Whom? A Clinical Review of Psychotherapy Research* (New York: Guildford Press).

Rubin, J.H. (1998) *'Contested Narratives: A Case Study of the Conflict Between a New Religious Movement and its critics'*. Available online from http: //www.perefound.org/jr_cn.htm (accessed 11 March 2002).

Rutters, P (1989) *Sex in the Forbidden Zone: When Men in Power – Doctors, Clergy, Teachers, and Others – Betray Women's Trust* (Los Angeles: Jeremy Tarcher).

Ryan, R.M. and Deci, E.L. (2000) 'Self-Determination Theory and the Facilitation of Intrinsic Motivation, Social Development and Well-Being', *American Psychologist*, 55: 68–78, cited in Chirkov, V. Ryan, R.M. Kim, Y. and Kaplan, U. (2003) 'Differentiating Autonomy From Individualism and Independence: A Self-Determination Theory Perspective on Internalization of Cultural Orientations and Well-Being', *Journal of Personality and Social Psychology*, 84 (1:) 97–110.

Saliba, J.A. (1995) *Perspectives on New Religious Movements* (London: Geoffrey Chapman).

Sanders D. and Wills, F. (2003) *Counselling for Anxiety Problems*, 2nd edition (London: Sage publications).

Schnurr, P.P. and Green, B.L. (2004) 'A Context for Understanding the Physical Health Consequences of Exposure to Extreme Stress', in Schnurr, P.P. and Green, B.L. (2004) *Trauma and Health: Physical Health Consequences of Exposure to Extreme Stress* (Washington DC: American Psychological Association).

Schnurr, P.P., Rosenberg, S.D. and Friedman, M.J. (1993) 'Change in MMPI Scores from College to Adulthood as a Function of Military Service', *Journal of Abnormal Psychology,* 102: 288–96, cited in McNally, R.J. (2003) *Remembering Trauma* (London: The Belknap Press of Harvard University Press).

Schuldberg (2000-2001) 'Six Subclinical Spectrum Traits in Normal Creativity,' *Creativity Research Journal* 13 (1):5-16.

Schwartz, L.L. (1985) 'Leaving the cults,' *Update: A Journal of New Religious Movements* 9: 3–12.

Scott, M.J. and Stradling, S.G. (2001) *Counselling for Post-Traumatic Stress Disorder,* 2nd edition (London: Sage Publications).

Scully, D., Kremer, J., Meade, M. M., Graham, R. and Dudgeon, K., (1998) 'Physical exercise and psychological well being: a critical review' *Br J Sports Med,* 32: 111-120. Available online from http://bjsm.bmj.com/content/32/2/111.full.pdf (accessed 22 April 2014).

Sell, D.M. (2000) 'Personality and Religiousness in the Family,' paper presented at Annual Meeting of the Society for the Scientific

Study of Religion and Religious Research Association, Doubletree Post, Oak Hotel Houston, October 21ˢᵗ 2000 Available online from www.cesnur.org/2001/thefamily.htm (accessed 29 January 2002).

Sexual Offences Act (2003) 'Section 74 Consent' (p. 48). Available online from http: //www.legislation.hsmo.gov.uk/acts/acts2003/30042--b.htm (accessed 8 February 2005).

Shaw, D. (1ˢᵗ March 2007) *Spring Cleaning; Mental Health Notes.* Available online from http://www.danielshawlcsw.com/spring_clean.htm (accessed 08 April 2010).

Siddique, H. (2010) James Bulger killing: the case history of Jon Venables and Robert Thompson. Available online from http://www.guardian.co.uk/uk/2010/mar/03/james-bulger-case-venables-thompson (accessed 28 August 2012).

Singer, M.T. (1986) 'Consultation with Families of Cultists,' in Wynne, L.I., McDavid, S.H. and Weber, T.T. (eds), *The Family Therapist as Systems Consultant* (New York: Guildford Press).

Singer M. T. and Lalich, J. (1996) *Crazy Therapies* (San Francisco: Jossey-Bass Publishers).

Singer, M.T. (1995) *Cults in our Midst* (San Francisco: Jossey-Bass Publishers).

Singer, M.T. and Ofshe, R. (1990) 'Thought Reform Programs and the Production of Psychiatric Casualties,' *Psychiatric Annals* 20: 188–93.

Sirkin, M.I. (1990) 'Cult Involvement: A Systems Approach to Assessment and Treatment,' *Psychotherapy* 27: 116–23.

Siskind, A. (1999) 'In Whose Interest? Separating Children from Mothers in the Sullivan Institute/Fourth Wall Community', in Palmer, S.J. and Hardman, C.H. (eds) *New Religions and Children* (London: Rutgers University Press).

Siskind, A. (2001) 'Child-rearing Issues in Totalist Groups' in Zablocki, B. and Robbins, T. (eds) *Misunderstanding Cults: Searching for Objectivity in a Controversial Field* (London: University of Toronto Press).

Siskind, A. (2003) *The Sullivan Institute/Fourth Wall Community: The Relationship of Radical Individualism and Authoritarianism* (Westport, CT: Praeger Publishers).

Siskind, A. (2010) Grandparents and the Second Generation, personal account presented to Annual conference of the International Cultic Stuides Association, Jul 1-3, New York, US.

Smith, P. B. and Bond, M. H. (1993) *Social Psychology Across Cultures.* (Cambridge: Cambridge University Press).

Smith, M.G. and Fong, R. (2004) *The Children of Neglect.* (East Sussex, Brunner-Routledge).

Steinberg, L. (1993) *Adolescence* (New York: McGraw-Hill), cited in Brigid, D., Wassell, S. and Gilligan, R. (1999) *Child Development for Child Care and Protection Workers* (London: Jessica Kingsley Publishers).

Stein, A. (1997) 'Mothers in Cults: The Influence of Cults on the Relationship of Mothers to Their Children,' *Cultic Studies Journal* 14 (1): 28-37. Available online from https://docs.google.com/file/d/0B4dmoPK1tYNjS2hXNXg1R3RNakU/edit?pli=1 (accessed 21 April 2014).

Stevens, R. (1983.) *Erik Erikson* (Milton Keynes: The Open University Press), cited in Worth, P.J. (2000) *'Localised Creativity: A Life Span Perspective.'* (Unpublished PhD Thesis, Milton Keynes, The Open University).

Stone, M.H. (1992) 'Religious Behaviour in the Psychiatric Institute 500,' in Finn, M. and Gartner, J. (ed.) *Object Relations Theory and Religion: Clinical Applications* (Westport, CT: Praeger).

Szalavitz, M. and Perry, B. D. (2010) *Born for Love* (New York, US: William Morrow an imprint of Harper Collins Publishers).

Szimhart, J., (2012) *Book Review: Child of the cult* by Nori Muster, (e-book, 63 pages). Available online from http://jszimhart.com/book_reviews/child_of_the_cult_by_nori_muster (accessed 16 Jan 2013).

Szurko, C. (1995) 'Can Yoga be Reconciled with Christianity,' in Watt, J. (ed.) *The Church, Medicine and the New Age* (London: Churches' Council for Health and Healing).

Szurko, C. (2002) *"Extremist Authoritarian Sects": What are They?'.* Available online from http: //www.dialogcentre.org.uk/eas.html (accessed 14 November 2002).

Tajfel, H. (ed.) (1978) *Differentiation Between Social Groups: Studies in the Social Psychology of Inter-Group Relations* (London: Academic Press).

Tajfel, H. and Turner, J. (1979) 'The Social Identity Theory of Inter-Group Relations,' in Worchel, S and Austin, W.G. (eds) *The Social Psychology of Inter-Group Relations* (Chicago: Nelson Hall).

Tamm, J. (2009) *Cartwheels in a Sari* (New York, USA: Harmony Books).

Tangney, J.P. and Dearing, R. L. (2002) *Shame and Guilt* (London: The Guildford Press).

Taylor, D. (1982) 'Becoming New People: The recruitment of young Americans into the Unification Church,' in R. Wallis (ed.) *Millennialism and Charisma* (Belfast: The Queens University).

The Independent, (2014) The human brain is the most complex structure in the universe. Lets do all we can to unravel its mysteries. Wednesday 2nd April 2014, available online fromhttp://www.independent.co.uk/voices/editorials/the-human-brain-is-the-most-complex-structure-in-the-universe-lets-do-all-we-can-to-unravel-its-mysteries-9233125.html (accessed 01 June 2015).

Theroux, L (2011, 31st March) *'Louis Theroux: Westboro Baptist Church revisited'* Online available from http://www.bbc.co.uk/news/magazine-12919646 (accessed 19 April 2011).

Thomas, P.M. (2003) 'Protection, Dissociation, and Internal Roles: Modeling and Treating the Effects of Child Abuse', *Review of General Psychology,* 7 (4): 364–80.

Thomas, P.M. (2005) 'Dissociation and Internal Models of Protection: Psychotherapy with Child Abuse Survivors', *Psychotherapy: Theory, Research, Practice, Training,* 42 (1): 20–36.

Thoresen (2002) *'Psychosocial Effects of Forgiveness Training with Adults' Stanford University,* Available online from http://www.forgiving.org/Result_Summaries_2006/Carl_Thoresen.pdf
(accessed 24 February 2011)

Tobias, M.L. and Lalich, J. (1994) *Captive Hearts, Captive Minds* (Alameda, CA: Hunter House).

Triandis, H.C. and Gelfand, M.J. (1998) 'Converging Measurement of Horizontal and Vertical Individualism and Collectivism', *Journal of Personality and Social Psychology*, 74 (1): 118–28.

Turner, J.C. and Oakes, P.J. (1997) 'The Socially Structured Mind', in McGarty, C. and Haslam, S.A. (eds) *The Message of Social Psychology* (Oxford: Blackwell Publishers).

Tylden, E. (1995) 'Psychological Causalities,' in Watt, J. (ed.) *The Church, Medicine and the New Age* (London: Churches' Council for Health and Healing).

van der Kolk, B.A. (1996b) 'The black hole of trauma.' In van der Kolk, B.A., McFarlane, A.C. and Weisaeth, L. (eds) *Traumatic Stress: The Effects of Overwhelming Experience on Mind, Body, and Society* (New York: The Guilford Press), cited in Scott, M.J. and Stradling, S.G. (2001) *Counselling for Post-Traumatic Stress Disorder*, 2nd edition, (London: Sage Publications).

van Eck Duymaer van Twist, A. (2007) *'Growing Up in Contemporary Sectarian Movements: An Analysis of Segregated Socialization'* Unpublished PhD Thesis, The London School of Economics and Political Science, University of London, England.

Vitello, P. (2010) *'Christian Science Church Seeks Truce with Modern Medicine'* New York Times Online. Available online from http://www.ny-times.com/2010/03/24/nyregion/24heal.html?pagewanted=all&_r=0 (accessed, 1 April 2013).

Wall, E. (2008) *Stolen Innocence: Growing up in a polygamous sect, becoming a teenage bride, and breaking free,* (London: Harper Element).

Walsh, Y. Russell, R. and Wells, P. (1995) 'The Personality of Ex-cult Members,' *Personality and Individual Differences* 19: 339–44.

Ward, D. (2000) 'Domestic Violence as a Cultic System,' *Cultic Studies Journal* 17: 42–55.

Weissman, M.M., Bland, R.C., Can Ino, G.J., Greenwald, S., Hwu, H.-G., Joyce, P.R., Karam, E.G., Lee, C.-K., Lellouch, J., Lep Ine, J.-P., Newman, S.C., Rub, M., Ipec, IO-ST, Wells, J.E., Ickramaratne, P.J.W., Wittchien, H.-U., Yeh, E.-K. (1999) 'Prevalence of suicide ide-ation and suicide attempts in nine countries' *Psychological Medicine, 29, 9-17.* Available online from http://psylux.psych.tu-dresden.de/ i2/klinische/studium/literatur/367.pdf (accessed 30 August 2012).

Werner, E. (2005). Resilience and Recovery: Findings from the Kauai Longitudinal Study. Focal Point: Research, Policy, and Practice in *Children's Mental Health: Resilience and Recovery,* 19(1), 11-14.

West, L.J. (1993). 'A Psychiatric Overview of Cult-related Phenomena,' *Journal of the American Academy of Psychoanalysis,* 21: 1–19.

West, L.J. and Martin, P.R. (1994) 'Pseudo-Identity and the Treatment of Personality Change in Victims of Captivity and Cults' in Lynn, S.J. and Rhue, J.W. (eds) *Dissociation: Clinical and Theoretical Perspectives* (New York: Guilford Press).

Wetherick, N.E. (2002) 'Psychology, Psychologism and Logic' *Theory and Psychology* 12 (4): 489–507.

Whitsett, D. and Kent, S.A. (2003) 'Cults and Families,' *Families in Society: The Journal of Contemporary human Services* 84 (4): 491–502.

Wilson, E. (1992) 'Fashion and the Postmodern Body ', in J. Ash and E. Wilson (eds), *Chic Thrills: A Fashion Reader* (London: Pandora).

Winocur, N., Whitney, J., Sorenson, P., Vaughn, P. and Foy, D.W. (1997) 'The Individual Cult Experience Index: The Assessment of Cult

Involvement and Its Relationship to Post-cult Distress,' *Cultic Studies Journal*, 14 (2): 290–306.

Wooden, K., (1981) *The Children of Jonestown* (US, McGraw-Hill Paperbacks)

Woolfe, R. and Dryden, W. (1996) (eds) *Handbook of Counselling Psychology* (London, Sage Publications).

Worth, P.J. (2000) 'Localised Creativity: A Life Span Perspective.' (Unpublished PhD Thesis, The Open University, Milton Keynes).

Yeakley, F.R. Jr. (ed.) (1988) *The Discipling Dilemma* (Nashville, TN: Gospel Advocate Co.)

Zablocki, B. (1997) 'Cults: Theory and Treatment Issues,' paper presented to AFF Conference, Philadelphia, PA, May 31, 1997, cited in Langone, M.D. (2003) 'Terms on using the term cult.' Available online from http: //www.cultinfobooks.com/infoserv_aff/aff_termcultp2.htm (accessed 23 April 2003).

Zablocki, B. (1998) 'Hallmarks, Hooligans, and Hostages; Three Aspects of Children in Cults,' paper presented to Annual Conference of the American Family Foundation, May 29–31, Philadelphia, PA.

Zablocki, B. (2001) 'Towards a Demystified and Disinterested Theory of Brainwashing,' in Zablocki, B. and Robbins, T. (eds) *Misunderstanding Cults: Searching for Objectivity in a Controversial Field* (London: University of Toronto Press).

Zablocki, B. (2005) 'What Factors Place Cultic Groups at Risk for Becoming Harmful? Paper presented at International Cultic Studies Association Conference 'Psychological Manipulation,

Cultic Groups and Other Alternative Movements', 14–16 June, University of Madrid, Spain.

Zadro, L., Williams, K.D. and Richardson, R. (2004). 'How Long Can You Go? Ostracism by a Computer Is Sufficient to Lower Self-Reported Levels of Belonging, Control, Self-Esteem, and Meaningful Existence', *Journal of Experimental Social Psychology*, 40: 560–7

INDEX

THE COVER OF THIS BOOK

The painting that was used for the cover of this book is entitled: *Monotone to Colour.* It was part of the inspiration for the poem below:

MANIFEST MONOCHROME TO MAGICAL MULTICOLOUR

Aggravated arse-licking to assured autonomy
Boxed boredom to blossoming boldness
Calculated conformity to credible creativity

Constricting confinement to crazy chaos
Damaging dependence to deep delight
Endless enmity to euphoric emancipation

Frowning focus to flowing freedom
Grave groaning to grunge greatness
Horrible hurt to helpful healing

Insidious ideology to incredible insight
Jaded jail to jumping jubilance
Knock-kneed to knowledge-knowing

Lonely limitations to lilied liberty
Manifest monochrome to magical multicolour
Noisy nonsense to naive nonchalance

Orchestrated organisation to organic originality
Pained powerlessness to peaceful pleasure
Quantum quota to quirky questions

Restricted rigidity to released rights
Sobering slavery to substantive solitude
Tumultuous training to thoughtful thinking

Unpleasant utterings to unrestricted utopia
Vague valley to valued vicissitude
Winter want to winged wonder

Exemplary xenophobe to x-axis
Yucky yesteryear to yummy yippee
Zealot zone to Z score

Made in the USA
San Bernardino, CA
11 November 2016